Sloterdijk's Anthropotechnics

Peter Sloterdijk is an internationally renowned philosopher and thinker whose work is now seen as increasingly relevant to our contemporary world situation and the multiple crises that punctuate it, including those within ethical, political, economic, technological, and ecological realms.

This volume focuses upon one of his central ideas, anthropotechnics. Broadly speaking, anthropotechnics refers to the technological constitution of the human as its fundamental mode of existence, which is characterized by the ability to create dwelling places that 'immunize' human beings from exterior threats while at the same time instituting practices and exercises that call on humanity to transcend itself 'ascetically'. The essays included in this volume enter a critical dialogue with Sloterdijk and his many philosophical interlocutors in order to interrogate the many implications of anthropotechnics in relation to some of the most pressing issues of our time, including and especially the question of the future of humanity in relation to globalism and modernization, climate change, the post-secular, neoliberalism, and artificial intelligence.

The chapters in this book were originally published as a special issue of *Angelaki*.

Patrick Roney earned his Ph. D. in Comparative Literature from the University of Wisconsin-Madison, USA, and taught in the Philosophy department at Koç University, Istanbul, Turkey, as Associate Professor until his retirement in 2018. At present he teaches in the Liberal Arts Department at the Peabody Institute of Johns Hopkins University, Baltimore, USA. His research interests include aesthetics and the philosophy of art, with a particular focus on the sublime and the postmodern, the modern lyric, as well as phenomenology and environmental ethics. He has published numerous essays both in literature and in philosophy in journals such as the *African American Review, Research in Phenomenology, The South African Journal of Philosophy,* and several others.

Andrea Rossi is Postdoctoral Fellow in the Department of Philosophy at Koç University, Istanbul, Turkey. His principal research interests lie at the intersection of twentieth- and twenty-first-century Continental philosophy and political theory, with a special focus on the question of political and economic subjectivity. He is the author of *The Labour of Subjectivity: Foucault on Biopolitics, Economy, Critique* (2015), and co-editor with Diana Stypinska of *Pastoral Power Today* (forthcoming).

Angelaki: New Work in the Theoretical Humanities
Series Editors: **Charlie Blake**, *University of Brighton, UK*
Pelagia Goulimari, *University of Oxford, UK*
Salah el Moncef *(Consultant Editor), University of Nantes, France*
Gerard Greenway *(Managing Editor), Oxford, UK*

New Work in the Theoretical Humanities is associated with *Angelaki: Journal of the Theoretical Humanities*, a leading international interdisciplinary journal that has done much to consolidate the field of research designated by its subtitle and which has been at the forefront of publication for three decades. This book series publishes generous edited collections across the humanities as informed by European philosophy and literary and cultural theory. It has a strong interest in aesthetics and art theory and also features work in those areas of the social sciences, such as social theory and political theory, that are informed by *Angelaki's* core disciplinary concentration. This broad latitude is disciplined by a strong sense of identity and the series editors' long experience of research and teaching in the humanities. The *Angelaki* journal is well known for its exceptionally substantial special issues. **New Work in the Theoretical Humanities** publishes vanguard collections on current developments in the energetic and increasingly international field of the theoretical humanities as well as volumes on major living thinkers and writers and those of the recent past. Volumes in this series are conceived as broad but integrated treatments of their themes, with the intention of producing contributions to the literature of lasting value.

Nuclear Theory Degree Zero
Essays Against the Nuclear Android
Edited by John Kinsella and Drew Milne

Tranimacies
Intimate Links Between Animal and Trans* Studies
Edited by Eliza Steinbock, Marianna Szczygielska and Anthony Clair Wagner

Ontogenesis Beyond Complexity
Edited by Cary Wolfe and Adam Nocek

Sloterdijk's Anthropotechnics
Edited by Patrick Roney and Andrea Rossi

The Pulse of Sense
Encounters with Jean-Luc Nancy
Edited by Marie Chabbert and Nikolaas Deketelaere

For more information about this series, please visit: www.routledge.com/New-Work-in-the-Theoretical-Humanities/book-series/ANG

Sloterdijk's Anthropotechnics

Edited by
Patrick Roney and Andrea Rossi

LONDON AND NEW YORK

First published 2022
by Routledge
2 Park Square, Milton Park, Abingdon, Oxon, OX14 4RN

and by Routledge
605 Third Avenue, New York, NY 10158

Routledge is an imprint of the Taylor & Francis Group, an informa business

Foreword, Introduction, Chapters 1–9 and Untitled © 2022 Taylor & Francis
Chapter 10 © 2021 Robert Hughes. Originally published as Open Access.

With the exception of Chapter 10, no part of this book may be reprinted or reproduced or utilised in any form or by any electronic, mechanical, or other means, now known or hereafter invented, including photocopying and recording, or in any information storage or retrieval system, without permission in writing from the publishers. For details on the rights for Chapter 10, please see the chapter's Open Access footnote.

Trademark notice: Product or corporate names may be trademarks or registered trademarks, and are used only for identification and explanation without intent to infringe.

British Library Cataloguing-in-Publication Data
A catalogue record for this book is available from the British Library

ISBN13: 978-1-032-19370-0 (hbk)
ISBN13: 978-1-032-19371-7 (pbk)
ISBN13: 978-1-003-25885-8 (ebk)

DOI: 10.4324/9781003258858

Typeset in Minion Pro
by codeMantra

Publisher's Note
The publisher accepts responsibility for any inconsistencies that may have arisen during the conversion of this book from journal articles to book chapters, namely the inclusion of journal terminology.

Disclaimer
Every effort has been made to contact copyright holders for their permission to reprint material in this book. The publishers would be grateful to hear from any copyright holder who is not here acknowledged and will undertake to rectify any errors or omissions in future editions of this book.

Contents

Citation Information   vii
Notes on Contributors   ix

Foreword   1
Patrick Roney and Andrea Rossi

Introduction: Sloterdijk's Anthropotechnics   3
Patrick Roney and Andrea Rossi

1 Alone with Oneself: Solitude as Cultural Technique   9
  Thomas Macho translated by Sascha Rashof

2 Anthropotechnics and the Absolute Imperative   22
  Patrick Roney

3 Of an Enlightenment-conservative Tone Recently Adopted in Philosophy   38
  Serge Trottein

4 Specters of Religion: Sloterdijk, Immunology, and the Crisis of Immanence   51
  Gary E. Aylesworth

5 Sartre and Sloterdijk: The Ethical Imperative. You Must Change Your Life   66
  Christina Howells

6 Ascetic Worlds: Notes on Politics and Technologies of the Self after Peter Sloterdijk   77
  Andrea Rossi

7 The Limits of the Spheres: Otherness and Solipsism in Peter Sloterdijk's Philosophy   92
  Antonio Lucci

8 Anthropotechnical Practising in the Foam-world 109
   Oliver Davis

9 Staying with the Darkness: Peter Sloterdijk's Anthropotechnics
   for the Digital Age 124
   Andrea Capra

10 The Unknown Quantity: Sleep as a Trope in Sloterdijk's
   Anthropotechnics 142
   Robert Hughes

   Untitled (Negative Exercises) 156
   Andrea Rossi

   Index 159

Citation Information

The chapters in this book were originally published in the journal *Angelaki*, volume 26, issue 1 (2021). When citing this material, please use the original page numbering for each article, as follows:

Foreword
   Patrick Roney and Andrea Rossi
   Angelaki, volume 26, issue 1 (2021) pp. 1–2

Introduction
   Sloterdijk's Anthropotechnics
   Patrick Roney and Andrea Rossi
   Angelaki, volume 26, issue 1 (2021) pp. 3–8

Chapter 1
   Alone with Oneself: Solitude as Cultural Technique
   Thomas Macho and Sascha Rashof
   Angelaki, volume 26, issue 1 (2021) pp. 9–21

Chapter 2
   Anthropotechnics and the Absolute Imperative
   Patrick Roney
   Angelaki, volume 26, issue 1 (2021) pp. 22–37

Chapter 3
   Of an Enlightenment-conservative Tone Recently Adopted in Philosophy
   Serge Trottein
   Angelaki, volume 26, issue 1 (2021) pp. 38–50

Chapter 4
   Specters of Religion: Sloterdijk, Immunology, and the Crisis of Immanence
   Gary E. Aylesworth
   Angelaki, volume 26, issue 1 (2021) pp. 51–65

Chapter 5
   Sartre and Sloterdijk: The Ethical Imperative. You Must Change Your Life
   Christina Howells
   Angelaki, volume 26, issue 1 (2021) pp. 66–76

Chapter 6
Ascetic Worlds: Notes on Politics and Technologies of the Self after Peter Sloterdijk
Andrea Rossi
Angelaki, volume 26, issue 1 (2021) pp. 77–91

Chapter 7
The Limits of the Spheres: Otherness and Solipsism in Peter Sloterdijk's Philosophy
Antonio Lucci
Angelaki, volume 26, issue 1 (2021) pp. 92–108

Chapter 8
Anthropotechnical Practising in the Foam-world
Oliver Davis
Angelaki, volume 26, issue 1 (2021) pp. 109–123

Chapter 9
Staying with the Darkness: Peter Sloterdijk's Anthropotechnics for the Digital Age
Andrea Capra
Angelaki, volume 26, issue 1 (2021) pp. 124–141

Chapter 10
The Unknown Quantity: Sleep as a Trope in Sloterdijk's Anthropotechnics
Robert Hughes
Angelaki, volume 26, issue 1 (2021) pp. 142–155

Untitled
Negative Exercises
Andrea Rossi
Angelaki, volume 26, issue 1 (2021) pp. 156–159

For any permission-related enquiries please visit:
http://www.tandfonline.com/page/help/permissions

Notes on Contributors

Gary E. Aylesworth is Emeritus Professor of Philosophy and former Chair of the Philosophy Department at Eastern Illinois University, Charleston, USA. He also serves as Co-Director of the International Philosophical Seminar, which takes place in Alto Adige/Südtirol, Italy, and is Executive Committee Member for The Association for Philosophy and Literature. He has published articles on postmodernism, Heidegger, Nietzsche, hermeneutics, deconstruction, and other topics in contemporary Continental philosophy.

Andrea Capra is Ph.D. student in the French & Italian Department of Stanford University, USA. He holds a master's degree in Modern Italian Literature from the University of Milan, Italy. His research focuses on the phenomenology of horror and takes Giacomo Leopardi as its main philosopher. In addition, Andrea's field of research also touches on the philosophy of technology.

Oliver Davis is Professor of French Studies at Warwick University, Coventry, UK. He has published extensively on the work of Jacques Rancière and is currently writing a historically informed philosophical critique of the bureaucratic ideal in Modern France.

Christina Howells is Emeritus Professor of French at the University of Oxford, UK, and Fellow of Wadham College. Her research is interdisciplinary and explores Continental philosophy, literary theory, and twentieth-century French literature.

Robert Hughes is Associate Professor of English at Ohio State University, Columbus, USA, where he teaches courses in comparative American and Continental literature and philosophy of the nineteenth century. He has published a co-edited collection *After Lacan: Clinical Practice and the Subject of the Unconscious*, and a monograph *Ethics, Aesthetics, and the Beyond of Language*, treating Romantic American and post-Romantic Continental intersections of ethics and aesthetics.

Antonio Lucci is Guest Professor of Religious Studies at the Free University in Berlin, Germany. Previously, he held positions at the Humboldt University (Berlin, Germany), the Forschungsinstitut für Philosophie (Hannover, Germany), the Internationales Forschungszentrum Kulturwissenschaften (Vienna, Austria), the NABA (Milan, Italy), the University of Trieste and Rome 'La Sapienza', Italy. His research focuses on three main areas: the history of asceticism in philosophy and religion, the concept of biopolitics in contemporary Continental philosophy, and the aesthetic of new media.

Thomas Macho served from 1993 to 2016 as Professor of Cultural History at the Institute for Cultural Studies of the Humboldt University of Berlin, Germany. Since his retirement in 2016, he has been Director of the International Research Centre for Cultural

Studies (IFK) at the University of Art and Design Linz in Vienna, Austria. In 2019, he was awarded the Sigmund Freud Prize for scholarly prose by the German Academy for Language and Poetry, and in 2020, the Austrian State Prize for Cultural Journalism.

Sascha Rashof completed her Ph.D. thesis in Media Philosophy, with a focus on Sloterdijk's anthropotechnics, at the Centre for Cultural Studies at Goldsmiths, University of London, UK, which was funded by the Arts and Humanities Research Council. She has a background in cultural journalism, taught media and cultural theory at a number of universities, and currently coordinates research projects across the University of the Arts London, UK.

Patrick Roney teaches in the Liberal Arts Department at the Peabody Institute of Johns Hopkins University, Baltimore, USA, after having taught for more than 20 years in the departments of Liberal Arts and Philosophy at Koç University in Istanbul, Turkey. His research includes several areas of Continental philosophy, including aesthetics and the philosophy of art, German Idealism, and phenomenology, as well as literary modernism and the avant-garde.

Andrea Rossi is Research Fellow in the Department of Philosophy at Koç University, Istanbul, Turkey. His research interests lie at the intersection of twentieth- and twenty-first-century Continental philosophy and political theory, with a special focus on the question of political and economic subjectivity.

Serge Trottein is researcher at the CNRS (National Center for Scientific Research), UMR 8230, ENS/PSL Research University, Paris, France, and Co-Director of the IPS (International Philosophical Seminar). His field of research is philosophical aesthetics from the Renaissance to the Enlightenment, and to Postmodernity.

FOREWORD

patrick roney
andrea rossi

SLOTERDIJK'S ANTHROPOTECHNICS

This special issue intends to introduce the English-speaking world to one of the most significant and far-reaching aspects of Peter Sloterdijk's thought, *anthropotechnics*. Although a number of introductions and commentaries on Sloterdijk's works already exist in English, there is as of yet no sustained discussion of anthropotechnics despite of its relevance not only to Sloterdijk's *oeuvre*, but especially to the several crises that now punctuate our contemporary world situation more generally. It is high time, we believe, that this notion, which Sloterdijk has now been elaborating for over twenty years, becomes part of the conversation about questions concerning the future of humanity in a world marked by globalization and its attendant developments – technological, political, economic, scientific, and ecological – and its discontents, its crises, and possibilities.

Like most of Sloterdijk's key terms, anthropotechnics defies easy conceptualization. While generally referring to the technological manipulation of man, its ramifications far exceed the domain of *techne*. At stake in Sloterdijk's use of the concept is, among other things, the constitution of the human and humanity's being-in-the-world, its ability not only to modify but especially to exercise and transcend itself ("whoever goes in search of humans," he writes, "will find acrobats"), and the possibility to mediate human interiority with the nonhuman "outside," the unknown and its dangers, or, in a word, with the "monstrous" that encircles us, ever more pressingly so since the end of classical metaphysics.

The essays included in this issue address and interrogate these problems across several domains, including the existential-ontological, the ethical, the religious, and the political, and in relation to the question concerning technology in general and new technologies in particular. In doing so, they enter into a dialogue, often critical, with Sloterdijk as well as his many interlocutors, from Kant, Nietzsche, Heidegger, Sartre, and Jaspers to Foucault, Luhmann, and Latour. Across these various engagements, our hope is that this special issue will help not only to shed more light on the often difficult and elliptic nature of Sloterdijk's thought, but that it will serve to open up the ways in which the idea of anthropotechnics invites us to re-think some most pressing issues of our time, including and especially the question of the future of humanity in relation to globalism and modernization, climate change, the post-secular, neoliberalism, and artificial intelligence.

The idea for this issue first came into being at the annual meeting of the *International Philosophical Seminar* in the summer of 2017 directed by Serge Trottein and Gary Aylesworth, which was dedicated to a reading of two of Peter Sloterdijk's recent works, *You Must Change Your Life* and *The Art of Philosophy*. Since then, this issue has expanded to include contributions from other international authors involved in the study of Sloterdijk's thought. In addition, we are delighted to publish here for the first time the translation of an essay entitled, "Alone with Oneself: Solitude as Cultural Technique" by Sloterdijk's long-standing friend and collaborator, Professor Thomas Macho.

Issue image: Cherimus, Du mußt dein Leben ändern *(Montalvo Arts Center, California, December 2019).*

The works of Peter Sloterdijk (b. 1947) have become more readily available in recent years to the English-speaking world,[1] and so too has the recognition that his thought represents a major contribution to the ongoing discussions about globalization and its discontents, some of which are becoming increasingly catastrophic, particularly at this moment in time. Although often identified as philosophical or theoretical in nature, a survey of Sloterdijk's corpus reveals a voluminous writing with a far wider scope, one that includes among its foci art and aesthetics, ecological concerns, most notably climate change, religion and its history, the crisis of liberal democracies and the political overall, an extensive attempt at Nietzschean-inspired diagnoses of the ills of modernity and modernization, and the development of a new topological history of human in-dwelling or "en-housing" [*Ge-häuse*] that goes by the name of *Spherology* (*Bubbles, Globes, Foams*; see Rashof). This list of subjects here does not even touch on Sloterdijk's multifarious styles of writing. Oftentimes philosophical and interrogative but also very often oriented around the construction of a narrative, some which are quite grand, Sloterdijk's styles are interspersed with polemical, playful, and provocative elements.[2]

Nonetheless, there are clear elements of continuity and lines of thought within this oeuvre, one of which is without a doubt the notion of anthropotechnics (see especially Sloterdijk, *You Must Change*; *Art of Philosophy*; *Nach Gott* 210–28; "Anthropo-technology"). It is our contention that far from being one of several occasional topics found in Sloterdijk's work, anthropotechnics is central to his ever-expanding diagnoses of modernity and its

INTRODUCTION

patrick roney
andrea rossi

SLOTERDIJK'S ANTHROPOTECHNICS

history – a history that now finds itself in a profound crisis. Our aim in this issue is to foreground and to initiate what we hope will be a deeper engagement with the many aspects and implications of this *problematique*.

Like most of Sloterdijk's key terms, anthropotechnics defies easy conceptualization. As a first approximation, it refers to that cluster of phenomena pertaining to the technological modification of the human at both the physical and psychological levels. Its scope, however, encompasses a much broader set of issues and perspectives that are at once sociological, anthropological, ethical, philosophical, and political, and which in fact aim to cast light – a different, a diagonal light – on the history of human culture as a whole. The contours of anthropotechnics emerge in Sloterdijk's work through a patient, if seemingly unsystematic accumulation of historical analyses and a multiplication of theoretical viewpoints elaborated over more than two decades, most of which would be impossible to reconstruct here.[3] Instead, our aim will be to outline a general horizon of concerns that will begin, following Sloterdijk's own suggestion, with the characterization of anthropotechnics as a "manoeuvre" (*You Must Change* 4), one whose purpose is to actively intervene into the current Western and indeed world situation where, under the pressure of modernization, peoples are increasingly and "dangerously" exposed to the deterritorializing forces of globalization, of ecological crisis, and of technologies such as genetic engineering and artificial intelligence. Anthropotechnics is as much a practice and a provocation as it is a theory, something that we would like to explore, in particular, in relation to three of its central theoretical moments, which are also the ones around which most of the essays in this issue revolve. These are respectively, the *technological*, the *ascetic*, and the *immunological* constitution of humanity.

Sloterdijk's first mention of the term "anthropotechnics" occurred in the late 1990s, in a piece that created an immediate controversy, "Rules for the Human Park" (*Not Saved* 193–216; Couture 77–84). The text was meant in part as an intervention into ongoing debates over the new technologies of genetic engineering and the "indistinct" and "frightening" questions that they raise concerning humanity's future. Here, it had already become apparent how much Sloterdijk's approach to the ethico-political implications of these and other anthropo-technologies would differ from those of some other prominent authors who have taken part in that debate. Rather than point to the threats posed by biogenetics to individual autonomy, human nature, or the *humanitas* of man, as one finds in different ways in the work of Habermas, Fukuyama, or Sandel, Sloterdijk focused, in a deliberately polemical way, on the notion and practice of breeding (*Züchten*) – a most eerie word to a German ear – in the specific sense of the ways in which technology embodies and enhances human plasticity, i.e., the human capacity for self-formation. To quote one of his later texts, "humans encounter nothing strange when they expose themselves to further creation and manipulation, and they do nothing perverse when they change themselves auto-technologically" (Sloterdijk, "Anthropo-technology" 16). Anthropotechnics can thus be characterized in a preliminary way as an ontological determination of the co-constitution of *anthropos* and *techne* and their historical permutations rather than as a traditional theory of human nature as *animal rationale* (cf. Duclos, "Anthropotechnics").

Even though Sloterdijk is not alone in his attempt to link the human and the technological from the ground up (see, e.g., Simondon; Stiegler; Haraway), still the scope that he gives to their relation proves to be much wider than is the case in many recent philosophies of technology. Technology, for Sloterdijk, includes not only material artifacts, machines, media, or other types of technical "exo-somatization," but also, more broadly, any cultural practice aimed at consciously transcending and remodeling the human being, his self-understanding and stance in the world. Anthropotechnics belongs, in other words, to a wider constellation centered around the notion of *askesis* as a *technology of the self*, that is, as a set of *praxes* or, if one prefers, of arts of life, as articulated most notably in the works of Michel Foucault and Pierre Hadot. Here lies a second fundamental dimension of anthropotechnics: it functions as a *general ascetology*, a new science in which the history of ascetic practices in all of their disparate manifestations becomes visible not in terms of a more conventional perspective that focuses on abnegation and self-renunciation, but "positively," as a system of anthropotechnical praxes that embody the fundamental ethical imperative to go beyond one's existing conditions towards a new state of being that appears as either impossible or "monstrous" in relation to the habits, the norms and the enclosed protective systems of everyday social life.[4]

Anthropotechnics as a general ascetology thus paves the way for a historical analysis where "charioteers and scholars, wrestlers and church fathers, archers and rhapsodists come together, united by shared experiences on the way to the impossible" (Sloterdijk, *You Must Change* 64). It forms a narrative of the multifarious ways in which human beings, both individually and collectively, have shaped, "bred," and cultivated themselves, from the beginnings of advanced civilizations – when the first "acrobats," "the wise men, the illuminated, the athletes, the gymnosophists, the sacred and profane teachers" made their appearance (194) – to the contemporary industry of self-enhancement and genetic engineering. Even the latter can and must be grasped as part of "a broad tableau of human 'work on oneself'" (10) rather than as unnatural threats to our *humanitas* created by a new breed of institutionalized Dr Frankensteins. Genetic engineering is but the latest ring in a long chain of cultural experimentations, broadly understood, by means of which human beings step into the open of the world and immunize themselves against possible harm coming from the outside.

This last mention of anthropotechnics and ascetology as a general practice of stepping into the opening of the environing world or alternatively, as a practice of *world-formation*, introduces the third and final moment that we wish to highlight here: anthropotechnics as part of a *general immunology*. This theme, which occupies a large portion of Sloterdijk's writings since the 1990s and culminates in the great spatial-ontological investigations of the *Spheres* trilogy,[5] bears a strong affinity with Heidegger's existential analysis of Dasein as *unheimlich*, as not-being-at-home in the world, although it is by no means the same. One can get a better sense of Sloterdijk's approach from his remark that "human beings are living beings that do not come to the world, but rather come into the greenhouse" (*Not Saved* 120). The world, in the sense of the sheer outside, is not an especially hospitable place, and *pace* the survivalist mindset, human beings that are exposed to it for too long do not last. Greenhouses – literally, those climatically controlled, enclosed, protective spaces that foster life and growth – are our natural dwellings. Humans need incubators, shelters, and artificial containers – in short, material and symbolic immunity scaffoldings – to protect themselves from a world that they are not well equipped at birth to inhabit. They are somehow compelled to form their world rather than simply expose themselves to its sheer facticity – the world is never given in such a brute manner. Hence, anthropotechnics appears a branch of a general immunology, as a comprehensive system of layered immunity structures that includes the biological, the social, and the symbolic. The latter is the specific focus of anthropotechnics, which may accordingly be defined as the study of

> the symbolic or psycho-immunological practices on which humans have always relied to cope – with varying success – with their vulnerability through fate, including mortality, in the form of imaginary anticipations and mental armour [and] the methods of mental and physical practising by which [they] have attempted to optimize their cosmic and immunological status in the face of vague risks of living and acute certainties of death.[6]

As should hopefully be clear by now, immunology, particularly at the symbolic level, entails more than just a prophylactic insulation from external dangers. The life of practice is never just a matter of survival or adaptation, as a crude form of pragmatism or biologism would have it; practice requires a controlled yet creative exposition to the outside (Duclos, "Falling"). In the interplay between the defensive retreat to an inside and the ecstatic opening to the world, the human looks out towards new horizons in the form of "vertical attractors," to use the language of *You Must Change Your Life*, through which s/he may discover a different life. For Sloterdijk, immunology underlies, in this sense, the most basic dynamics of human culture:

> In order to cope with the self-endangerments that increase for sapiens-beings from their unique biological position, they have produced an inventory of procedures for the formation of the self, which we discuss today under the general term "culture," [which encompasses] all those ways of ordering, techniques, rituals, and customs with which human groups have taken their symbolic and disciplinary formation "into their own hands." (*Not Saved* 126–27)

Not only technology, but also politics, ethics, religion, art, and athleticism, to name but a few, might be reinterpreted accordingly, since life as a whole is only "the success phase of an immune system" (449).

The main coordinates of Sloterdijk's anthropotechnical maneuver are thus delineated: the human, whose essence is technological, and whose technological essence impels it to transcend itself ascetically, is at the same time the subject who, through practice, must form the world it inhabits to shelter itself from the abyss of sheer exteriority.

Through this conceptual framework, we are now in a position to gesture, however tentatively, to the dangers as well as the opportunities associated with Sloterdijk's diagnosis of modern anthropotechnics, and of the "Great Catastrophe" that he evokes at the end of *You Must Change Your Life*, which looms on our horizons today as never before. The crises that we are experiencing may be regarded as technological, ascetic, and immunological, which are now unfolding at virtually every level, including the viral, social, environmental, economic, and political. In a purely schematic way, modernity for Sloterdijk appears torn between its attempt to expand and democratize the life of practice, and the dilution, if not the sheer erasure, of its vertical dimension – i.e., the prospect of a radical transformation, a *metanoia*, a leap to the most improbable as the condition of possibility of any asceticism (*You Must Change* 315–435; *Nach Gott* 211–16). Never has humanity been as enthused by the prospect of a total and permanent transformation as in our age, but Sloterdijk is also aware that up until now this has failed to produce anything other than "a cybernetic optimization system," where we "are guaranteed all human rights – except for the right to exit from facticity" (*You Must Change* 437). Despite his recognition of the essentially technological essence of man, Sloterdijk does not ignore how recent technologies – which, needless to say, extend well beyond biogenetics – tend to be mobilized primarily as "life-augmenting and life-increasing accessories" that direct life and the imperative to change one's life only to the flat, horizontal perspective of enhancing or making more comfortable our existing life rather than transforming it. Divested of its vertical dimension and therefore of its ecstatic opening to the outside, immunity turns, to draw on the insights of another author who has long been preoccupied with similar questions, into auto-immunity (Esposito).

However vaguely, Sloterdijk seems nonetheless to detect a new paradigm looming on the horizon – or the need or the hope for one – which he refers to as "co-immunity." In the face of the utter impossibility that things could still go on just as they have been for the last half century or more, humanity is, and will increasingly be called upon to realize "that shared life interests of the highest order can only be realized within a horizon of universal co-operative asceticisms," ones that transcend "all previous distinctions between own and foreign," and "the classical distinctions of friend and foe" (Sloterdijk, *You Must Change* 451–52). What this might entail, apart from an ill-defined, environmentally tinted cosmopolitanism remains an open question. Sloterdijk's contention here seems to be simply that the crisis itself, whose religious overtones he stresses throughout *You Must Change Your Life*, may give rise to a new verticality, a new "unconditional overtaxing" in the form of an "absolute imperative" (442) – a dimension which modern, and above all contemporary anthropotechnics, would seem to have forsaken long ago. What is certain, though, is that like any ascetic exercise, this new imperative would not evince a clear and certain aim, but would, at the very most, be heard as a call to "rehearse the most improbable as the most certain" – "*certum est quia impossibile*," as Tertullian wrote (*You Must Change* 334). At its most incisive, Sloterdijk's anthropotechnics represents an attempt to reawaken this call – a call to which this issue and the essays contained in it have tried critically to pay heed, as a tribute, so to speak, to its necessary improbability.

notes

1 Cf., for example, Couture; Elden; Schinkel and Noordegraaf-Eelens.

2 On Sloterdijk's philosophical styles, see Hoban.

3 For a genealogy of the concept of "anthropotechnics" in Sloterdijk, see Lucci.

4 For a critical appraisal of Sloterdijk's ascetology, see Ahmadi.

5 For an introduction to this theme, see Mutsaers, ch. 5.

6 Sloterdijk, *You Must Change* 9. Ascetology is in this sense only a branch of General Immunology, which also encompasses the study of biological and social immunity, the second of which Sloterdijk explores at length in the *Spheres* trilogy.

bibliography

Ahmadi, Amir. "Peter Sloterdijk's General Ascetology." *Critical Horizons* 18.4 (2017): 333–46. Print.

Couture, Jean-Pierre. *Sloterdijk*. Cambridge: Polity, 2015. Print.

Duclos, Vincent. "Anthropotechnics: On the Relationship between Technology and Humanity according to Peter Sloterdijk." *Sociétés* 131.1 (2016): 41–49. Print.

Duclos, Vincent. "Falling into Things: Peter Sloterdijk, Ontological Anthropology in the Monstrous." *New Formations* 95 (Jan. 2019): 37–53. Print.

Elden, Stuart, ed. *Sloterdijk Now!* Cambridge: Polity, 2012. Print.

Esposito, Roberto. *Immunitas: The Protection and Negation of Life*. Cambridge: Polity, 2011. Print.

Foucault, Michel. *The Hermeneutics of the Subject*. New York: Picador, 2005. Print.

Fukuyama, Francis. *Our Posthuman Future: Consequences of the Biotechnology Revolution*. New York: Picador, 2003. Print.

Habermas, Jürgen. *The Future of Human Nature*. Cambridge: Polity, 2003. Print.

Hadot, Pierre. *Philosophy as a Way of Life: Spiritual Exercises from Socrates to Foucault*. Hoboken: Wiley-Blackwell, 1995. Print.

Haraway, D. "A Cyborg Manifesto: Science, Technology and Socialist-Feminism in the Late Twentieth Century." *Feminism/Postmodernism (Thinking Gender)*. Ed. L. Nicholson. Routledge: London, 1989. 50–57. Print.

Hoban, Wieland. "The Language of Give and Take: Sloterdijk's Stylistic Methods." *Sloterdijk Now!* Ed. Stuart Elden. Cambridge: Polity, 2012. 114–32. Print.

Lucci, Antonio. "L'animale Acrobatico. Origini e Sviluppo del Concetto di Antropotecnica nel Pensiero di Peter Sloterdijk." *Esercizi Filosofici* 7 (2012): 78–97. Print.

Mutsaers, Inge. *Immunological Discourse in Political Philosophy. Immunisation and its Discontents*. London: Routledge, 2016. Print.

Rashof, Sascha. "Spheres: Towards a Techno-Social Ontology of Place/s." *Theory, Culture & Society* 35.6 (2018): 131–52. Print.

Sandel, Michael J. *The Case against Perfection: Ethics in the Age of Genetic Engineering*. Cambridge, MA: Harvard UP, 2009. Print.

Schinkel, Willem, and Liesbeth Noordegraaf-Eelens, eds. *In Medias Res. Peter Sloterdijk's Spherological Poetics of Being*. Amsterdam: Amsterdam UP, 2011. Print.

Simondon, Gilbert. *On the Mode of Existence of Technical Objects*. Minneapolis: U of Minnesota P, 2017. Print.

Sloterdijk, Peter. "Anthropo-technology." *New Perspective Quarterly* 21.4 (2004): 12–19. Print.

Sloterdijk, Peter. *The Art of Philosophy: Wisdom as a Practice*. New York: Columbia UP, 2012. Print.

Sloterdijk, Peter. *Bubbles: Spheres Volume I: Microspherology*. Los Angeles: Semiotext(e), 2016. Print.

Sloterdijk, Peter. *Foams: Spheres Volume III: Plural Spherology*. Los Angeles: Semiotext(e), 2016. Print.

Sloterdijk, Peter. *Globes: Spheres Volume II: Macrospherology*. Los Angeles: Semiotext(e), 2014. Print.

Sloterdijk, Peter. *Nach Gott*. Frankfurt: Suhrkamp, 2017. Print.

Sloterdijk, Peter. *Not Saved. Essays after Heidegger*. Cambridge: Polity, 2017. Print.

Sloterdijk, Peter. *You Must Change Your Life*. Cambridge: Polity, 2014. Print.

Stiegler, Bernard. *Technics and Time Vol. 1. The Fault of Epimetheus*. Palo Alto: Stanford UP, 1998. Print.

I

In scholarly as well as literary texts, solitude is often described as a state, as a suffering and passion, as more or less tragic fate (cf., exemplarily, Rakusa or Dreitzel). In the following considerations, I want to try to examine solitude from a contrary perspective. "Solitude" shall (firstly) figure as a title for processes that are actively initiated and not suffered; it shall (secondly) be thematised as an indeed ambivalent, yet not just painful, but also sensuous experience; and it shall (thirdly) be perceived as both context and cause of the practice of cultural techniques – and precisely not as pathos formula for contingent events or fatal circumstances. By the way, I use the expression "cultural techniques" by following Marcel Mauss and his notion of "techniques of the body," and of course with regard to Foucault's analyses of "technologies of the self" ("Technologies"; cf. Foucault, *The Care of the Self*; Foucault and Sennett).

What do techniques of solitude consist in? They can very generally be characterised as "doubling-up techniques," as self-perception strategies. The one who is not merely abandoned by everyone (what ordinarily leads to death), but survives, conquers and designs his "abandonment," performs some kind [*Art*] of relation to himself. By perceiving his solitude, without becoming mad, he splits into two figures at least: as a being that is alone *with itself* – and thus is actually "two." In this regard, the most famous mayor of Bordeaux postulates, "We have a soul that can be turned upon itself; it can keep itself company; it has the means to attack and the means to defend, the means to receive and the means to

thomas macho

translated by sascha rashof

ALONE WITH ONESELF
solitude as cultural technique

give" (de Montaigne 177). The soul turns upon itself, it becomes the sun (*sol*) of its *solitudo*, a *medium* in the process of *meditatio*. Solitude as a "doubling-up" strategy indeed has to be learned and practised – like all cultural techniques. For

> there are ways to fail in solitude as well as in company. Until you have made yourself such that you dare trip up in your own presence, and until you feel both shame and respect for yourself, *let true ideals be kept before your mind*, keep ever in your mind Cato, Phocion, and Aristides, in whose presence even fools would hide their faults; make them controllers of all your intentions; if these intentions get off the track, your

reverence for those men will set them right again. (182f.)

– Montaigne cites Seneca (as so often), who he prefers to the philosophy of Pliny and Cicero, which is "ostentatious and talky." In his XXVth letter to Lucilius, Seneca namely wrote,

> There is no real doubt that it is good for one to have appointed a guardian over oneself, and to have someone whom you may look up to, someone whom you may regard as a witness of your thoughts. It is, indeed, nobler by far to live as you would live under the eyes of some good man, always at your side; but nevertheless I am content if you only act, in whatever you do, as you would act if anyone at all were looking on; because solitude prompts us to all kinds of evil. And when you have progressed so far that you have also respect for yourself, you may send away your attendant; but until then, set as a guard over yourself the authority of some man, whether your choice be the great Cato, or Scipio, or Laelius – or any man in whose presence even abandoned wretches would check their bad impulses. (185)

This sounds like contemporary psychology, as the translation of "dignatio tui" with "respect for yourself," suggests. While Montaigne speaks about "examples" though, which the soul shall "dwell on," it remains doubtful whether Seneca, plagiarised by him, really wanted to give advice for the formation of a well-functioning "conscience," of a "super-ego," which – named after a prominent idol – should have diminished the dangers and risks of solitude. The cited text passage from the XXVth letter in no way compels such associations. It talks of a "guard" ("custos"), an appointment of a teacher ("paedagogus") or spectator ("tamquam spectet aliquis"); it talks of protection and intervention. The exercise advocates the imagination of a personal guardian spirit, of a "third man," which at the same time monitors the solitary excesses of the "cogitationes"; it is reminiscent of the Roman cult of "geniuses," who used to be worshipped as some sort of personal "doubles" – on each birthday, for example (Censorinus; cf. Schmidt; Macho, "Himmel"). In addition, Seneca's letter recapitulates as a maxim what it at once performatively puts into effect: namely, the representation of the interlocutor Lucilius, who creates and constitutes the "auctoritas custodi" of Seneca the author in the first place. But what should the imagined personality save its "creators" from – Cato/Lucilius, Lucilius/Seneca? What did the "omnia mala" of "solitudo" consist in? What was the solitude person seduced to? To despair, insanity, suicide? The dietetics of the invention of a mental "witness" or "guard" hardly served the resistance against melancholy (which was only demonised in the middle ages – as *acedia*) or even the resistance against autoerotic desires (which would only be cast out in the nineteenth century), but rather the order and discipline of soliloquy, of inner dialogues. Not for nothing it says: "omnia nobis mala solitude *persuadet.*" Solitude "speaks," it cajoles and persuades, which is what its potential harmfulness consists in. The solitary person runs the danger to get, literally, "talked to death" – and indeed by oneself. In solitude, even a "good man," so Plato already argued in the tenth book of *The Republic*, would be "doing many things which he would be ashamed of any one hearing or seeing him do."

For the one who is alone exposes himself to too many voices: regardless of whether he perceives them as his own or as foreign voices. Through the "Ta eis heauton," the "self-admonitions" of the emperor-philosopher Marcus Aurelius, composed in the Greek language, Pierre Hadot demonstrates how the building work of a "citadelle intérieure" was erected against inadequate forms of *phantasia* and *dianoia*. Following Epictetus, Marcus Aurelius differentiated between "objective" and "subjective" representations: whilst the objective representation (*phantasia kataléptiké*) correlated with reality, the subjective representation issued comments and evaluations, as elaborate as unnecessary. In the sense of the recommended "self-limitation" exercises, it now depends on limiting every inner speech to the objective, realistic *phantasia*; merely physicalistic "protocol sentences" should be pronounced in the mind. In the *Meditations*, Marcus Aurelius wrote,

> Don't tell yourself anything more than what your primary representations tell you. If you've been told, "So-and-so has been talking behind your back," then this is what you've been told. You have *not*, however, been told that "Somebody has done a wrong to you." (Hadot, *The Inner Citadel* 103)

Pierre Hadot comments on these sentences as stages of a process:

> In the first place, we have the exterior event: someone announces to Marcus that so-and-so has been saying negative things about him. Next, we have the representation produced within him, which is called "primary" because as yet, nothing has been added to it. In the third place, there is the discourse which enunciates the contents of this primary representation: "So-and-so has been saying negative things about you"; this is what is announced by the primary representation. Finally, there is yet another enunciation, which is no longer content merely to describe the situation, but emits a value-judgement: "I have been wronged" [...] Thus, both Marcus and Epictetus draw a clear distinction between "objective" inner discourse, which is merely a pure description of reality, and "subjective" inner discourse, which includes conventional or passionate considerations, which have nothing to do with reality. (*The Inner Citadel* 103f.)

The ideal of the Stoic – the hoped-for effect of long-term exercising – consequently consists in the freedom from the overwhelming power of things and relations that intrude consciousness by provoking inner images, voices and conversations. For "what troubles people is not things, but their judgements about things," Epictetus writes in the fifth paragraph of his "Enchiridion" (cited in Hadot, *The Inner Citadel* 107).

From these examples, it could be concluded: solitude techniques are strategies for the initiation and cultivation of self-perceptions (including the imagination of examples and "guiding voices"); they intend to achieve an incitation and disciplining – not the haphazard unleashing – of inner dialogues. Montaigne cites Tibullus, "In solitude be to thyself a throng" ("in solis tu mihi turba locis").[2] This "turba" had to be conquered; the techniques of its conquering had to be learned and practised. What was striven for was no "self-restraint" in the sense of modern civilisation theories, but the control of representations that – particularly as voices, but also as images and phantasies – populate the space of consciousness. The experience of freedom, which may have emanated from such disciplining exercises, culminated in the evidence that the "turba" of inner images and voices cannot storm the "ego core," the "citadelle intérieure."[3] This certainty (and the fortune of unaccountability associated with it) can only be understood if the contrasting experience is called into memory: the experience of being overwhelmed by events and affects that provoke an unwanted uproar of inner representations and dialogues. Such experiences were less alien to antiquity than to contemporary consciousness; "becoming possessed" by other powers, images or voices was plausible in multiple regards – and befell in no way only social outsiders, but also heroes and mythical idols: from the Delphic Pythia to Sybille von Cumae, from Ajax raving mad, who massacres a herd of sheep, to Heracles slaying wife and child, from the Homeric rhapsodist Ion to the Corinthian Bellerophon (Starobinski 9–80). Notoriously, Plato's Socrates still praised the "manic art," which was distorted by the more recent interpretation as the "mantic art" ("Phaedrus" 244b–d): for the poets are "the interpreters of the Gods by whom they are severally possessed" (*Ion* 534e).

2

"The greatest thing in the world is to know how to belong to oneself," remarks Montaigne (178); but even in his sixteenth century, this "thing" was a bit strange. The modern ideal of exclusive self-ownership – the enlightened insight that humans are able to determine and be in command of themselves because they can, and must, be regarded as sole owners of themselves – presumes, for example, that the definition of slavery prevalent since Aristotle is given up: namely, the notion that slaves function like bodily organs of their master, i.e., like their arms, legs or tongues (Aristotle 1254a–b). However, slavery was only forbidden in England in 1834 and – after the end of the civil war – the United States. The feudal principle of serfdom was also only abolished in the wake of the bourgeois revolutions in Europe – in 1861 in Russia; and the suicide attempt (for instance in England) was classified as a criminal act until 1961: which only makes sense as long as one can assume that the suicide wanted to damage "foreign property." To this day, a potential claim to the body and life of at least the male population is conceded to every state government: during "general mobilisation," the ideal of "self-ownership" is also retracted, and "desertion" is not uncommonly punished with death. To this day, many parents need to be taught that they do not "own" their children – and therefore must also not abuse them or prevent them from attending school; and since the implementation of new organ transplantation laws, the right of disposal of one's own body can be drastically limited. In a nutshell: humans only belong to "themselves" in exceptional cases. Most humans are never, and have never been, able to learn or practise the art of "belonging to themselves." The one who does not belong to oneself however belongs to another master, is their property and *eo ipso* a *possessed person*, a literally *foreign-determined subject*, which obeys the orders, rhythms and maxims of its leaders (cf. first section of Macho, "Zeichen" 225–29; cf. Macho, "Auferstehung" 34–36).

Solitude techniques were often practised to suspend a specific logic of "becoming possessed." Because of his hermitage in the forest lasting several months, Henry David Thoreau authorised the proposal of a "civil disobedience" against the state. Most solitude techniques did not intend any narcissistic "self-doubling," so to say as a permanent staging of autoerotic "mirror stages of self possession," but rather the defence against menacing obsessions and external claims of ownership. The one who was able to get used to talking to himself was able to neutralise the chain of commands of foreign voices by hearing his own voice – regardless of whether they came from priests, spirits, parents, teachers or leaders; he obeyed the internalised compulsions to submit of everyday "obedience" – a not just socially agreeable, but almost constitutive "possession" – through a state of alternative "possession." Marcus Aurelius wanted to erect the "citadelle intérieure" in order to protect his ego from all passions and to commit to the indomitable guiding principle (*hēgemonikon*) of the good *daimôn*: though he was in no way convinced to "own" this ego, and even Pierre Hadot is not sure whether the *agados daimôn* as inner voice has to be interpreted as a kind of divinity (in the tradition of ancestor and genius worship) or merely as an allegorisation of the ability to reason (*The Inner Citadel* 112–27). Lucilius was supposed to be "possessed" by Cato or Scipio in order to be able to practise (dangerous) solitude as art "to belong to oneself"; as it were, the ego, besieged by images and voices, was given a "higher self" as companion, witness, guardian, teacher, *daimôn* or genius. Epictetus spoke of this "higher self" as an "Other," which thwarts every real holder of power, "When you go to see some important personage, remember that there is an Other, watching what happens from above, and that it is better to please this Other than that man." Pierre Hadot comments,

> Like an inner voice, this Other has a dialogue with the guiding principle in the discussion which Epictetus imagines following this passage. It is, moreover, this same transcendent Other with whom Marcus Aurelius carries on a dialogue in the *Meditations*. (*The Inner Citadel* 122)

The talk of a "great Other" is reminiscent of a multitude of religious and spiritual practices: the discovery of the "inner witness" – of *purusa* – in Indian Sāmkhya yoga (cf.

Hiriyanna 106–28; Schweitzer 67–74); of course also of God's self-designation in the burning bush: "I am he who is" (*New Jerusalem Bible*, Exodus 3.14). In late antiquity, the early Christian desert monks, these "athletes of despair" (after an expression of Hugo Ball (18f.)), practised the development and differentiation of specific solitude techniques. The "Temptations of Saint Anthony" became particularly famous; in fact – entirely in contrast to their later reception history – they did not represent any feelings and sensations occurring more-or-less unplanned, but virtually projects of an agonal contest between monk and devil, effects of a grandiose crisis experiment, during which the anchorite went out ever further into the desert, lay down in burial caves for days and had several fights against evil spirits that offered him silver bowls, gold nuggets or female affection. I cite from "Life of Antony" by Church Father Athanasius:

> The [devil] would suggest foul thoughts and [Antony] counter them with prayers: the one fire him with lust, the other, as one who seemed to blush, fortify his body with faith, prayers, and fasting. And the devil, unhappy wight, one night even took upon him the shape of a woman and imitated all her acts simply to beguile Antony. But he, his mind filled with Christ and the nobility inspired by Him, and considering the spirituality of the soul, quenched the coal of the other's deceit. (197)

The comment of Athanasius seems to pity the "unhappy wight" as a hopelessly weaker opponent: as if Anthony had turned the evil spirit merely into a sparring partner in order to appropriately practise his own strength, endurance and fighting technique. The "great Other" of Anthony was of course called "Christ": the divine human replaced the empirical ego (as *sol* of *solitudo*). Only by concentrating on this new "agados daimôn," the hermit was able to resist the voices and images of the "evil demons."

Solitude techniques were practised as attention exercises, not as trance techniques; for the ancient philosophers – as for the saints of the desert – it was not about the heightening of mindfulness (*prosoche*), not about ecstasy. In contrast to an occasionally prevalent etymology of the word "*Einsamkeit*" [solitude] (which refers to experiences of unity, of *unio mystica*), the solitude experts cultivated the practice of a controlled "*Zweisamkeit*" [twosomeness], in which they were able to set themselves in relation to themselves, without becoming overwhelmed by the "turba" of inner representations and voices. In this sense, Plato's writings were not devised as fictive transcripts of conversations, but so to speak as "ideal dialogues";[4] in this sense, already Antisthenes – after the testimonial of Diogenes Leartius (Book VI) – responded to the question about the "advantage" of philosophy: "The ability to hold converse with myself." This ability was practised in the encounters with the "great Other," which – as a kind of double – could be personified in the Greek *daimôn*, the Roman genius, the Christian guardian angel. In the Kabbalistically inspired mysticism of numbers and letters by Abraham von Worms (from the year 1458), the magical invocation of demons and angels, though particularly of a personal guardian spirit, was still taught; and the author insisted "that a man should go into retirement in some desert or solitude, until the time of the Six Moons destined unto this Operation be fulfilled" (ch. 10). For "it is impossible," so an expert of ancient solitude techniques eventually formulated in the twentieth century,

> to receive the "truth" from oneself. When one feels it forming (this is an impression), one forms at the same moment *another self, an unaccustomed self*... and is proud of it – jealous of it ... (This is one limit of internal policy.) (Valéry, *Monsieur Teste* 37)

This "unaccustomed self," Paul Valéry concerned himself with during his entire intellectual life: he notoriously called it "Mr. Witness" – "Monsieur Teste." This "witness" represented Valéry's "auctoritas custodi": "M. Teste is my bogeyman; whenever I misbehave, I think of him" (*Cahiers* 57).

3

Certainly, the spectrum of solitude techniques has changed since Plato, Seneca, Marcus Aurelius, Paul or Anthony. Before I try to suggest indicators for these changes though, I want to recall to memory the wealth of techniques of "internal policy." Thus, we owe two lists of Stoic–Platonic exercises to Philo's tractates "Legum Allegoriae" (Hadot, *Philosophy* 84; cf. Philo, "Allegorical Interpretation" 52 (§ 18)) and "Quis Rerum Divinarum Heres" (cf. Philo, "Who is the Heir" 298 (§ 253)). These lists comprise: research (*zetesis*), thorough investigation (*skepsis*), reading, listening, attention (*prosoche*), self-mastery (*enkrateia*), indifference to indifferent things, meditations (*melétai*), therapies of the passions, remembrance of good things and the accomplishment of duties. Paramount among the meditations was the reflection on one's own mortality, the *meléte thanátu*. Since the Platonic "Phaedo" at least, this exercise was practised as a "change of perspective," a psychic *metastrophe*, which was about contemplating oneself as "dead" from the point of view of the "higher self," the "great Other," which was conflated with the universal – the law, the cosmos or God. In that sense, Socrates characterised his entire philosophical existence as the attempt to be "as nearly in a state of death as he could" (Plato, "Phaedo" 67d–e). The one who was able to see himself "dead" rescued himself onto the "other side," as it were: the "*I think*," which has to "accompany all my representations" (Kant, *Critique* 246 (B 132)), also succeeded in taking part in the representation of one's own demise. The early Christian thinkers argued in a similar way. "I face death every day" Paul wrote to the Corinthians (*New Jerusalem Bible*, 1 Cor. 15, 31–32); and Anthony in his last speech to the monks spoke "in the outer mountain": "Live as though dying daily. Give heed to yourselves, and remember the admonition you have heard from me" (St Athanasius 220). The one who was able to live in such a way remained an overpowered opponent to the demons (of whose expulsion the "Life of Antony" gives numerous examples): a free spirit, in continuous dialogue with the "great Other."

Meditations and prayers formed – sometimes in connection with breathing techniques[5] – the concrete figures of the dialogues with the spiritual "double." They were supported by ascetic practices, which took a prominent position amongst solitude techniques. The Stoic "citadelle intérieure" was mounted – just like the monastery – through a systematic disciplining of desire and affects. Sexual abstinence, physical deprivation and other purification rituals were often considered requirements for successful *meléte*; and occasionally a considerable degree of creativity was invested in the invention of experimental arrangements. These exercises had the task to establish and test the independence of individuals from the external world.

> For example, in Plutarch's *De Genio Socratis*, one gives oneself over to very hard sporting activities. Or one tempts oneself by placing oneself in front of many tantalizing dishes and then renouncing these appetizing dishes. Then you call your slaves and give them the dishes, and you take the meal prepared for the slaves. Another example is Seneca's eighteenth letter to Lucilius. He prepares for a great feast day by acts of mortification of the flesh in order to convince himself that poverty is not an evil and that he can endure it. (Foucault, "Technologies of the Self" 37)

Askésis (of diet, of sexuality or of sleep) was of course also practised amongst the Christian desert monks; later it formed the centre of numerous monastic rules. In 358, Basil the Great wrote from his hermitage to Gregory of Nazianzus that solitude was of greatest help:

> quieting our passions, and giving leisure to our reason to uproot them completely from the soul. Just as animals, if they are stroked, are more easily subdued, so desires, wraths, fears, and griefs, the venomous evils of the soul, if they have lulled to sleep by silence and have not been kept aflame by constant provocation, are more easily overcome by reason. Therefore,

choose a place such as ours, removed from association with men, so that nothing from the outside will interrupt the constant practices of the ascetic life. (St Basil 7)

Occasionally, it was attempted to infer the solitude techniques of antiquity from the effects of intoxicants consumed: hence the "temptations of Saint Anthony" emanated from the poisons of scorpions (which liked to stay in rock tombs), while, for example, the "escapism" of Marcus Aurelius occurred as the result of a veritable opium addiction. Entirely disregarding the arguments that Pierre Hadot (*The Inner Citadel* 250–57) is able to summon against Thomas W. Africa's thesis of the "opium addiction" of the emperor-philosopher, the impression of a confusion imposes itself: Marcus Aurelius was no Thomas De Quincey, and the anchorite in the Thebaid no Arthur Rimbaud. While for the experts of ancient solitude techniques it was about disciplining soliloquy, about an "ego limitation" through orientation towards the "great Other": and indeed in a culture which knew countless possibilities of "possession," the avant-gardists of the nineteenth and twentieth centuries sought a methodically controlled "delimitation" of the ego – in a culture which hoped to open up all "possessions" to therapeutic interest. The "great Other" of Baudelaire was therefore called Joseph Moreau de Tours; and the "great Other" of Rimbaud was called Charles Baudelaire. This "God" was referred to by the sixteen-year-old in his letter to Paul Demeny (from 15 May 1871) – which became famous as the second "Seer Letter" – in which he postulated the exceeding of any self-knowledge through a kind of poetic alchemy:

The first study of the man who wants to be a poet is the knowledge of himself, complete. He seeks out his soul, inspects it, tests it, learns it. As soon as he knows it, he must cultivate it; It seems simple: in every mind a natural development takes place; so many *egoists* call themselves authors, there are many others who attribute their intellectual progress *to themselves*! – But the soul must be made monstrous: in the fashion of the comprachicos, if you will! Imagine a man implanting and cultivating warts on his face. I say one must be a *seer*, make oneself a *seer*. The Poet makes himself a *seer* by a long, gigantic and rational *derangement* of *all the senses*. All forms of love, suffering, and madness. He searches himself. He exhausts all poisons in himself and keeps only the quintessences. (Rimbaud 377)

Rimbaud dreamed of a solitude technique of excesses and unleashing, which makes wood suddenly realise that it is a violin (or brass that it is a trumpet);[6] in contrast, the early Christian solitude technicians rather dreamed of a "divine plectrum," which uses the disciplined spirit of the pious monks as a "harp or lyre" (St Justin Martyr 383).[7]

Je est un autre: Rimbaud famously escaped. The myth of his biography wasn't based on the early poems alone, but also on that solitary-nomadic life which perhaps connected him more closely to the Egyptian desert monks, as the project of a poetic prophecy (not to mention the ecstasies of drug indulgence). For separation, departure, *anachōresis* and at least the imagination of another place are among the oldest solitude techniques. Solitude techniques are *heterotopic* practices. They project the desired (or feared) effects of solitude onto that foreign place in which we are alone. Solitude is, as it were, modelled as a "place of solitude"; and the history of solitude techniques can hence also be developed as the history of ideas of solitude places.[8] All uninhabited places where humans can only live poorly are solitude places: the rock caves of Anthony the anchorite, the seas of Odysseus (or of the misanthropic captain who took on the name of the cunning sailor), the deserts of the Syrian pillar saints, the forests of Percival or Dante (to the forests of Thoreau), the mountains (from Petrarch's *Mont Ventoux* to *Monte Verità*), the islands of Robinson or Rousseau, the deserted steppes of all "frontier" movements (be it in the East or West), the icy polar regions of research expeditions, the interstellar spaces of the cosmonauts. It is not uncommon for solitude places to be centres of an "inverted world," in which the dead are more powerful than the living, and the servants stronger than the masters; already the lively imagination of solitude places – in whose development the forest can convert to a desert,[9] the island to a cave, the sea to an ice zone – facilitates meditation: as if one's own centre was identical with uninhabitable emptiness, the "no-man's-land" of freedom, but also the realm of the "great Other" and all competing demons. In his "Observations on the Feeling of the Beautiful and Sublime" of 1764, Kant notes: "Deep solitude is sublime, but in a terrifying way. For this reason great and extensive wastes, such as the immense deserts of Schamo in Tartary, have always given us occasion to people them with fearsome shades, goblins, and ghosts" (*Observations* 16–17). Solitude techniques are *heterotopic* practices: notably, this assertion can be demonstrated through "The Spiritual Exercises of Saint Ignatius of Loyola." Already the first exercise starts with a

> composition, seeing the place. Here it is to be observed that in the contemplation or meditation of a visible object, as in contemplating Christ or Lord, Who is visible, the composition will be to see with the eye of the imagination the corporeal place where the object I wish to contemplate is found. I say the corporeal place, such as the Temple or the mountain where Jesus Christ is found, or our Lady, according to that which I desire to contemplate. In a meditation on an invisible thing, such as the present meditation on sins, the composition will be to see with the eyes of the imagination and to consider that my soul is imprisoned in this corruptible body, and my whole compound self in this vale [of misery] as in exile amongst brute beasts; say my whole self, composed of soul and body. (St Ignatius of Loyola 53–54)

The following places are presented with the further meditation exercises: the "synagogues, towns and villages through which Christ our Lord went preaching," the "cave of the Nativity," the "vast plain embracing the whole region of Jerusalem," another "plain, in the region of Babylon," the "road from Bethany to Jerusalem," the "road from Mount Sion to the valley of Jehoshaphat," the "holy sepulchre" or the "house of our Lady," particularly "her oratory" (77, 91, 101, 136, 141, 149).

4

Solitude places are usually characterised not just by the absence of humans, but also by uniformity and homogeneity: deserts, seas, forests, steppes or snowfields form (at first sight at least) monotonous surroundings in which one can get easily lost. But just this uniformity facilitates the appearance of demons, guises of the "great Other," angels and geniuses: in this regard, the wasteland [*Einöde*] functions like every flat stone, a tablet made of clay or wax, canvas, papyrus or a sheet of paper. The place of solitude allows, precisely through its appearance poor in differences, the most multifaceted, colourful performances of meanings and symbols which – as signs on an anonymous surface, as actors in the arena as it were – augment their semantic radiance in front of a neutral stage. Thus, Basil writes in the already-cited letter in praise of solitude (to Gregory of Nazianzus) that the exercises "of the heart" consisted in

> the unlearning of worldly teachings which previously held possession of the heart. Just as it is not possible to write in wax without first smoothing down the letters already engraved upon it, so it is impossible to impart the divine teachings to the soul without first removing from it the conceptions arising from worldly experiences. (1: 6)

Basil of course describes what he himself (like Seneca in the XXVth letter to Lucilius) is doing at the moment – he puts the recommendation of a "tabula rasa," which is symbolically represented by the desert, on a wax tablet; prayer and meditation are supplemented by writing and reading. Writing and reading are extraordinarily important solitude techniques (which are of course mentioned at the very beginning of Philo's lists already cited): possibly the "great Other," this "higher self" of self-interaction, can only be attained through writing anyway. This impression imposes itself by reading the observations of Marcus Aurelius: their common title – "ta eis heauthon" – refers to the genus of *hypomnémata*, of personal notes, and means in literal translation neither "meditations" nor "self-admonitions," but quite simply an address: "Writing concerning Himself" (Hadot, *The Inner Citadel* 21–34).

The *Soliloquies* and *Confessions* of Augustine are among the most important heirs of Marcus Aurelius's *hypomnémata*: basic texts of renewed forms of self-thematisation. In a key passage of the eighth book of his "confessions," Augustine tells of a conversion experience that resulted from reading. I am referencing the well-known, often commentated scene: Augustine sits in the garden, reads in the Pauline epistles; next to him is only his close friend Alypius, of whom it is said: "for I was no less secret when he was near." Augustine sinks into a "deep consideration" (*a fundo arcano alta consideratio*), in whose course his good and evil spirits (folly, vanity, sensuality, chastity) start to wrangle with each other; the passage in which the *antiquae amicae meae* pluck at the "fleshly garment" of the meditator is almost touching; they ask him sadly: *Dimittisne nos?* – and at once they menace: *a momento isto non erimus tecum ultra in aeternum*. Augustine feels torn, and indeed by the voices that he hears. An acoustic conflict is overtly described: *Et erubescebam nimis, quia illarum nugarum murmura adhuc audiebam, et cunctabundus pendebam* (in the translation of William Watts: "I blushed all this while to myself very much, for that I yet heard the muttering of those toys, and that I yet hung in suspense"). Augustine is not able to detach himself from the voices: *Ista controversia in corde meo non nisi de me ipso adversus me ipsum*. And quickly he leaves his friend because he feels a mighty "shower of tears" emerging. *Et ut totum effunderem cum vocibus suis, surrexi ab Alypio – solitudo mihi negotium flendi aptior suggerebatur – et secessi remotius, quam ut posset mihi onerosa esse etiam eius praesentia*. These "voices" (*vocibus suis*), which by the way don't sound anymore in the translation, belong to the "storm" which forces one into absolute solitude. Augustine throws himself under a fig tree in order to give the *flumina oculorum* free rein. At the peak of his emotional outburst, he hears the voice of a child (Augustine remarks explicitly: *quasi pueri an puellae, nescio*), which repeats in an insistent singing tune: *Tolle lege, tolle lege*. Augustine recognises immediately that this voice does *not* belong to his inner voices – he gets up, goes back to his friend and reaches for the Pauline epistles put aside. The passage suggests that Augustine perceived the voice of the book himself: as if the epistles with that (genderless) voice, which emerges in the process of reading, summoned him. He opens the book and, as is well known, reads the chapter that he first casts his eyes on: *et legi in silentio capitulum, quo primum coniecti sunt oculi mei* (St Augustine 445, 462f., 458f., 460f., 462f., 464f.). Augustine reads *in silentio*. This is important: after all the muttering and whispering of the voices, after the singing tune of the child's voice, the author of the *Confessions* reads *in silentio*. He reads silently – entirely unusual for a teacher of rhetoric who was astonished, on another occasion, that Ambrose was able to read without moving his tongue and lips.[10]

The passage, which Augustine eventually reads after this dramatically charged sequence of scenes, can actually only include a comment on the right voice. After the voices of the conflict between the *antiquae amicae meae* and the new virtues, after the surprising voice of the child, which as it were converts into the voice of the book – *Tolle, lege* – the voice of the apostle himself sounds *in silentio*. Its message concerns the "great Other": "Not in rioting and drunkenness, not in chambering and wantonness, not in strife and envying: but put ye on the Lord Jesus Christ; and make no provision for the flesh, to fulfil the lusts thereof" (St Augustine 465; cf. *New Jerusalem Bible*, Romans 13.13–16). The voice articulates a "calling" by deploying a new "higher self": a "guardian," like Seneca recommended to

Lucilius. This "guardian" Petrarch still wanted to hear again – almost one thousand years later – as he tells in his letter about the ascent to the top of *Mont Ventoux* (dated 26 April 1336). To his friend *Francesco Dionigi di Robertis* from *Borgo San Sepolcro* in Tuscany, an early humanist, Augustinian monk, professor of theology and philosophy at the Sorbonne in Paris, the poet writes of great perspectives.

> The Pyrenean range, boundary of France and Spain, was not visible, not because of any intervening obstacle, but because of the weakness of human vision. On the other hand I could clearly see the Cévennes to the right, and to the left the sea beyond Marseilles and Aigues-Mortes, all several days' journey distant. The Rhone itself lay under our eyes. (Petrarca 49)

Yet, notoriously the poet does not enjoy the view for long, but soon opens the *Confessions* of Augustine that he brought onto the mountain peak.

> While I was admiring all these features, now recognizing some earthly object, now uplifting my soul, like my body, it occurred to me to look at the *Confessions* of Augustine, the gift of your love. (I keep it always with me, for the sake of the author and of the donor. It's of pocket size, but its small volume contains infinite sweetness.)

There, he instantly discovers the moral objection against the aesthetic pleasure in viewing the landscape: "Men go to admire the high mountains and the great flood of the seas and the wide-rolling rivers and the ring of Ocean and the movements of the stars; and they abandon themselves!" (49). Petrarch closes the book in order to really open it in spirit; he turns away from the mountain – and his view towards the inside: "Then, sated with sight of the mountain, I turned my inward eye upon myself [...]" The word of Augustine silences him – and leads him to an extended letter passage about the acoustic circumstances of callings since Anthony, Athanasius or Augustine (49f.).

More recent revelations require alphabetisation. Thus, the "great Others," "witnesses" and "guardians" do not just originate in "spiritual exercises" or meditations, but also in the techniques of reading and writing (as the metaphorisation of solitude places already suggests). The letters "to oneself" – from Plato to Epictetus, from Seneca to Marc Aurel, from Augustine to Petrarch – create a strategic "doubling-up"; the "doubles" of every "Confessio": self-techniques refer to media techniques (and vice versa). The reader splits up into a talking and a listening self; the writer splits up into author and addressee of his texts (regardless of whether he composes dialogues or letters); when Montaigne cites Seneca's suggestion to imagine Cato or Scipio as companion in solitude, he envisages Nero's educator as his own "Monsieur Teste." Reading and writing as self-talk: to this day, it has remained unclear what Niccolo Machiavelli – after his political fall – actually did as soon as he entered his office (the *studio*). In his infamous letter to the Florentine envoy *Francesco Vettori* in Rome, he wrote about his life in exile on 10 December 1513:

> When evening comes, I go back home, and go to my study. On the threshold I take off my work clothes, covered in mud and filth, and put on the clothes an ambassador would wear. Decently dressed, I enter the ancient courts of rulers, who have long since died. There I am warmly welcomed, and I feed on the only food I find nourishing, and was born to savor. I am not ashamed to talk to them, and to ask them to explain their actions. And they, out of kindness, answer me. Four hours go by without my feeling any anxiety. I forget every worry. I am no longer afraid of poverty, or frightened of death. I love entirely through them. And because Dante says there is no point in studying unless you remember what you have learned, I have made notes of what seem to me the most important things I have learned in my dialogue with the dead. (Machiavelli 3)

It remains uncertain whether Machiavelli merely wanted to allegorically enhance the process of reading and writing – or whether he actually held solitary conversations with the ancient notables. Did the self, hurt by political disempowerment, have to be restored through systematic identification with the ancient "guardians" and "doubles"? Did the author of the "Principe" use to read aloud what he wrote down? Or did he read to himself what he hoped to give a written reply to – as a case study?

Advanced cultures are systems in which solitude can be practised and trained: as systems that not only facilitate a methodical individualism, but also the belonging to several social groupings. Therefore, advanced cultures are commonly also systems in which one can complain about large numbers of people – and desire solitude. Civilisation is the cultivation of the "ability to be alone" (cf. Marquard). This ability to be alone – as self-technical competence – correlates with the respective standards of communication technology. To put it bluntly: *Write to your neighbour as you would write to yourself.* Psycho-techniques ("meditations" in the literal sense) are media techniques (and vice versa). Friedrich Kittler has emphatically deciphered this relationship through the example of the Romantic "double" figures (cf. Kittler): precisely by blowing up the alleged identity of the empirical and transcendental ego (the old "guardian" self), the "doubles" (of Chamisso and Hoffmann to Meyrink) simply second the transition from a (acoustically dominated) system of poetry and reading to a (optically dominated) system of photography, film and the cinematographically conditioned gaze. The "new media" meanwhile establish new "guardians" and "witnesses": in the form of those "mother double" machines that also enable the mute to present his being-"in-myself" [*"inmich"-Sein*] (cf. Sellin). At least since Birger Sellin, a new epoch of specific solitude techniques – from the "Game Boy" to the "Walkman" – has irrevocably begun.

disclosure statement

No potential conflict of interest was reported by the author.

notes

1 The essay was originally published as "Mit sich allein. Einsamkeit als Kulturtechnik," *Einsamkeit. Archäologie der literarischen Kommunikation VI*, ed. Aleida and Jan Assmann (Munich: Fink, 2000) 27–44.

2 Cf. de Montaigne 17. Here, the author cites a verse from the *Elegies* [Liber III, XIX, 12], which by now are not attributed to Tibullus anymore.

3 Self-*limitation* – not self-*dissolution* – was the intent, by all means in the sense of Luhmann (41): "In jedem Falle gilt mithin: das Ich ist Selbstlimitation."

4 Cf. Hadot, *Philosophy* 91: "Platonic dialogues are model exercises."

5 Cf. particularly regarding the hesychastic breathing prayer (from *hesychia*, "sweet repose"), Lockhart 12–20.

6 Ibid. 371: "It is too bad for the wood which finds itself a violin," or 375: "If brass wakes up a trumpet, it is not its fault."

7 T.N. Even though included in the English translation of his writings, the "Exhortation to the Greeks," where this quote originates, is today no longer attributed to St Justin Martyr. The reference in the original German is to Pseudo-Justinus, "Mahnrede an die Hellenen," *Bibliothek der Kirchenväter*, Band XXXIII (Kempten: Kösel, 1917).

8 Cf. first attempts in Augé.

9 Cf. the highly instructive treatise of Jacques Le Goff, "The Wilderness in the Medieval West."

10 Ibid. 273: "But when he was reading, he drew his eyes along over the leaves, and his heart searched into the sense, but his voice and tongue were silent." Cf. also Manguel 42f.

bibliography

Aristotle. "Politics." *Aristotle in 23 Volumes, Vol. 21*. Trans. H. Rackham. Cambridge, MA: Harvard UP; London: Heinemann, 1944. Web. 22 Jan. 2020. <http://www.perseus.tufts.edu/hopper/text?doc=Perseus%3Atext%3A1999.01.0058%3Abook%3D1%3Asection%3D>.

Augé, M. *Orte und Nicht-Orte. Vorüberlegungen zu einer Ethnologie der Einsamkeit.* Trans. M. Bischoff. Frankfurt: Fischer, 1994. Print.

Ball, H. *Byzantinisches Christentum. Drei Heiligenleben.* Frankfurt: Insel, 1979. Print.

Censorinus. *The Birthday Book.* Trans. H.N. Parker. Chicago: U of Chicago P, 2007. Print.

de Montaigne, M. "Of Solitude." *The Complete Works of Montaigne.* Trans. D.M. Frame. Stanford: Stanford UP, 1957. Print.

Diogenes Laertius. *Lives of Eminent Philosophers.* Trans. R.D. Hicks. Cambridge, MA: Harvard UP, 1972. Web. 22 Jan. 2020. <http://www.perseus.tufts.edu/hopper/text?doc=Perseus%3Atext%3A1999.01.0258%3Abook%3D6>.

Dreitzel, H.-P. *Die Einsamkeit als soziologisches Problem.* Zurich: Arche, 1970. Print.

Foucault, M. *The Care of the Self: Volume 3, The History of Sexuality.* Trans. R. Hurley. London: Allen Lane, 1988. Print.

Foucault, M. "Technologies of the Self." *Technologies of the Self: A Seminar with Michel Foucault.* Ed. L.H. Martin, H. Gutman, and P.H. Hutton. Amherst: U of Massachusetts P, 1988. 16–49. Print.

Foucault, M., and R. Sennett. "Sexuality and Solitude." *London Review of Books* 3.9 (1981): 4–7. Print.

Hadot, P. *The Inner Citadel: The Meditations of Marcus Aurelius.* Trans. M. Chase. London: Harvard UP, 2001. Print.

Hadot, P. *Philosophy as a Way of Life: Spiritual Exercises from Socrates to Foucault.* Trans. M. Chase. Oxford: Blackwell, 1995. Print.

Hiriyanna, M. *The Essentials of Indian Philosophy.* London: Allen, 1978. Print.

Kant, I. *Critique of Pure Reason.* Trans. P. Guyer and A.W. Wood. Cambridge: Cambridge UP, 1998. Print.

Kant, I. *Observations on the Feeling of the Beautiful and Sublime and Other Writings.* Ed. P. Frierson and P. Guyer. Cambridge: Cambridge UP, 2011. Print.

Kittler, F. "Romanticism, Psychoanalysis, Film: A Story of Doubles." *The Truth of the Technological World: Essays on the Genealogy of Presence.* Trans. E. Butler. Stanford: Stanford UP, 2013: 69–83. Print.

Le Goff, J. "The Wilderness in the Medieval West." *The Medieval Imagination.* Trans. A. Goldhammer. Chicago: U of Chicago P, 1992. 47–59. Print.

Lockhart, R.B. *Halfway to Heaven: The Hidden Life of the Carthusians.* London: Darton, 1999. Print.

Luhmann, N. "Die Autopoiesis des Bewußtseins." Ed. A. Hahn and V. Kapp. *Selbstthematisierung und Selbstzeugnis: Bekenntnis und Geständnis.* Frankfurt: Suhrkamp, 1987. Print.

Machiavelli, N. *Selected Political Writings.* Trans. D. Wootton. Indianapolis, IN: Hackett, 1994. Print.

Macho, T.H. "Auferstehung der Toten. Notiz zur Logik der Besessenheit." *Perspektiven. Magazin für Stadtarchitektur und Lebensqualität* 3 (1992): 34–36. Print.

Macho, T.H. "Himmel als Abgrund. Fragment über den Geburtstag." *Manuskripte* 100 (1988): 223–30. Print.

Macho, T.H. "Zeichen aus der Dunkelheit. Notizen zu einer Theorie der Psychose." Ed. R. Heinz, D. Kamper, and U. Sonnemann. *Wahnwelten im Zusammenstoß. Die Psychose als Spiegel der Zeit.* Berlin: Akademie, 1993. 225–29. Print.

Manguel, A. *A History of Reading.* London: Flamingo, 1997. Print.

Marquard, O. "Plädoyer für die Einsamkeitsfähigkeit." *Skepsis und Zustimmung. Philosophische Studien.* Stuttgart: Reclam, 1994. Print.

Mauss, M. "Techniques of the Body." *Economy and Society* 2.1 (1973): 70–88. Print.

New Jerusalem Bible. London: Darton, 1985. Print.

Petrarca, F. "The Ascent of Mont Ventoux." *Letters from Petrarch.* Ed. M. Bishop. Bloomington: Indiana UP, 1966. Print.

Philo. "Allegorical Interpretation, III." *The Works of Philo.* Trans. C.D. Yonge. Peabody, MA: Hendrickson, 1997. Print.

Philo. "Who is the Heir of Divine Things." *The Works of Philo.* Trans. C.D. Yonge. Peabody, MA: Hendrickson, 1997. Print.

Plato. *Ion.* Trans. B. Jowett. Web. 11 Feb. 2020. <http://classics.mit.edu/Plato/ion.html>.

Plato. "Phaedo." *Plato in Twelve Volumes, Vol. 1.* Trans. H.N. Fowler. Cambridge, MA: Harvard UP; London: Heinemann, 1966. Web. 22 Jan. 2020. <http://www.perseus.tufts.edu/hopper/text?doc=Perseus%3Atext%3A1999.01.0170%3Atext%3DPhaedo%3Asection%3D67d>.

Plato. "Phaedrus." *Plato in Twelve Volumes, Vol. 9.* Trans. H.N. Fowler. Cambridge, MA: Harvard UP; London: Heinemann, 1925. Web. 11 Feb. 2020. <http://www.perseus.tufts.edu/hopper/text?doc=Perseus%3Atext%3A1999.01.0174%3Atext%3DPhaedrus%3Asection%3D244b>.

Plato. *The Republic.* Trans. B. Jowett. Web. 16 Jan. 2020. <http://classics.mit.edu/Plato/republic.11.x.html>.

Rakusa, I., ed. *Einsamkeiten. Ein Lesebuch.* Frankfurt: Insel, 1996. Print.

Rimbaud, A. *Complete Works, Selected Letters.* Trans. W. Fowlie. Chicago: U of Chicago P, 2005. Print.

Schmidt, W. *Geburtstag im Altertum.* Giessen: Töpelmann, 1908. Print.

Schweitzer, A. *Indian Thought and its Development.* Trans. C.E.B. Russell. London: Black, 1951. Print.

Sellin, B. *Ich will kein inmich mehr sein: botschaften aus einem autistischen kerker.* Ed. M. Klonovsky. Cologne: Kiepenheuer, 1993. Print.

Seneca, L.A. *Seneca: Epistles 1–65.* Trans. R.M. Gummere. London: Harvard UP, 1917. Print.

Starobinski, J. *Besessenheit und Exorzismus. Drei Figuren der Umnachtung.* Trans. H. Kossodo. Frankfurt: Ullstein, 1978. Print.

St Athanasius. "Life of Antony." *Select Works and Letters.* Ed. H. Wace and P. Schaff. Oxford: Parker; New York: Christian Literature, 1892. Print.

St Augustine. *Confessions, Books I–VIII.* Trans. W. Watts. Cambridge, MA: Harvard UP, 1995. Print.

St Basil. *Letters, Volume I (1–185).* Trans. Sister A.C. Way. Washington, DC: Catholic U of America P, 1965. Print.

St Ignatius of Loyola. *The Spiritual Exercises of Saint Ignatius of Loyola.* Trans. W.H. Longridge. London: Mowbray, 1950. Print.

St Justin Martyr [sic]. *Writings of Saint Justin Martyr.* Trans. T.B. Falls. Washington, DC: Catholic U of America P, 1965. Print.

Thoreau, H.D. *Walden or, Life in the Woods and On the Duty of Civil Disobedience.* New York: Harper, 1965. Print.

Valéry, P. *Cahiers/Notebooks 1.* Trans. P. Gifford, S. Miles, R. Pickering, and B. Stimpson. Frankfurt: Lang, 2000. Print.

Valéry, P. *Monsieur Teste.* Trans. J. Matthews. London: Routledge, 1973. Print.

von Worms, A. *The Book of the Sacred Magic of Abramelin the Mage, As Delivered by Abraham the Jew unto his Son Lamech, A.D. 1458.* Trans. S.L. MacGregor Mathers. London: Watkins, 1900. Web. 22 Jan. 2020. <https://www.sacred-texts.com/grim/abr/index.htm>.

I the theme: anthropotechnics and the absolute imperative

Peter Sloterdijk's *You Must Change Your Life*, subtitled *On Anthropotechnics*, is one of several recent books that has helped to reshape the discussion about the catastrophe that has befallen modern life and thought in an epoch marked by the predominance of globalization and planetary technology, twin developments that are in turn directly related to several others, including the growing ecological catastrophe, and questions and concerns over whether humanity is now transitioning from the era of the human to what has been called for lack of a better term, the "posthuman." If we do not err in seeing Peter Sloterdijk's book as a response to this growing catastrophe, then one of its noteworthy qualities is that it begins and ends with an imperative. These two imperatives, which are in effect two instances of a recurring imperative that Sloterdijk calls the "Absolute Imperative," express the fact of our distress in a modernity that not only has eliminated most if not all forms of otherworldly transcendence, religious or otherwise, in favor of the demand for unconditional development that punctuates a neoliberal existence; it is also a modernity that has become both wary and weary of the promise of progress that has, if anything, brought us ever closer to a future of no future. I use the word "catastrophe" not only in the sense of a disastrous event, but of an overturning of the status quo that, to be sure, may not be all that sudden, but whose effects are now felt at an accelerating pace. It is in relation to this state of affairs that one can ask whether and to what extent the tradition of philosophical thought, which has until

patrick roney

ANTHROPOTECHNICS AND THE ABSOLUTE IMPERATIVE

now provided the foundations for our ethics and politics, offers any effective response to our situation, particularly the tradition of humanism in its various guises, or whether the catastrophe that has befallen life and thought entails that this same tradition must also face its overturning. Is it not the case that we who live in this time must face a future for which we are unprepared – for the *unprecedented* in short? And must not thinking find new ways of responding to the unprecedented insofar as time enters into the heart of our ethical deliberations in terms of the growing realization that we may be out of time?[1] It is the "must" of these, my own variations on Sloterdijk's imperatives, that deserves attention.

Sloterdijk's formulation of the two imperatives that serve as bookends for his renowned and somewhat controversial tome (a controversy, I will say straight away, that does not interest me here) restates on the one hand perhaps the oldest ethic of the Western tradition, that of *askesis*, in terms of a new language that Sloterdijk calls *anthropotechnics*. On the other hand, it offers us an imperative, uttered in the sublime style, that speaks directly to the unprecedented nature of our present. Both are characterized as imperatives that are, in a word, *absolute*. The first is expressed in the title itself and is taken from one of Rilke's most striking poems, the "Archaic Torso of Apollo" (in German: *Archaischer Torso Apollos*) – striking, I might add, for its abruptness. It is a line that literally cuts into verse that is cast largely into the subjunctive mood and that plays on the presence of an absence and vice versa: the broken torso of the god, the fragment of a past to which we moderns no longer belong, still "holds fast and shines" with a presence that "otherwise would stand deformed and curt" (*sonst stünde dieser Stein enstellt und kurz*). It is, as Sloterdijk names it, an aesthetic imperative; it is a *command* (*ein Befehl*) that comes from the thing itself, the stone. The second iteration of the imperative comes after a sustained meditation on the consequences of modernity's drive to shape all of existence according to the horizontal dimension of world-and-self-improvement, an "ethic" that has devolved into the empty drive for development without end. In the realm of technology, human beings now find themselves threatened both in their being and in their continued existence by the imminent dangers of biotechnology, particularly in the form of human cloning, artificial intelligence, and climate change. Sloterdijk's second imperative reads, "the only fact of universal ethical significance in the current world is the diffusely and ubiquitously growing realization [*Einsicht*] that things cannot continue in this way" (*You Must Change* 442). He characterizes it both as sublime and absolute in a way that seems to echo both the Kantian sublime on the one hand and a "Zarathustrian" sublime on the other: it is a call "to everyone and no one," and, "Whoever hears the call without defenses will experience the sublime in a personally addressed form. The sublime is that which, by calling to mind the overwhelming, shows the observer the possibility of their engulfment by the oversized" (443).[2] In this dual aspect, both Nietzschean and Kantian, the imperative seems to call upon us in a very individual way to bear witness to the overpowering might of Nature in a new sense – two senses in fact: first of all, with the advent of biotechnology, and second, with climate change. Both are part and parcel of the growing realization that we, contemporary human beings, have entered into an age where "Nature" (the scare quotes are meant to draw attention to the now untenable metaphysical dualism to which it belongs) and the Human have become indistinguishable, and where the agency of "Nature" has become a critical factor of our politics. This new epoch is one that has often been referred to as the Anthropocene.[3] This final imperative also exhorts us individually to go beyond ourselves, beyond the human in particular, towards that which characterizes the human in its essence, namely, the extreme, the excessive, the ecstatic – the specific terms that Sloterdijk employs are *das Ungeheuer*, "the monstrous" in the sense the immense or the immeasurable, and *Unheimlichkeit*, the "not being at home" that is so central to Martin Heidegger's existential analytic of Dasein.

the penultimate imperative: gelassenheit

What is it that distinguishes these imperatives as absolute, and who or what authorizes them? My aim in this essay is not only to address these questions, but to show what is at stake in posing them. They are not, I maintain, idle ones. My hope is not only to gain a greater understanding of the strange and indeed "monstrous" nature of the imperative that Sloterdijk addresses to everyone and no one, but also to determine whether and to what extent an *absolute* imperative represents an effective response, perhaps the only one left to us in this, our time. If "we" who are everyone and no one are indeed out of time; if the ones who utter, who receive and who act on the imperative are as yet undecided, then *how* does Sloterdijk's idea of anthropotechnics make the saying, hearing and acting on this imperative a possibility? Are "we" any closer to hearing what needs to be heard once the anthropotechnical maneuver reaches our ears? One of my claims in this essay is that anthropotechnics is not merely a new theory, borne out of the desire to resuscitate a philosophical anthropology, but an intervention – Sloterdijk calls it a "manoeuvre" (*Manöver*) – and a response to the extreme *Unheimlichkeit* of our contemporary being-in-the-world.

Characterizing his efforts as I have in terms of the *Unheimlichkeit* of Dasein's *In-der-Welt-sein*, it should be obvious that Sloterdijk's relation to, indeed, his *Auseinandersetzung* with Heidegger's thought is of primary concern here. As any reader of Sloterdijk is aware, Heidegger represents one of his primary interlocutors. My focus will be on the Heidegger of the question concerning technology and of the *Kehre*, a "turn" not so much away from or against technology but towards establishing a free relationship to it. Since for Heidegger, technology is a mode of Being's unveiling and veiling in a modernity that could stretch on indefinitely, the "turn" to which he appeals does not amount to an overcoming of technology for the sake of founding a different order of being, as if that were within Dasein's powers, as it is a matter of preparation – the preparing of a space in which the technological could indeed be *heard* in a different way. This Heidegger named *Gelassenheit*. The relevance of this to the discussion here is that Sloterdijk also sees Heidegger's *Gelassenheit* as an imperative, perhaps the last one within the metaphysical tradition but which also indicates a transition towards a decentered mode of presencing, that is, towards a plural ontology of being-in-the-world as, to use his phrase, "being-in-foam."[4] If, as Sloterdijk has traced out across his many works, Christianity had found the authority for its imperative in God, Kant in the moral person, and Rilke in the thing itself – that is, the stone – then Heidegger had found it in Being, although here the authority does not take the form of a command but of a hint that may or may not be heard by Dasein.

My treatment of Sloterdijk's confrontation with Heidegger over his response to technology will interrogate the reasons why he finds *Gelassenheit* as a response to technology fundamentally flawed, and why *anthropotechnics* as a "maneuver" presents a far better one. To briefly mention the point of disagreement, *Gelassenheit* remains tied to the Christian idea of grace, since it implies that the saving power can only come from outside, from Being, and that our only task is to prepare a space for Being's possible advent. This despite the fact that it was Heidegger's existential ontology that had struck the decisive blow against otherworldly transcendence, or "world-flight" (Sloterdijk, *You Must Change* 439). In a time when we are out of time, Sloterdijk refuses to follow the path of *Gelassenheit*, at least in part, not only because it fails to address the urgency of our situation, but also because it does not think the essence of technology as world-disclosing adequately enough. To do so is the task of anthropotechnics, and the question concerning what is at stake in Sloterdijk's enunciation of an absolute imperative has a direct connection to a rethinking of the very essence of technology, a rethinking that exceeds Heidegger's thought even as it follows in his footsteps. "Anthropotechnics" names in effect the co-immunitary constitution of human beings as our mode of being-in-the-world, and in so doing recasts our history in terms of technologies both past, present, and future that are themselves modes of dwelling.

The rest of the essay will proceed in two parts. The first will address the nature of the absolute imperative uttered in the final pages of *You Must Change Your Life* and show whether and how it can be distinguished from both the categorical imperative of Kantian ethics, and Rilke's aesthetic imperative that appeals to the force of the Dionysian most closely associated with Nietzsche. Art, to speak to the latter for a moment, is the saving power that emerges once the appeal to otherworldliness has lost it power and the time of the overman, who shall remain true to the Earth, is on the horizon. By contrast, the absolute imperative is one that alone authorizes: "The only authority that is still in a position to say 'You must change your life!' is the global crisis," whose authority he describes as "real" and, he continues, "As it possesses the aura of the monstrous, it bears the primary traits that were previously ascribed to the transcendent powers" (Sloterdijk, *You Must Change* 444). These words indicate what direction this inquiry needs to follow. If it is indeed a matter of authority and of what authorizes, and if the collapse of all previous transcendent powers has already taken place – including and especially the end of all metaphysical systems[5] – then what is the nature of this authority and *who*, if anyone, is its author in the era of the death of the Author, when authorship has long been in retreat, becoming more or less a matter of intellectual property? If the call comes from the imminence of a future catastrophe that is already upon us, how then is it absolute?

The second part will continue to pursue these questions by addressing the "last Author" to appear in the history of metaphysics: Heidegger's notion of Being itself, or better to say, Being as it is thought in relation to the ontological difference. What will be discussed in this part are the merits of Sloterdijk's attempt to position Heidegger's appeal to Being itself as the final obstacle to a fully adequate response to the absolute imperative. If, as Heidegger suggested, the aim of the question concerning technology is to place ourselves in a free relationship to the essence of technology,[6] Sloterdijk's contention is that Heidegger fails to think the more essential possibilities of acting within a technological existence nearly enough, instead opting for the active-passivity of letting beings be, *Gelassenheit*. The aim of this discussion will be to ask whether Sloterdijk's rethinking of the essence of technology as anthropotechnics make the new form of a time-immemorial imperative possible, one that will be heeded in our time. An imperative without author that commands absolutely? A monstrous imperative indeed.

II from the categorical to the ecological imperative: kant and jonas

Any reader of the *Spheres* trilogy is aware that Sloterdijk's rewriting of a new, anthropotechnical history of human being amounts largely to the narration of a series of scenes. Accordingly, in *You Must Change Your Life* this rewriting focuses on a succession of ascetic practices ranging from the ancient to the modern that are themselves punctuated by imperatives. Anthropotechnics, the "legitimate successor to metaphysics" takes the form of a General Immunology and produces in effect a new definition of the essence of human being as *Homo immunologicus*: human beings are those who must build a "world," who must "en-house" themselves by means of three systems of protection – biological, sociocultural, and symbolic. These immune systems negotiate the many and malleable relations between an "inside" and an "outside." Whether or not Sloterdijk would accept my suggestion that a new idea of human essence emerges from his thinking is not certain, since for him *practice* is the category around which everything turns and which *over*-turns the very concept of essence. In addition, his further claim is that this postmetaphysics also represents the "real theory of 'religions'" (Sloterdijk, *You Must Change* 451); that is to say, religious practices are seen as various instances of the human will-to-verticality through which they secede from the everyday. One of the important features of modernity however, as Sloterdijk points out so often, is the transposition of the vertical movement back into the world, a move that complicates it considerably. Nowhere is this more the case than in Kant's moral theory, whose categorical imperative casts the vertical dimension solely in terms of pure reason, a reason that is both practical in essence, and human.[7]

Despite its significance, what is remarkable about Sloterdijk's treatment of the categorical imperative and Kant's moral philosophy in general is how little he has to say about it. It is mentioned often, but almost always as a foil for the idea of the absolute imperative. The absolute imperative is one that "exceeds the options of the hypothetical and the categorical" (Sloterdijk, *You Must Change* 25). Rather than a call to act according to the unconditional as dictated by pure reason, the absolute imperative rests on "the authority to a different life in this life. The authority touches on a subtle insufficiency within me that is older and freer than sin; it is my innermost not-yet" (26). At first blush, this repeats Kant in another form: substitute the "vertical" or the "monstrous" for pure practical reason's unconditional desire – the desire to transcend our sensible, pathological appetites – and the categorical imperative is preserved. Nevertheless, Sloterdijk is at pains to distance himself from Kant, and it is not so much what is said about the categorical imperative, which is in truth very little, but what is not. Neither in *You Must Change Your Life* nor in any other of his published works can one find any sustained discussion. The only place where it receives any kind of attention is in a short lecture entitled, "Absoluter and kategorischer Imperativ," which is included in the collection *Nach Gott*, and even there Kant's imperative is mentioned only to be quickly dismissed in favor of an updated form of the imperative, found in the work of Hans Jonas, that is deemed more appropriate for our time.

After characterizing our age as "ein Zeitalter der globalen Sorge und uberdies ein Zeitalter der Desorientierung" (*Nach Gott* 301), Sloterdijk briefly interprets the categorical imperative in what seems to be Hegelian terms. It is, he writes, Kant's attempt to reconcile the egoism of private interest with the claims of the public good, a reconciliation that will make a bourgeois society possible (302). That is all. He then briefly moves on to its Marxist rendering, and then to its reformulation by Hans Jonas as an ecological imperative, and it is Jonas' imperative that occupies most of the rest of the lecture.

Before addressing Jonas' reformulation, it is important to consider the significance of this lacuna. Sloterdijk sums up the problem with the categorical imperative thus: "In einer kantischen und einer marxistischen Welt weiß man prinzipiell immer genau, was zu tun ist […] Das Richtige ist nur zeitweilig aufgeschoben, kann aber nie inaktuell werden" (*Nach Gott* 303).[8] In other words, under the aegis of the Enlightenment idea of progress, time does not matter; the future, though it may be *aufgeschoben* – deferred or delayed – is both present and certain. However, in the age of global crisis and disorientation, that certainty has vanished and the future becomes a source of profound anxiety.

Consider for a moment what is left out of this cursory treatment of Kant's imperative. Kant's formulation of the basic law of pure practical reason, "So act that the maxim of your will could always hold at the same time as a principle of a universal legislation (Gesetzgebung)" (45), places the emphasis squarely on reason's capacity to be self-legislative, and in and through the act of giving the law to itself human reason affirms its *autonomy*. Yet as is widely recognized, there is a second formulation of the imperative which runs, "Act so that you treat humanity, whether in your own person or in that of another, always as an end and never as a means only" (Kant 96 (V. 429)). "Humanity in the person" – the end that determines the will is not an external one but is rather the human being's own essence, the human being as person whose "personality" consists in the capability for being responsible. As Heidegger points out in his treatment of Kant's imperative, what is truly at stake is that the willing oneself as an *ought* discloses at the same time the essence of human freedom. Practical freedom is self-legislation, a fact whose ontological implications are not to be missed: "Freedom now reveals itself as the *condition of the possibility of the factuality of pure practical reason*" (Heidegger, *Freedom* 200). The essence of human being is none other than the essence of freedom in which we are disclosed to ourselves as persons who are capable of an originary self-binding – being responsible. Moreover, this originary capacity not only makes human beings manifest to themselves as persons, but makes possible the disclosure of being-in-the-world, and specifically, of beings *qua* beings encountered within it: "Freedom is the condition of the possibility of the manifestness of the being of beings, of the understanding of beings" (205).[9]

Why is it that Sloterdijk ignores such a central aspect of Kant's thought, namely, the question of human freedom and its relation to self-and-world-disclosure? One of the reasons seems to lie in his deployment of the anthropotechnical "maneuver" in which the question of freedom is translated into the language of general immunology, and into the set of anthropotechnical and specifically vertical praxes that, when seen from this perspective, form a history that goes by the name of a "General Ascetology." Hans Jonas' reworking of Kant's law of pure practical reason into an ecological imperative serves the purpose. This raises several questions: does Jonas' reworking preserve the question of freedom as an originary self-binding? And does Sloterdijk's appeal to the monstrous, *das Ungeheuer*, comprehend human being in the mode of self-responsibility or is this form of self-disclosure abandoned for the sake of another, quite different form of manifestness, call it the "immunized human being"? In short, is immunization still grounded upon freedom and is freedom still the condition of its possibility?

Let me recall Sloterdijk's definition of the absolute imperative. It is the call that comes from my "innermost not-yet" that, because of the insufficiency of my own finitude, compels me to transgress the status quo and its immune systems that provide me a dwelling place, a home. Hans Jonas, who writes under the shadow of the growing ecological crisis, reformulates Kant's imperative thus: "Act in such a way that the effects of your actions can be reconciled with the permanence of true human life on earth"[10] (Sloterdijk, *You Must Change* 448). What does Sloterdijk find so compelling about Jonas' idea? First, it forces us to acknowledge that there are deadlines (*Fristen*) in which, ecologically speaking, a different law other than the law of pure practical reason asserts itself: the law of irreversibility. Second, the fact that life on earth is now subject to the law of irreversibility shifts the locus of responsibility from self-legislation to general immunology. Life is a successful immune system [*die Erfolgphase eines Immunsystems*; Sloterdijk, *Nach Gott* 304]. This, he claims, is an axiom, one that repeats Jonas' claim that before any other imperatives, there must be an ontological imperative stating that, first and foremost, there *must be* mankind. Responsibility thus lies in preserving and developing successful immune systems that assure the continued survival of humanity, which are in effect combinations of private immunity and co-immunity structures. In the era of ecological catastrophe, our primary responsibility lies in the creation and preservation of the latter, that is, a "global solidarity system" based on "an ethos of global protection" (307). In the final pages of *You Must Change Your Life*, Sloterdijk affirms the value of Jonas' imperative as a "forward-looking philosophy" that binds me individually to a harsh and "overtaxing" form of responsibility that in effect represents a new and concrete instance of the monstrous: *act in such a way that you must estimate the effects of your actions on the ecology of the global society*. What Jonas' imperative accomplishes, in Sloterdijk's words, is to raise the categorical imperative to the absolute. Thus it seems in the end that what distinguishes between them is that "humanity" in Kant is replaced by "co-immunity," and so it is the absence of co-immunity structures on a global scale that describes our plight and prescribes the ends of our praxis – that is, our *imperative*. The coming battle, one that has already started, is the battle for global co-immunity.

One can thus describe Sloterdijk's absolute imperative as one where my innermost not-yet calls on me not to actualize my freedom *qua* the free binding of myself to the law, but to activate my agency for the sake of creating a global network of co-immunity in the wake of the imminent threat to human survival on earth. Although it may appear as if freedom has dropped out of the equation, I would suggest that it has instead taken on a Nietzschean coloring that could be characterized as the freedom of invention. The pithy saying, "Whoever goes in search of humans will find acrobats" (Sloterdijk, *You Must Change* 13), expresses this brilliantly. Although it would be too much for me to address Sloterdijk's deep and extensive affinities for Nietzsche's thought in this essay, I can at least indicate how he builds on Nietzsche's idea of the will the power as a will to free and innocent creation, and translates it into the language of anthropotechnics: the invention of new, one could say "monstrous" practices and technologies are needed to elevate humanity to a new level of shared survival. Sloterdijk affirms this unequivocally as the will to create new ascetic practices: "Another cycle of secessions may begin in order to lead humans out once again – if not out of the world, then at least out of dullness, dejection, and obsession, but above all out of banality" (441).

Sloterdijk's affinities with Nietzsche raise the question as to just how closely he follows in Jonas' footsteps. Jonas is no Nietzschean; he explicitly rejects Nietzsche's Overman as the basis for an ethics of technology.[11] Examining Jonas' basic position more in detail, it is easy to see what Sloterdijk finds attractive there, for Jonas' starting point is that traditional ethics, including Kantian ethics, fails to address the fundamental changes brought about by modern technology. This is the case insofar as the premises of traditional ethics are (a) human nature is immutable, (b) the human good is determinable, and (c) the range of human action is restricted to proximate human beings and not distant ones (Jonas 1). Technology has not only invalidated all of these premises but has introduced new ones, namely, (a) our ability to shape human beings genetically, (b) the distinction between good and evil becomes ever more undecidable, and (c) its effects take place over a very long period of time on a global scale.[12]

Consequently, traditional ethics is powerless to establish ethical norms in the age of technoscience; the latter has, in fact "destroyed the very idea of norm as such" (Jonas 22). Technological progress has put the very future of humanity at stake, and ethics can therefore no longer rest on the reciprocity of rights and duties, according to which my duty is the counterpart of another's right and vice versa. Ethics must therefore rest on the aforementioned axiom that there *be* a humanity; that is, it is an ontological premise that gives rise to a principle of action: act for the sake of self-preservation that must now be extended to the level of the species.

My contention is that Sloterdijk follows Jonas up to that point, however, the shift to anthropotechnics introduces a Nietzschean perspective that would mean in effect that the survival of the species cannot serve as the foundation for an ethics of technology. True, human beings need immune structures and cannot survive without them, however, the form of the absolute imperative today must of necessity be one that breaks with the stultifying repetitions of everyday life that have come to punctuate a modern, indeed neoliberal existence. The truism that humans are creatures of habit has only been amplified by a consumer economy. "Humans live in habits, not territories. Radical changes of location first of all attack the human rooting in habits" (Sloterdijk, *You Must Change* 407). On the one hand, globalization is responsible for the growing destruction of our *habitus*; on the other, it is no longer possible for us moderns to preserve the prevailing form of life as long as those forms remain within the modern *habitus*, meaning that new forms have to be invented. "The ethical distinction brings about the catastrophe of habits" (410), and at no time is this more the case than now.

In sum, the apparent reason why Sloterdijk rejects the categorical imperative is because it rests on the authority of pure practical reason as self-legislative. In the wake of the ever-accelerating development of technology, the *being* of our very humanity has been put into question, if indeed it has become a question at all;

this in turn places serious obstacles in the way of establishing ethical norms that would set proper limits on the "good" use of technology. We must therefore turn to another sort of human being – the human as acrobat – that is marked by a will to inventiveness that brings us to another form of the imperative, the aesthetic.

III the aesthetic imperative

As previously mentioned, Sloterdijk opens *You Must Change Your Life* with the claim that the aesthetic imperative, exemplified by Rilke's poem, represents the new form of the absolute imperative that appears at the beginning of the twentieth century (cf. page 23 of this essay). The virtues of the "command from the stone" are identified straightaway: art becomes an experiment of "allowing oneself to be told something" – that is, if there is a command at all, it is to expose us to a "non-enslaving experience of rank differences" (Sloterdijk, *You Must Change* 19). Works of art gain their non-coercive authority by proving themselves through self-exposure, "the powerless superiority of the work," which issues from "this singular thing that turns to me by demanding my full gaze" (19, 20). Insofar as it is a command that issues from the thing itself, the aesthetic imperative calls upon me to allow myself to be spoken to; thus our hearing the command depends on our capacity to transform our relation to things from one that represents them as objects that stand over and against a subject to one that lets the torso of Apollo come towards us as that stands there in all of its exemplary radiance and that *sees us*. It appears then that the reason why neither the religious nor the deontological forms of the absolute imperative can be heard in modernity is due to their coercive nature; both seek to bind us in the form of an unconditional *ought* that originates from the realm of the supersensible. By contrast, the superiority of art consists precisely in the way that it authorizes without appeal to an Author that lies outside the world. Singular beings in their sheer presence and their depth, brought to a stand in the work of art, alone command, and the command is less of a *Befehl* in the strict sense of an order, as it is a call, an appeal, *eine Appellkraft*.

It would seem then that art embodies a different kind of imperative, one that gathers up all previous religious, ethical, and ascetic imperatives and reduces them to an utterance that comes from no other place than beings themselves (Sloterdijk, *You Must Change* 25). Yet for all its apparent virtues, Sloterdijk ends his book by denying the power of the aesthetic imperative. "Today, the authoritative voice can scarcely be heard in works of art" (444). Why is this the case? Again, no explicit answer to the question is offered, and so the reasons have to be ferreted out from his other writings, but even there one will find few statements addressing the issue directly. This is no less true of an entire volume of lectures and essays dedicated to Art and the arts that bears the title *The Aesthetic Imperative*. Nonetheless there are a few clues one can find in a chapter on Nietzsche entitled "I Tell You: One Must Still have Chaos in One."[13]

In this brief essay, Sloterdijk affirms Nietzsche's idea of the will to power as art in the form of a command to experiment. "The world has become an experiment," and Nietzsche's *Zarathustra* is nothing less than the expression of this state of the world (Sloterdijk, *The Aesthetic Imperative* 249). This aesthetic response to modernity is then translated into anthropotechnical terms: "chaos is the authority of the monstrosity which creates conflict for people who usually exist in an ordered and finite situation" (250). And not only does it create conflict, this chaos-within-oneself constitutes the source for all creation. Quoting *Zarathustra*, "I tell you: one must still have chaos within one, to give birth to a dancing star" (250). There is a shift here whose drastic nature should not be missed: not chaos in general, but chaos as an original force within oneself, a perpetually restless drive to go over (*übergehen*), is named as the true source of authority. It seems therefore that the will to experiment corresponds to the appeal issuing from my finitude: the call from above actually originates from within, from my "innermost not-yet," which calls upon me to unleash the monstrous, that is, to go over from the static character of everyday existence to a different, future self. The appeal of art and the authority of a different life thus seem to merge, yet the implication seems to be that by the end of the century this incessant will to creativity had reached a closure. Sloterdijk's remarks in this particular piece are often gnomic, if not cryptic. Modernity, the incessant call of the monstrous, reaches a point of saturation when Zarathustra's appeal is addressed to everybody. "But I can see a time coming, the time when nobody will have anything left in them that is evil, messy and unpredictable [...] The history of improvements will reach its conclusion" (251–52). Might Sloterdijk be suggesting that monstrosity has been largely incorporated into the engine of modernity? In a way, yes; for what has become of the aesthetic imperative? It has become athletics: "The statement, 'You must change your life!' can now be heard as the refrain of a language of getting in shape." It is, as he says, the "coach discourse" (*You Must Change* 28).

In the absence of a clear argument, what evidence is there for this conclusion? At a historical level, one could argue from the fate of modernist and Avant-garde artistic experimentation. Not only has the Avant-garde more or less disappeared as an oppositional and indeed revolutionary force, but anti-art and counterculture have been absorbed into advanced capitalist and particularly consumer culture (a history that would be far too long in the telling for this essay). Sloterdijk offers his own version of this when he identifies the rigorous training of *Homo artista* with the reduction of life to the horizontal dimension. Here, the aesthetic imperative devolves into training, and training in turn becomes part of a global fitness exercise that finds its highest expression in sports. Accordingly, the age finds its highest exemplars among elite professional athletes.[14] Far from taking part in the re-enchantment of the world, art has become a call to get in shape.

As thought-provoking as this explanation may be of why the absolute imperative can no longer be heard in art, this alone wouldn't lend much credence to Sloterdijk's conclusion. A second reason can be adduced however from the concluding essay to Sloterdijk's volume written by Peter Weibel. There he suggests that Sloterdijk's real aim is to break the alliance between ethics and aesthetics, an alliance where the aesthetic imperative constitutes in effect the categorical imperative in disguise. "Aesthetic pleasure can only function if it does not have to obey any commandment or prohibition. For this reason Sloterdijk opposes an aesthetic imperative derived from Kant and his categorical imperative" (Weibel 319). This view is very much worth considering. Weibel's point is that any sort of command that comes from art must remain non-coercive, the very point made by Sloterdijk in his discussion of Rilke. Ultimately, there can be no "aesthetic imperative," because such an imperative could never accomplish its aim. And so when reading the final line of Rilke's poem, one would have to conclude that "you must change your life" can only be construed as an interruption of the poem that comes from the outside and in doing so, abruptly brings it to an end.[15]

But there is more. In another essay, Sloterdijk transposes art into the realm of immunology: art belongs, he writes, to the compensatory social system insofar as it possesses a symbolic role. In anthropotechnical terms, art "would be something like an immune system that society concedes to individuals" (Sloterdijk, *Aesthetic Imperative* 288). That is its role, which in a way is not so far removed from its devolution into sports and athleticism. He even goes so far to say that the arts "have represented the most important complex of quasi-meditative exercise systems in the modern tradition" (297). Against this recasting of artistic practice as an ascetic ideal, the long-standing negative and utopic thrust of modern art that is based principally on the unbreakable alliance and beauty and freedom, expressed as a radical break with the existing world, its objects and its instrumentalized language, negates itself.

A utopian art is an art that ends in self negation.

Having dispensed with a modernist aesthetics *qua* radical negativity, it seems there is but one possibility left for the future of art, and that is to embrace its role as – and Sloterdijk does not hesitate in the least to use the term – a "meditative cybernetics" (*Aesthetic Imperative* 303). What sort of monstrosity is this?!

Before examining this final idea, let me gather together the various strands of this discussion of the aesthetic imperative. From Hans Jonas' translation of the categorical imperative into an ontological imperative that posits human survival (that there be human beings) as its basic axiom, an imperative that seems more suited to a technological era, I moved to consider the aesthetic imperative as that which addresses, in my view at least, the shortcomings of Jonas' ethics. The command from the stone consists of a non-coercive appeal that issues from things themselves but which, in our time, can no longer be heard for two reasons. First, because artistic practice has become indistinguishable from the now institutionalized drive for self-improvement and self-enhancement through training, and second, because the time of the alliance between aesthetics and deontological ethics is past. The only imperative coming from art is not to obey any commandment other than *jouissance*. Art is functional, anthropotechnical; the workings of contemporary art lie in the direction of an increased mental wakefulness to the various possibilities of being-in-the-world that are bound up with the new technologies of communication and intelligence – and by that is meant, both literally and figuratively, *artificial intelligence*. Returning for a moment to Sloterdijk's pithy utterance, "Whoever goes in search of humans will find acrobats," it is now clear that in ours, the time of the advent of the Great Catastrophe, art must assume the role of a most particular kind of exercise: through the cultivation of a "wakefulness," it readies us for the emergence of the new technologies of intelligence: "If the main event in history is human intelligence itself, the emergence of a superior intelligence will become the condition for history to go on [...]" (*Aesthetic Imperative* 302). Meditative cybernetics can thus be described as a releasement *from* the instrumental relation to technology that is part and parcel of humanism, *to* a free, that is, non-coercive relation that, like the torso of Apollo, guides us by "letting things happen" rather than by seeking to predict an exact future, and by "trusting intelligent impulses" as new forms of communication (302). The extraordinary transformation of the aesthetic imperative into an affirmation of a new relation to technology is one where technological "things" themselves, imbued with intelligence, speak. One could even say without much exaggeration that artificial intelligence machines have taken the place of Rilke's torso: we now have or will soon have such self-standing beings *qua* embodied intelligences that see us and call upon us to change our lives!

By way of conclusion, the question concerning art and following the path from the categorical to the aesthetic imperatives has led finally to the question concerning technology, particularly Heidegger's meditation, which stands at the very center of the anthropotechnical maneuver; for what is meditative cybernetics if not a form of technological *Gelassenheit*?

IV the absolute imperative and the question concerning technology

In this final part of my essay I wish to briefly address the way in which Sloterdijk positions Heidegger's response to the question concerning technology as the last attempt to found the absolute imperative upon an authority that originates, in effect, from the outside, which in this case corresponds to Being itself in terms of the ontological difference, as radically other than beings, or Being as the Open [*das Offen*] or the clearing [*die Lichtung*] of the "there" [*da*], or finally, Being as that from which a call issues forth and which calls for a thinking response [*Was heißt denken?*]. Despite acknowledging Heidegger's achievement in both the dismantling of Europe's various humanisms and bringing the finitude of Dasein and of Being-as-presencing to the fore, Sloterdijk is nonetheless troubled by Heidegger's "crypto-Catholic" rhetoric of Grace that finds salvation in Being alone: as with God, so Being alone has the power to save, and our task here on earth is to respond to the call of Being so that presencing can happen again.[16] Being speaks, but does so only by way of hints [*Winke*], a way that exceeds any form of scientific or historical prediction or envisaging. Its arrival is a matter of resolute and restrained anticipation, not representation.

By no means does Sloterdijk reject Heidegger's conception of Being as world-disclosure, but there is, he contends, something unthought that results from Heidegger's refusal to consider animality as constitutive of Dasein's being-in-the-open which, when considered, leads to a different conception, one that implicates human being in the technological from the beginning: "There is a history of the human being's stepping out into the clearing that is resolutely ignored by Heidegger [...]" (*Not Saved* 205). That history is twofold. There is, on the one hand, a *natural history* of the human being as the animal that becomes capable of having a world, and a *social history* of tamings [*Zähmungen*] and immunity structures that together construct enclosures, *Gehäuse* – that is, the forms of enhousing in and through which human beings "domesticate" the clearing.

This shift marks Sloterdijk's departure from Heidegger. It is one that relates directly to the question concerning technology, for when Sloterdijk employs terms like "domestication" and *Gehäuse* to describe the way that human beings enter into the clearing, he does so for the purpose of developing a new ontology of the human as always already technological. Sloterdijk names this new relation as "ecstase-technology" (*Not Saved* 96), implying that *Lichtung*, the ecstatic entering-into-the-clearing, or world-disclosure, is essentially technogenic. In order to bring this new ontology of ecstase-technology into relief, it is necessary to understand where and in what way Sloterdijk differs from Heidegger regarding the essence of technology.

Briefly, when Heidegger names the essence of technology as *das Ge-stell* (usually translated as "enframing"), the "*Ge-*" prefix is used to imply that it is both the final mode of the disclosure of beings *qua* beings that belongs to the epoch of metaphysics and the one that gathers them all together as forms of setting-in-place [*stellen*], from Plato's *eidos* where being is understood as permanence, to Descartes' "representations" as being-represented by a subject. In the working out of this history, being as permanent presence dissolves in favor of a mode of disclosure that sets upon beings [*stellen*], including and above all humanity itself, and challenges them [*Herausfordern*] to supply the maximum energy at minimal cost. As supplies, beings "are" only insofar as they form a *standing-reserve* [*Bestand*]. Heidegger's thought concerning the essence of technology culminates in his later work in the ideas of replaceability [*Ersetzbarkeit*] and consumption [*Verbrauch*]. This entails on the one hand that both substance and "objectness" as ontological determinations dissolve into replaceability, which is itself an ontological determination that orders beings in such a way that anything can take the place of anything. "Today being is being-replaceable," and replaceability exists for the sake of "plan-driven consumption" (Heidegger, *Four Seminars* 62). Thus, Heidegger's thought culminates in the accord between our modern consumer-driven global economies and the nihilation of beings insofar as they "are" nothing but a standing reserve. In terms of language, replaceability is accomplished in the form of cybernetics, which reduces all language to the ordered exchange of information.

Appearances to the contrary, Heidegger's questioning never devolves into an anti-technology diatribe. The result of his inquiry reveals an essence that is, as he puts it, "in a lofty sense ambiguous." Working out the meaning of this statement has proven difficult to say the least. My interpretation here should be taken as provisional, and is based on certain passages from the *Four Seminars*.

On the one hand, the danger of technology appears as the imperative of progress: progress demands that everything serve the needs of the ever-new that must, according to its own logic, be replaced by the "ever-newer" (Heidegger, *Four Seminars* 73). Yet at the same time, infinite replaceability is continually spurred on by the will to appropriate the inexhaustible outside towards which Dasein is always already ecstatically oriented. "Ek-statically being the there" (71) means being-outside, for something always exceeds any mode of presencing, including technology. Modes of presencing are themselves finite, and if, in addition to beings *qua* replaceable, the *Ge-stell* discloses anything at all, it is the extremity to which human beings are subjected when their essential determinations are reduced to the roles of producer, self-producer, maximizers and self-maximizers (74). In the midst of this extreme and inexorable imperative, the possibility for a renunciation [*Verzicht*] of the cycle of production and consumption may arise, as long as one does not reduce Heidegger's use of *Verzicht* to ascetic renunciation, which it is not. Renunciation is rather a preparatory step, literally a stepping into a space where the human is open to the outside, "to what is not man," to the *Da* of Dasein, which does not serve, as Heidegger so often emphasizes, as a definition of human being as much as it indicates a departure from the metaphysical determination of the human as *animal rationale* and a transition into the space of the "between" of the event of appropriation [*Ereignis*].[17]

Two things are noteworthy here. First, Heidegger makes no appeal to an imperative. Imperatives are calls for action. Nothing says that we *must* enter into this "between-domain," partly because it is not a relation that humanity has the power to *will* itself into. On the contrary, the imperative lies on the side of technology. Thinking can, by contrast, *prepare* a way of entry into the domain of the "There" (the *Da*), by renouncing the imperatives of production and consumption, but the *event* of our stepping into a new domain can only take place in conjunction with what comes from outside, that is, from Being. Second, this casts a different light on the notion of *Gelassenheit*. *Pace* Sloterdijk, *Gelassenheit* is not an imperative but a response, and more specifically, it is a possibility of co-responding. Nothing says that humanity must take this step, and nothing says that the technological mode of presencing couldn't go on indefinitely. All sorts of innovative solutions to the world's current crises can be and hopefully will be found, but if they are not accompanied by a transformation of the essence of the human to *Dasein*, that is, to the transitional space of a being-open to that which approaches from the outside, then the *Gestell* – enframing, perhaps with a more "human" face – will persist.

Sloterdijk's response to Heidegger's meditation on the essence of technology is summed up in a single sentence that brings together being-in-the-world with anthropotechnics in the most striking fashion: "What Heidegger calls 'en-framing' [*Ge-stell*] and understands as a dire sending of Being is initially nothing other than the en-housing [*Ge-Häuse*] that accommodates human beings and by means of such accommodation imperceptibly fabricates [*herstellt*] them" (*Not Saved* 119). En-framing is but an instance of en-housing? *Gestell* is *Gehäuse*? So it seems! This turns the entire question concerning technology around; rather than the final, epochal mode of metaphysical presencing, technology is projected backwards into the inception of the clearing. There is, as Sloterdijk claims, a "real story of the clearing": en-housing, which has finally been uncovered by the anthropotechnical maneuver.

The implications of Sloterdijk's wholesale translation of the essence of technology into the praxis of anthropotechnics are far-reaching. It means first of all that the natural history of humanity's entering into a world (see above) does not refer to "world" or "worlding" as the opening of a space of appearance as much as it corresponds to the "environing world," an *Umwelt* that is already enclosed as a shelter against the pressures of the outside. There is no world without building. En-housing makes possible the nearness of the world *as* greenhouse and the remoteness of the outside. Second, it means that the clearing itself [*Lichtung*] is always already technological. To build is to fabricate [*herstellen*] a dwelling, which serves as a preserve, an incubator, even as an external uterus.[18] Remarkably, it is biological birth as the birth into spatiality (into the Open) out of the containedness in the mother that makes enhousing both possible and necessary.

In addition to projecting *Gehaüse* backwards to the very origin of coming-to-the-world, Sloterdijk's translation also transforms the essence of truth in the same manner. Instead of the primordial notion of truth as pure disclosure, or the very openness of existence, which Thomas Sheehan designates as *aletheia*-1,[19] the primordial meaning of truth arises from the natural history of the human being's conquest of natural distance by learning to throw, to aim, and to hit a target with a stone, then a spear, and everything thereafter. Each of these actions require the synthetic operation of attending to a thing, of clearing the space around it, and setting it in front of an expansive horizon. "From these operations truth is read off *primordially* as accurateness [...]" (Sloterdijk, *Not Saved* 117). And accuracy is in turn directly related to success, i.e., to hitting the mark. This implies that the primordial meaning of *aletheia* has become radically pragmatic; it is a function of success. And this in turn marks the change of perspective from temporality in Heidegger to spatiality in Sloterdijk. Whereas Heidegger has uncovered the care-structure as the primordial characteristic of Dasein's being-in-the-world, Sloterdijk displaces Dasein's being-ahead-of-itself in favor of an interpretation of *Being-in* as dwelling within a constructed incubator. In this way, the meaning of being-outside-oneself is changed into the imperative for *taming* the outside by bringing it inside and rendering it harmless (i.e., immunization). What disappears from Sloterdijk's reworking is the sheer outside of Dasein's most extreme possibility for being, the temporality of being-towards-death. Dasein is ecstatic most of all in its being-towards its own impossibility, which it can never overcome, be certain of, or tame.

Finally, in the wake of this translation, what then becomes of *Gelassenheit* as a response to the danger of technological self-destruction? What had been proposed by Heidegger as a preparation for entry into the *Da*, the "between" where the sending of Being may happen differently, has been translated into the *preparation for* and the *releasement of* the technologies of enhousing, which have now reached such a level of sophistication that they have become embodied intelligences that are themselves constitutive of the spheres that surround and shelter us; such is the act of "worlding." *Gelassenheit* thus becomes a preparatory exercise, making us ready for the advanced technological transformation that has now come to light thanks to the anthropotechnical recasting of human history. *Gelassenheit* has, in effect, been turned into an imperative to change our lives in such a way as to welcome that which has not yet become manifest, and ready ourselves for the further discovery of new forms and structures of enhousing. This is how we should respond to the crisis.

V conclusion: technologized animals?

Sloterdijk's anthropotechnics, which now appears as an almost complete translation of the question concerning technology, gives rise to an unsettling question: has the new practice of anthropotechnics made possible the free relation to the essence of technology that Heidegger had originally sought, or has it instead led to a greater entanglement in enframing? Has replaceability been displaced? There are reasons to believe that it has not. If the primary aim of overcoming the present global crises is, per Hans Jonas, the survival of the human race, then it is hard not to see in this a repetition of what Heidegger had identified as the triumph of the "technologized animal," the one for whom technology replaces and indeed *becomes* the instincts, and for whom all culture is transformed in a "battlefield technology for the sake of a will that no longer wills any goal." For, as Heidegger continues, "the preservation of a people is never a possible goal but is only a condition of the setting of a goal," even if that people is the entire human species (*Contributions* 78).

Now it would be simply erroneous to reduce Sloterdijk's thought to such a crude principle. As previously discussed, it is not merely survival as much as it is the free invention that is called for by one's "innermost not-yet" that matters. It is the call of the vertical dimension, but one that is new and distinct because it arises within and is wedded to *Homo technologicus* as the sole ground of authority left to us.

So much is at stake here, which is best expressed in the form of a question about the very possibility of being human: in confronting the crises of the present, has anthropotechnics opened a possibility for rethinking the being of the human in relation to technology from the ground up, or does anthropotechnics leave intact the metaphysics of man as the "rational animal," which has now devolved into the "technological animal," one who looks at climate change as nothing more than a life-threatening problem to be solved by the invention of new technologies that will help us bring this bit of chaos under control?

Although I am certainly aware of the potential errors of presenting the question as an either-or, since the result of my analysis has been to show that anthropotechnics cannot be construed as a repeat of a traditional humanist subject by any means, my hope is that it will at the very least bring some recognition of the tremendous potential of Sloterdijk's anthropotechnics for addressing one of the most decisive issues of our time, and open up possibilities for further investigation on what has only begun.

disclosure statement

No potential conflict of interest was reported by the author.

notes

1 There are three senses in which one can say that we are of time. In each case, it is the sense of a future that has already arrived and will keep arriving.

The senses I have in mind are: (1) the urgency of our situation in light of the growing ecological disaster; (2) being out of time also relates to Sloterdijk's *spherology*: insofar as being in the world consists of living in spheres that domesticate relations between an inside and an outside, the breakdown of immunological structures that have housed human beings has left us exposed to the de-territorializing tendencies of globalism without recourse. On this see Jean-Pierre Couture's discussion of the geographical question in Sloterdijk, especially pages 58ff.; (3) more distantly, being out of time also indicates the emptying of time because of its reduction by means of contemporary communications technology to simultaneity and latency.

2 "Erhaben ist, was durch Vergegenwärtigung des Überwältigenden dem Beobachter die Möglichkeit seines Untergangs im Übergroßen vor Augen stellt [...]" (Sloterdijk, *Du Mußt* 701). The emphasis on the position of the spectator before the overwhelming bears an unmistakable reference to Kant's dynamic sublime, where it is Nature as might (*Macht*) and as dominion (*Gewalt*) before which the spectator stands and feels his impotence. Whether Sloterdijk actually follows Kant down the path from an aesthetics of beauty to that of the sublime is unclear, since Sloterdijk never addresses Kant's aesthetics to my knowledge.

3 Cf. Bruno Latour, *Facing Gaia* and *The New Climatic Regime*. Sloterdijk shares much in common with Latour, although one must not minimize the differences. Latour's is more of a political objective: to outline the new "climatic regime" as a new political formation. Sloterdijk does not refer to the political in terms of specific regimes very often, much preferring the philosophical-anthropological idea of Anthropotechnics. Sloterdijk remains more committed to the philosophical and particularly to a continuous *Auseindandersetzung* with Heidegger that certainly has its political implications, but is, as I intend to show, more dedicated to the condition of *dwelling*.

4 Cf. Sloterdijk, *Foams* 59.

5 Cf. The Prologue to *Foams*, where metaphysics is described as macrospherology, that is, as an all-encompassing circle, an absolute orb that represented nothing less than a total immune structure that housed all microspheres within itself, organized around its center (17).

6 "We shall be questioning concerning technology," Heidegger writes, "and in so doing we should like to prepare a free relationship to it. The relationship will be free if it opens our human existence (*Dasein*) to the essence (*Wesen*) of technology" (*Technology* 17).

7 Unless otherwise noted, I follow Sloterdijk's particular use of the term "modernity" that emphasizes three characteristics: first, that in contradistinction to the ancient, the modern era is distinguished by the mobilization of human powers for the sake of work and production (*You Must Change* 211–12); second, modernity makes room for two tracks of ascetic practice, namely, adapting oneself to the labor of creating a better world (323) and self-realization (326); and finally, "progress" does not mean a process of secularization but rather the de-verticalization of existence (371).

8 "In a Kantian or Marxist world one knows in principle always exactly what to do [...] The right thing is only temporarily delayed but can never become irrelevant" (translation mine).

9 Although I cannot trace the extent of Heidegger's reading of Kant here, his point is that according to the usual way for beings to become manifest as objects that are subject to the law of causality, "objectness" is a mode of comportment (*Verhalten*) that has the character of a "letting something stand-over-against as given." This mode of comportment is only possible if an originary self-binding exists in the form of the giving of a law to oneself (Heidegger, *Essence of Human Freedom* 205).

10 This is Sloterdijk's rendition of Jonas' imperative. In his own text, Jonas reformulates the imperative several times. See, for instance, Jonas 11 and 43–44.

11 Cf. Jonas 157–58.

12 Cf. Jonas 1 and 117ff.

13 Sloterdijk, *The Aesthetic Imperative* 249–52.

14 Cf., for example, Sloterdijk, *You Must Change* 27–28, 337, and 417–18.

15 It is a pity that Sloterdijk chose not to address Kant's *Critique of Judgment* here or anywhere else that I am aware of. Doing so could have led to a much more fruitful discussion of how and in what way art might command, whether by means of a moral imperative or otherwise. Kant attributes to judgments of beauty a "free liking" (*freie Wohlfgefallen*) that is demanded of everyone not in the form of an imperative, but as a *sensus communis*, a common sense that consists solely in the expectation that each and every one of us will agree that the free liking that accompanies the aesthetic presentation of an object is universally communicable and thus potentially shared or shareable by all. Far from mimicking the moral imperative, the aesthetic contains no imperative save for the demand that everyone consent to judgments of beauty which are in turn based on the pleasure of free-play of the faculties before pure appearances. The discussion of the relation of aesthetics and ethics in Kant is vast and long-standing. Cf. the works of Paul Guyer, Henry Allison, Frederick Beiser, Hannah Arendt, Dieter Henrich, and many, many others.

16 "The concept (or the model) of grace returns in Heidegger – transformed into the kinetic schema of releasement [*Gelassenheit*]" (Sloterdijk, *Not Saved* 39).

17 Cf. Heidegger, *Contributions to Philosophy* 23ff.

18 These are in fact Sloterdijk's own terms. The latter relates directly to his project in *Spheres, Vol. I: Bubbles* which identifies the pairing of mother and infant as archetype of all forms of existential spatiality.

19 See Sheehan 75ff.

bibliography

Couture, Jean-Pierre. *Sloterdijk*. Key Contemporary Thinkers Series. Cambridge: Polity, 2016. Print.

Heidegger, Martin. *Contributions to Philosophy. Of the Event*. Trans. Richard Rojcewicz and Daniella Vallega-Neu. Bloomington: Indiana UP, 2012. Print.

Heidegger, Martin. *The Essence of Human Freedom. An Introduction to Philosophy*. Trans. Ted Seller. London: Continuum, 2002. Print.

Heidegger, Martin. *Four Seminars*. Trans. Andrew Mitchell and François Raffoul. Bloomington: Indiana UP, 2003. Print.

Heidegger, Martin. *The Question Concerning Technology and other Essays*. Trans. with an Introduction by William Lovitt. New York: Harper, 1977. Print.

Heidegger, Martin. *Über den Humanismus*. Frankfurt: Klostermann, 2000. Print.

Jonas, Hans. *The Imperative of Responsibility. In Search of an Ethics for the Technological Age*. Trans. Hans Jonas with the collaboration of David Herr. Chicago: U of Chicago P, 1984. Print.

Kant, Immanuel. *Groundwork to the Metaphysic of Morals*. Trans. and analyzed by H.J. Paton. New York: Harper, 1964. Print.

Latour, Bruno. *Facing Gaia. Eight Lectures on the New Climatic Regime*. Trans. Catherine Porter. Cambridge: Polity, 2017. Print.

Sheehan, Thomas. *Making Sense of Heidegger. A Paradigm Shift*. The New Heidegger Research Series. Lanham, MD: Rowman, 2015. Print.

Sloterdijk, Peter. *The Aesthetic Imperative. Writings on Art*. Trans. Karen Margolis. Cambridge: Polity, 2017. Print.

Sloterdijk, Peter. *Du Mußt dein Leben Ändern. Über Anthroptechnik*. Frankfurt: Suhrkamp, 2009. Print.

Sloterdijk, Peter. *Nach Gott*. Frankfurt: Suhrkamp, 2018. Print.

Sloterdijk, Peter. *Nicht Gerettet. Versuche Nach Heidegger*. Frankfurt: Suhrkamp, 2001. Print.

Sloterdijk, Peter. *Not Saved. Essays after Heidegger*. Trans. Ian Alexander Moore and Christopher Turner. Frankfurt: Suhrkamp, 2017. Print.

Sloterdijk, Peter. *Spheres I. Bubbles. Microspherology*. Trans. Wieland Hoban. Los Angeles: Semiotext(e), 2011. Print.

Sloterdijk, Peter. *Spheres II. Globes. Macrospherology*. Trans. Wieland Hoban. Los Angeles: Semiotext(e), 2014. Print.

Sloterdijk, Peter. *Spheres III. Foams. Plural Spherology*. Trans. Wieland Hoban. Los Angeles: Semiotext(e), 2016. Print.

Sloterdijk, Peter. *You Must Change Your Life. On Anthropotechnics*. Trans. Wieland Hoban. Cambridge: Polity, 2013. Print.

Weibel, Peter. "Afterword: Sloterdijk and the Question of Aesthetics." *The Aesthetic Imperative*. Cambridge: Polity, 2017. 304–20. Print.

directions

You must change your life, Peter Sloterdijk writes.[1] What does this mean? Is he serious? And who in fact utters these words? Who is here talking to whom? Is he really talking to someone? Is this a command, an order, an imperative, or just a reminder, an observation, a simple remark, a mere acknowledgment or report? Sloterdijk plays here the role not only of the philosopher, but also the writer, the playwright, or the director: to understand what he writes also means to understand his direction(s), in every sense of the word – the orders he gives, the staging he creates, and the path he takes. Where Sloterdijk is heading, in which direction, is what we must discover if we are to make sense of what we are reading, of the performance presented to us.

To signal directions and to explain what is at stake in a book is normally the purpose of an introduction, which *You Must Change Your Life* does not lack: 105 pages in the English edition, that is, fifteen pages called "Introduction," followed by "The Planet of the Practising," a series of five chapters offering mostly literary examples (Rilke, Nietzsche, Unthan, Kafka, and Cioran), and ending with two more examples (Coubertin and Hubbard) in a so-called "Transition" (*Übergang*, and the whole book is after all about *übergehen*, going beyond), a trans-ition whose title repeats the first thesis of the Introduction: "Religions Do Not Exist." It is as if *You Must Change Your Life* started with another book, on a slightly different subject – religions and their existence –, containing nevertheless a whole chapter explaining its title: Chapter 1, about Rilke's poem, which is not yet Chapter 1, since the

serge trottein

OF AN ENLIGHTENMENT-CONSERVATIVE TONE RECENTLY ADOPTED IN PHILOSOPHY

work itself has not yet begun. In fact, the book contains so many *hors d'œuvres* or *parerga* that one wonders whether the reader will ever reach its core, if there is one, or head in the proper direction, if there is one, for such an exercise. For the first part itself begins with a program (*Programm*), the second one with a backdrop (*Prospekt* in German, *perspective* in the French edition[2]), the third one with a prospect (*Perspektive*), the whole book ending not with a single conclusion (referring to who knows which introduction?), but with a double one: a retrospective (*Rückblick*), followed by an outlook (*Ausblick*, *perspective* again in French), thus with all kinds of ways of looking into, through, back, or forward to something that may well remain to be defined, or even to be found. You must change your life, but how, in which way? Anticipating what future? Or looking back, retrospectively, toward what command? Given this multiplication of perspectives, it is not difficult to become quickly disoriented and to lose what at first seemed to be the guiding thread of the analysis.

More intriguing still are the first theses encountered by the reader: not only that this book is about technics, anthropotechnics, but also about a turn (*Wende*), and even a return, a revenant, a specter, therefore also a manifesto, an explicitation via a translation: these are all "key terms" that contain "the present book *in nuce*," as Sloterdijk writes, mentioning only the word[3] "explicit." Explicit, he continues, refers to a rotation, a maneuver, an enterprise, that of rendering explicit the implicit, which Sloterdijk defines as "Enlightenment-conservative."

The translation suggested here of the religious, spiritual and ethical facts into the language and perspective [*Optik*] of the general theory of practising [*Übungstheorie*] defines itself [*versteht sich*] as an Enlightenment-conservative enterprise [*ein aufklärungskonservatives Unternehmen*[4]] – a conservatory one [*ein konservatorisches*], in fact, in the matter itself. It rests on a twofold interest in preservation: firstly, it declares its allegiance to the continuum of cumulative knowledge that we call Enlightenment,[5] and which, despite all rumours of having entered a new "post-secular" state, we in the present continue as a context of learning [of modern times – *moderner Zeiten*] meanwhile spanning four centuries; and secondly, it takes up the threads, some of them millennia old, that tie us to early manifestations of human knowledge about practice and animation – assuming that we are prepared to follow on from them [relate to them – *an ihnen anzuknüpfen*] in an explicit fashion.

With this, we have introduced the key term for everything that will be read in the following: the world [*sic*] "explicit," applied to the objects in question, contains the present book *in nuce*. The aforementioned rotation of the intellectual-historical stage [*Drehung der geistesgeschichtlichen Bühne*] means nothing other than a logical manoeuvre to render explicit circumstances that, in the masses of tradition, are present in "implicit" – that is, inward-folded and compressed – forms. If Enlightenment in a technical sense is the programmatic word for progress in the awareness of explicitness, one can say without fear of grand formulas that rendering the implicit explicit is the cognitive form of fate.[6]

How an enterprise can be Enlightenment-conservative is what I have tried to understand, and what I would like to render a little more explicit, or rather make clearer in this essay. For one could say that because of his emphasis on the explicit and the implicit, Sloterdijk's notion of *Aufklärung* is more Leibnizian than Kantian, and therefore could be considered more characteristic of a certain pre-Enlightenment or premodernity than of Enlightenment or *Aufklärung* itself. Although *Aufklärung* can also have the meaning of clearing up, elucidating, solving (a mystery), making public (informing citizens), or even of information (as in *Aufklärungsbuch*, a book on sex education), or reconnaissance (observation and study of an enemy), the main metaphor at the heart of the concept is that of clarification, shedding light on what remained rather obscure or in the background (*mettre en lumière*, bringing to the fore), which admittedly often does not go without the reintroduction of new obscurities, the creation of a chiaroscuro on the object or situation it meant to clear up. No light can be shed on a subject without simultaneously obscuring it in places and casting shadows: a definition, so to speak, of the postmodern process already at work within the modernity of *Aufklärung*. It is for the reader to decide whether this essay begins to render explicit what is merely implicit in Sloterdijk's text, or whether it also casts light on his project amidst unavoidable fresh obscurity.

to the inconceivable practitioners of theory

You must change your life, Sloterdijk writes. Whom does he address? What audience? Are we, as philosophers, part of this audience? Apparently we are, since a second book, *The Art of Philosophy. Wisdom as a Practice*, is dedicated to this particular subject, philosophers and other practitioners of theory, a book explicitly presented as an extension or application of the first one. Unfortunately, the meaning of its title is not much clearer; like the other title, it needs at least to be rendered explicit if we want to understand Sloterdijk's project. Many of these reflections, in a way, will have no other purpose than to develop what is implied and at stake in these two somewhat misleading titles.

Whereas the first title is as enigmatic as it is provocative, the second one hides in its banality the intriguing character of the original: *The Art of Philosophy. Wisdom as a Practice* is supposed to be the English translation of *Scheintod im Denken – Von Philosophie und Wissenschaft als Übung*. In the guise of a justification, an introductory "translator's note" provides a few hints, referring vaguely to Kafka as well as "the present debate on the conditions of scholarship," and summarizing the author's argument with an analogy between the practice of science and athletic training. No explanation is given for why *Scheintod* (literally apparent or simulated death, also translated as suspended animation) has been replaced by *art*, or thinking and science by *wisdom*. At least Sloterdijk himself is a little more explicit in his Introduction ("Theory as a Form of the Life of Practice"), written in order to reassure his reader, as he explains in a rather tongue-in-cheek mode: knowing in advance what to expect relieves unnecessary tension (could it be a vertical tension?) and allows serenity (*Gelassenheit*), and dividing one's ideas in four instead of three, seven, or ten sections shows one addresses philosophers rather than theologians, since "the classical philosophical quaternity [...] is based on the assumption that to tell the truth one must be able to count up to four" (*Art of Philosophy* 2), but apparently not much higher if one does not want to fall back into theology, if I may add.

What should we then expect that would allow us to keep our serenity? First a general talk about philosophy or academic science, represented by two "founding figures," Husserl and Socrates, and secondly, a propaedeutic exploration of "the conditions of the possibility of theoretical behavior" (Sloterdijk, *Art of Philosophy* 2). But these two sections may well be in fact irrelevant or off topic, since only the third (and maybe fourth) sections "go to the heart of today's topic," namely, "the formation or self-generation of the disinterested person" (2), finally assassinated under bizarre circumstances. The whole inquiry certainly seems to end as a detective story, but before we jump to the conclusion, Sloterdijk warns us that "one other preliminary remark seems necessary," a "comment in advance" (3), the key in fact to its understanding: we need to be "serious about the term 'practice' in all its implications (including as exercise or training)" (5). Let us be serious then, all the more serious since this remark introduces and establishes the link between two works, *Suspended Animation in Thought* and *You Must Change Your Life*. To be serious about practice means to keep in mind what Sloterdijk is aiming at, which he finally sums up here in a few words: "to restore the high status of practice" (6).

Practice, Sloterdijk explains, "has been neglected by theoretical modernism, if not wantonly pushed aside and scorned" (*Art of Philosophy* 5–6), hence its low status for modernity. Yet the situation of practice described by Sloterdijk is much worse than that of a low status: from at least the Middle Ages onward, practice has not only been neglected, it has become invisible, and even inconceivable:

> In *You Must Change Your Life!* I show in some detail how the traditional approach to classifying human action, that is, the familiar distinction between the *vita activa* and *vita contemplativa* that initially related

only to monks, was linked with the effect of making the dimension of practice as such invisible, if not actually inconceivable. As soon as we accept the ingrained difference between "active" and "contemplative" as if it were an exclusive and total alternative, we lose sight of a substantial complex of human behavior that is neither merely active nor merely contemplative. I call this the life of practice. (6)

Practice then is a kind of in-between, a "mixed domain," which in spite of its medieval and modern invisibility has nevertheless a name, of older origin, like "classical askesis," inevitably mentioned by Sloterdijk in that same context of invisibility. Its definitions continuously shift: practice is exercise, then training, then constitution, virtue, virtuosity, competence, excellence or fitness, ultimately identified to the *askesis* of Greek or Christian athletes. Sloterdijk insists, "The moment we force exercising into distinguishing between theory and practice or the active and contemplative life, we lose sight of its intrinsic value [...] This structuring of the practical field [...] makes the dimension of the practicing life invisible" (*Art of Philosophy* 7).

To force practice or exercising to find its place between theory and ... itself would indeed be a tour de force if practice did not also refer to Greek *praxis*, hence revealing the essential ambiguity of what is here the key term. By pulling practice toward asceticism, Sloterdijk strives to present himself as a Nietzschean philosopher, as is obvious in the very next passage, as in many others throughout his writings:

> My book tries to give an impression of the extent, weight, and variety of forms of the life of practice. I quote Nietzsche's evocative remark that, seen from the universe, the planet earth of the metaphysical age must appear almost like the "ascetic star." On this star, the struggle of the discontented nation of the ascetic priests against their inner nature is "one of the most widespread and enduring facts there are." [Here a note, note 2, gives the reference to Nietzsche's *Genealogy of Morals*.] The time has come to cast off life-stultifying asceticism and acquire once again the positive arts of affirmation that have been obsolete for too long. (*Art of Philosophy* 7)

The danger with an author as prolific as Sloterdijk is to give in to precipitation. For what exactly is he doing here? He is describing one large book from the surface of a smaller one, which appears as one of its satellites. And he starts with two remarks by Nietzsche, which offer us a perspective and a fact. To have the right perspective on life or on the human condition, we need to zoom out, as it were, to see our planet from very far away, from a global point of view, which is going to be Sloterdijk's starting point. Hence the title of the first part of *You Must Change Your Life*: "The Planet of the Practising." But this first part of planet Anthropotechnics (the other name of *You Must Change Your Life*) is not really its first part, nor is it its introduction either: it is somewhere in-between in Sloterdijk's universe, almost invisible in spite of its size, as if it had been forced to find its place between theory (the object of the small satellite) and itself as the first part, which makes it literally inconceivable, like its inhabitants.

However, the Nietzschean perspective adopted makes this planet appear as the ascetic star, and reveals a fact, "one of the most widespread and enduring facts there are": asceticism. It is so widespread and enduring, in fact, that the book cannot be exhaustive, and can only give an impression of its extent, weight, and variety. It is widespread, but invisible, and in order to make it conceivable, Sloterdijk must increase its extension to the maximum, thus ultimately departing from Nietzsche's treatment of the concept.

the metaphysical age and the aristotelian planet

Another point of departure, that is, of separation from Nietzsche concerns no longer space, but time: from a Nietzschean perspective one could perceive "the planet earth of the metaphysical age," whereas now the time has come to "cast off life-stultifying asceticism and acquire once again [something] that [has] been obsolete for too long": in other terms, we stand at a turning point, where something is going to return from the past and allow us to overcome metaphysics, to go beyond stultifying routine and rules toward a renaissance of life and free play. That something is said here to be "the positive arts of affirmation," which will require further clarification, as will the delimitation of the metaphysical age preceding the revolution to come.

For the moment, note that the metaphysical age begins at least as far back as the Middle Ages, i.e., the epoch of the "distinction between the *vita activa* and *vita contemplative*," which had the effect of making the dimension of practice invisible. Why? Because it privileges the opposition of *theoria* and *praxis*, over lower-ranked human activities like *technè* and *poiesis*. Now this opposition goes back to an even earlier epoch that Sloterdijk does not exclude from his domain of investigation. On the contrary Sloterdijk writes that in *The Art of Philosophy* his "aim is to show why the idea that the thinking person has to be a kind of a dead person on holiday is just inseparable from the ancient European culture of rationality, particularly classical, Platonic-inspired philosophy" (3). Thus, the metaphysical age may well include antiquity, it needs at least to be thought in Platonic terms (and Nietzsche also tended to identify the history of philosophy with the history of platonism). But if it is platonism whose history Sloterdijk here proposes to narrate or rewrite, the concepts he uses are from Aristotelian origin, and if in the imperative *You Must Change Your Life* each word has its importance, change is here what is at the base of all definitions or redefinitions leading to the rediscovery of practice. For what distinguishes *theoria* from the rest is that it is concerned by things that do not change, are immortal or eternal or literally super-natural, that belong to the "supralunar" world; nature, *physis*, is the domain of change, of growth, of generation and corruption, where *technè*, *praxis*, or *poiesis* are found. Whether you must change it or not, life *is* change. Your life is going to, will necessarily change, whether you wish it or not, whether someone tells you to change it or not. In this (Aristotelian) context, both words mean the same thing and *You Must* is superfluous: the imperative has not yet found its place. Human beings do not have a choice, they live in the sublunar world, that of *physis*, which means that they cannot keep from living according to nature, whatever activity they need or decide to perform, and whatever art they try to practice. What distinguishes all these arts and activities (*technai*) is their aim: if their aim is outside themselves, then they are productions, *poiesis*; if their aim is inside or none other than themselves, they are examples of *praxis*. Therefore, the domain of *praxis* is that of ethics and politics, of those who act, and the domain of *poiesis* that of artisans and artists, those who make things. At least that is how the specter of human activities seems to configure itself on the Aristotelian planet, where Sloterdijk appears to have resided before traveling to a farther planet or satellite. From this more distant point of view, distinctions vanish as quickly as the extension of the concepts increases, forcing them to overlap and invade each other's territory. One concept in particular tends to occupy the whole field, that of technics, whose aim is internal as well as external when its object or objective becomes the *anthropos*, human being, itself: hence the term *anthropotechnics*, which is the subject of the first book and of which the second book offers to its readers another detailed example. Seen from beyond the moon, planet earth becomes the ascetic planet inasmuch as its inhabitants seem no longer to have distinctive and varying activities, but only one: practice, *la pratique*, which encompasses *praxis* as well as *poiesis*. By virtue of a highly invasive extension, the ascetic planet has become the planet of the practicing, virtue has become virtuosity, even science or *theoria* can be thought under the category of training. Practicing used to be invisible in the platonic tradition, where *theoria* served as a model; a simple quarter turn rotation or distancing, and everything else becomes invisible in its turn, the end of oppositions meaning also the end of hierarchies. Once all activities are reduced to a single activity, how and using what criteria can one type of practice still be considered superior to others? We have acquired a new way of defining man or the human condition in general, but we have lost all means of ranking, evaluating, or even preferring one way of living above others, we have lost the very condition of possibility of any morals or ethics, and of any politics. Modern Aristotelianism or a certain Aristotelian modernity, by virtue of its extension, has erased the platonism of tradition.

turns and returns, or extensions and rotations?

Extension, and not only the word *explicit* as indicated in the introduction of *You Must Change Your Life* (6), is in fact one of the key terms of Sloterdijk's enterprise; besides, it is extension that makes explicit what used to be implicit, and thus invisible. Extension is not however a historical process: practice does not invade little by little all sectors of human life over the course of history, from the religious asceticism of the Middle Ages or even more remote epochs, starting not only with Plato, but even earlier with the pre-Socratics, who, sleepless in Ephesus, were already practicing the "art of philosophy," to the contemporary culture of competition, sports, and coaching. No change has occurred, there will always have been practice and anthropotechnics, just more or less invisible or masked, depending on the adopted perspective or planet from which these phenomena are viewed. This is phenomenology, not a history, or a philosophy of history.

And yet, from the very beginning, from the subtitles and the title, Sloterdijk speaks of anthropotechnics as a "turn," and of life not just as change, but as submitted to an imperative. It is the *turn* and the *you must* that we now need to understand if we are to make sense of the theoretical practice in which Sloterdijk engages in these two books.

It would take too long to catalog all the twists and turns of Sloterdijk's text, and even longer to comment on each of them, an exercise I leave to careful readers. The turns multiply in so prolific a way that they end up becoming little more than rhetorical expressions. Each time a new theme or author is introduced, its appearance has to take the form of a turn, even if it is later explicitly denied. One example occurs on the very first page, at the beginning of the introduction of *You Must Change Your Life*, which starts explaining the anthropotechnic turn by invoking not one but two revenants, a true and a false returnee, the specter of religion and the specter of communism:

> A spectre is haunting the Western world – the spectre of religion. All over the country we hear that after an extended absence, it has now returned and is among the people of the modern world, and that one would do well to reckon seriously with its renewed presence. Unlike the spectre of communism, which, when its *Manifesto* appeared in 1848, was not a returnee but a novelty among imminent threats, the present case [*der aktuelle Spuk*] does full justice to its revenant nature.[7]

However, two pages later, we learn that the revenant in question, the true one, may be equally false: the return or the specter of religion is not going to mark history, because it is just a story, a fiction, *ein Märchen, une fable*, a myth:

> Let us recall: Marx and Engels wrote the *Communist Manifesto* with the intention of replacing the myth of a spectre named communism with their own aggressive statement of true communism. Where the mere fear of ghosts had predominated, there would now be a justified fear of a real enemy of existing conditions. The present book likewise devotes itself to the critique of a myth, replacing it with a positive thesis. Indeed, the return of religion after the "failure" of the Enlightenment must be confronted with a clearer view of the spiritual facts. I will show that a return *to* religion is as impossible as a return *of* religion – for

the simple reason that no "religion" or "religions" exist, only misunderstood spiritual regimens [...] The false dichotomy of believers and unbelievers becomes obsolete and is replaced by the distinction between the practising and the untrained, or those who train differently. (Sloterdijk, *You Must Change* 3)

Just as practice, as we have seen, cannot be opposed to theory, which is simply another kind of practice, the untrained cannot be opposed to the practicing for they are only "those who train differently." The opposition and the return are mere fables. And the following paragraph reaffirms this, while paradoxically but characteristically clinging to the vocabulary of the return:

Something is indeed returning today – but the conventional wisdom that this is religion making its reappearance is insufficient to satisfy critical inquiries. Nor is it the return of a factor that had vanished, but rather a shift of emphasis in a continuum that was never interrupted. The genuinely recurring element that would merit our full intellectual attention is more anthropological than "religious" in its implications – it is, in a nutshell, the recognition of the immunitary constitution of human beings. After centuries of experiments with new forms of life, the realization has dawned [*hat sich die Einsicht abgeklärt*] that humans, whatever ethnic, economic and political situation might govern their lives, exist not only in "material conditions," but also in symbolic immune systems and ritual shells. It is their fabric that we shall discuss in the following. (Sloterdijk, *You Must Change* 3)

Again, these statements do not constitute a philosophy of history, whether old or new, but rather a *Darstellung*, a new presentation, or at least an explicitation, an *éclaircissement*, a clarification or a different lighting on things, that is, something having to do with Enlightenment, in every sense of the word.

Going back one last time to the "preliminary remark" concluding the introduction of *The Art of Philosophy*, we find in the brief summary of *You Must Change Your Life* given by its author the confirmation of the ahistorical and extensive aspect of Sloterdijk's enterprise: his anthropological or anthropotechnical perspective extends to the past, but not to the point of opening toward a revolutionary, or simply different future. Sloterdijk summarizes his book thus:

In *You Must Change Your Life!* I began by focusing on the ancient systems of practice related to the emergence of ethics in [...] the first millennium BC [...] In the modern age in Europe, there was a tendency to group these systems together under the misleading heading of "religions" without considering that "religion" was a Romano-Christian term transposed to these phenomena [...] For the moment, the only question that concerns us is whether we can broaden our insight into the structures of the explicit and implicit life of practice revealed in ancient ethics to the area of theoretical behavior. If I were not sure of an affirmative answer, I would have to break off my investigation at this point. (*Art of Philosophy* 8–9)

Both books are then first of all extensions of the field of practice. One last digression (but can it still be considered one when there are so many?) refers to what could have been the subject of yet another book, or satellite of the ascetic planet, this time about art history reconsidered and reformulated "as a history of artistic or virtuoso asceticism." Sloterdijk writes

We could then see every phenomenon on this field more or less from a side view and, alongside the familiar history of art as a history of completed works, we could obtain a history of the training that made it possible to do art and the asceticism that shaped artists. (*Art of Philosophy* 9)

Here again, Sloterdijk does not call for a rewriting of art history, but only proposes a side view, a para-history of art, so to speak, where the work of art has been replaced by the training of the artist. How this proposal can "restore the high status of practice" remains nonetheless problematic when one realizes the surprising result created by the change of perspective:

If we assume, as Belting has plausibly suggested, that the tradition of European pictorial culture began with the icon painting of the Hellenized Christian cult, from the start we encounter a form of image-making practice in which art and asceticism represent a perfect unity. The icon painter works with endless repetition all his life, executing a single basic repertoire of a very few motifs in the belief that he is nothing more than the instrument of a supernatural image-light that pours into the work through his hand, always with the basic assumption that the authentic original picture could project itself into the visual world even without human mediation, although this occurs extremely seldom. A direct outpouring of this kind would be a divine photographic slide [...] Christ was such a slide [...] his image on Veronica's veil was also a slide [...] This process set the stage for the steady expansion of artistic methods, as well as for inflated ideas about the importance of the artist. The self-referentiality of artistic excellence increased inexorably until the watershed at the beginning of the modern age that led to the decline of consciousness about practice in the visual arts. (Sloterdijk, *Art of Philosophy* 10)

This is perhaps going a little too far, since in the middle of this experiment and of all these assumptions the in-between that the practicing artist is supposed to be ends up disappearing, i.e., moving down from the status of a technician to that of a mere instrument or *organon* of the (already) divine image which the artist no longer reproduces but only projects. The artist is here considered as little more than a slide projector – hardly a rehabilitation of his or her status.

To keep anthropotechnics from falling into anthropo-organology, as it were, one should probably be careful not to exaggerate the rotation required for the side or backward view, the *per-* or *retro*-spective, to appear. No turn is really effected over the course of history; not unlike Kant's Copernican revolution, the anthropotechnic turn is a strategic move performed by the anthropologist, neither a complete revolution, nor a reversal (by 180 degrees), but a quarter turn: "Now it is a matter of turning the whole stage by ninety degrees until the religious, spiritual and ethical material becomes visible from a revealing new angle" (Sloterdijk, *You Must Change* 5). Again, *The Art of Philosophy*, in its proposed reformulation of art history and of the history of science as histories of artistic and scientific asceticism, explicitly asks this rhetorical question: "What would happen if we rotated the conceptual stage ninety degrees in both cases?" (9).

conserving modernity

Now we perhaps can better understand the intriguing passage quoted at the beginning of this reading, and in which Sloterdijk defines his enterprise as conservative: instead of making or announcing a revolution, it relies on a displacement, a translation, an extension, a quarter circle rotation from *praxis* to practice, from Aristotle to Nietzsche and Heidegger, establishing neither a new philosophy of history nor a political program or manifesto for a radical social transformation, but a revised human geography of our planet. Sloterdijk's enterprise is conservative in the sense of "Nietzsche's Antiquity Project" as defined in the chapter following that on "Rilke's Experience" – that is the second of its "twofold interest in preservation" (*You Must Change* 6). But it is on its first interest in preservation that I would like lastly to shed some light, that which defines it as an Enlightenment-conservative enterprise, declaring

> its allegiance to the continuum of cumulative knowledge that we call Enlightenment, and which, despite all rumours of having entered a new "post-secular" state, we in the present continue as a context of learning [of modern times – *moderner Zeiten*] meanwhile spanning four centuries.

Enlightenment is obviously here just another name for modernity, which Sloterdijk thinks as a *continuum* (not a series of turns and returns, as the succession of the following chapters might lead us to believe), a continuum extending from the Renaissance to the present, for at least four centuries, and much longer in fact, as is revealed or clarified later in the Nietzsche chapter. This is a continuing modernity, without postmodernity, a modernity of which Sloterdijk claims to be the guardian and even the curator – in French *le conservateur* (cf. page 1). It is, by the way, this same *conservateur* who, in the last section of the last chapter, will complain about the catastrophe of the plastic arts and conclude with the following alternative:

> Like the doping-corrupted sport system, the art system is at a crossroads: either it goes all the way on the path of corruption through imitation of the extra-artistic effect in the world of exhibitions and collections, exposing art once and for all as the playground of the last human [obviously not what Sloterdijk calls for], or it remembers the necessity of bringing creative imagination back to the workshops and re-addressing the question of how one should distinguish between what is worthy and what is unworthy of repetition. (Sloterdijk, *You Must Change* 435)

Such is the note on which the book itself closes, that is, before the final *Rück-* and *Ausblicke*, retrospective and outlook, forming, so to speak, its horizon. Beyond the undeniable condemnation of contemporary art in Nietzschean, but also very traditional, conservative or even reactionary terms (the playground of the last human, art which no longer is art but imitation of the extra-artistic scene, where the virtuoso artist has disappeared, selfishness, absence of imagination, etc.), the book ends with a hope presented as a necessity or a must: in order to avoid the end of art, to prevent art from falling irremediably into corruption, we must go back to the workshops, to repetition, to exercise, to practice. But the necessity of this problematic final return (or shall we say: conservation attempt) cannot hide the question – which seems to have been postponed until this last moment – of *which* repetition, *which* practice. It has even become a doubly moral question, in its form (how one *should* distinguish), as well as in its content (what is worthy and unworthy). The whole problem has now become how to articulate this hidden question, which allows such definitive judgments about art, with the general ascetology and theory of practice that Sloterdijk develops throughout his book.

Although it concerns art, this question is not a strictly aesthetic question; nor is it strictly ethical, at least not in the sense of an ethics as deeply rooted in ontology as Sloterdijk's, "an ethics that does not have values, norms and imperatives at its centre, but rather elementary orientations in the 'field' of existence" (like Heidegger's moods or *Stimmungen*, he adds (*You Must Change* 161)), and which he also names "First Science" or "First Theory" (164), with capitals in the English and French translations. This first theory however contains already, as ethics, the problem it is supposed to solve, namely, that of hierarchy and predominance of the worthy over the unworthy, of one opposite over the other one, or in still other terms, the problem of the articulation of theory and praxis. It suffices to read the very awkward deduction of the imperative from Heraclitus's fragment on ethos in Chapter 3, "Sleepless in Ephesus": what Heraclitus says about *ethos* presupposes the predominance of thought over non-thought, i.e., of *sophronein*, diversely translated as *Verständig-Sein*, good sense, or *être-sage*, being-wise; therefore, his ethics must contain the thesis "*sophronein* exists," *es gibt sophronein*, which, in its turn, must contain more than its "propositional content" (adding each time in your mind all the necessary quotation marks). Hence the conclusion: "It is an authoritative, spurring and tonic statement that confronts its addressees with the challenge: 'Give precedence to *sophronein*!' The oldest version of the metanoetic imperative already demands that humans distinguish between the upper and lower within themselves" (164). And if that was not clear enough, Sloterdijk explicitly adds in the next sentence that "the primal ethical directive 'You must change your life!' becomes acute in the pre-Socratic word *sophronein* – and with a manifestly practice-theoretical tendency" (164–65).

With this fragment we discover, surprisingly, a second torso, the torso of a text this time, as little archaic as the first one and from about the same years, between the sixth and the fifth century, a textual torso which may not see the philosopher as the other saw the poet, but certainly makes heard a voice. We still do not know exactly who is speaking to whom, but we distinctly hear the same imperative, the same sentence, twenty-five centuries later, even though transmitted through Rilke, then Sloterdijk. The experiences of the poet and of the philosopher are similar, the directive they both hear is identical: ontology must contain ethics, and ethics must contain a moral imperative. The problem lies in the meaning of this *must*: a probability or a necessity, and if a necessity, a merely physical one or rather a moral obligation? How does one go from the horizontality or immanence of life and practice to the verticality and transcendence of the moral imperative? *You must change your life!* is not the answer to this problem, just its implicit formulation: life is change, then why add this dimension of moral necessity? And why is it so necessary to show that it has always been there since the beginning?

specters of kant

After all, *change your life!* is already written in the imperative. Therefore, *you must* seems to be no more than a superfluous addition, a repetition. Yet, inasmuch as it makes the implicit explicit, it is essential to Sloterdijk's *Aufklärung* project. We know that he defines his enterprise as a *konservatorisches Unternehmen*, the task of a curator attached to the preservation of a continuum of knowledge, a context of learning called the Enlightenment. What a close reader soon learns is that such an *Aufklärung* appears in a mostly Kantian light. Along with Heidegger and Nietzsche, Kantian specters also haunt Sloterdijk's discourse, and they confer to the title voice a specific tone, that echoes other tones recently adopted in philosophy.

References to Kant's vocabulary are not difficult to find, from the critique to the three or four questions leading to anthropology, to the imperative. After his first *Critique of Cynical Reason*, Sloterdijk gives here his Critique of Immunitary Reason.[8] In the very last chapter of his book, he raises three questions, whose syntax cannot fail to remind us of the three questions mentioned by Kant at the end of the *Critique of Pure Reason*, in the second section of the "Canon of Pure Reason":

> All interest of my reason (the speculative as well as the practical) is united in the following three questions:
>
> 1. *What can I know?*
> 2. *What should I do?*
> 3. *What may I hope?*
>
> The first question is merely speculative [...]
> The second question is merely practical [...]
> The third question, namely, "If I do what I should, what may I then hope?" is simultaneously practical and theoretical [...][9]

In his lectures on logic, speaking then of the "field of philosophy in its cosmopolitan meaning," Kant adds a fourth question, to which the first three relate: what is man? and he indicates where to find their answers, namely, in metaphysics, ethics, religion, and anthropology. Sloterdijk seems here to adopt the cosmopolitan perspective, that is the one that puts the emphasis on anthropology, and, as we know, he privileges the third question: if I act as I ought to do, if I change my life as I should, what may I hope? – a question "at once practical and theoretical" in a much more intricate way, as we have seen with the extension of practice, than what Kant was referring to; therefore we also know that its answer cannot be strictly religion, but anthropotechnics.

One should moreover mention the existence of another link between Sloterdijk's general theory of practice and the Kantian enterprise that he is trying to conserve, of which he claims to be the curator: the method or the scheme of extension that is so pervasive in Sloterdijk's book has a certain analogy, if not more, with universalization in the construction of the categorical imperative. To sum up very briefly and loosely what Kant explains with great precision in the *Foundations of the Metaphysics of Morals*, the reason why morality has to take the form of a categorical imperative is that it cannot be dependent on exterior motives, however high or noble they may be. If it were dependent on something else (the pursuit of the common good, the fear of God, the need to become a better person, etc.), it would not be categorical, but hypothetical. Therefore, the moral imperative has no content, and is pure and absolute in that sense, absolutely detached from any conditions or determinations which would make our actions "pathological," to use another Kantian term from this context. As an absolute imperative, if it is one, *You Must Change Your Life* can have no other content than itself. How then do I know what I should do?

To answer this question, one needs to find, to use Sloterdijk's terms, "a sensible motif [a reasonable means] with whose aid the gulf between the sublime imperative and the practical exercise can be bridged" (*You Must Change* 449). This bridge, for Sloterdijk, is General Immunology. In Kant's *Critique of Practical Reason*, and more specifically in its Typic, it is the universality of law that serves as a schema, or a mediated representation in a kind of schematism analogous to that of the *Critique of Pure Reason*, except that the imagination of the first Critique is here replaced by the understanding, since there can be no sensible motives for moral action. Let us remember that the categorical imperative does not tell us what to do; its first formulation is: "Act as if the maxims of your action were to become through your will a universal law of nature," and only understanding, the dominant faculty in the domain of the knowledge of the laws of nature, can be of help in such a context. If the understanding is unavailable, then only the sublime remains. Understanding is the faculty of the universal, under which the multiplicity of the sensible, in time and space, is subsumed and synthesized in order to form concepts and thus knowledge. By forming the concept of practice through its maximal extension to the whole domain of human activity, Sloterdijk makes use of a procedure which is analogous to the schematism of practical reason. From that perspective, *You Must Change Your Life* can be reformulated thus: live your changing life as if everything you do, any exercise you practice, could be thought as a universal law of nature or of mankind. This requires thinking or considering things at a level or distance from where all local egotisms and determinations attaching us to our person, family, class, color, gender, province, or nation end up vanishing, allowing us to think globally and "a global co-immunity structure" to be born (451). On a more basic level, one could say that this implicit schematism, which I have tried to render explicit, is the moment where so-called verticality is born from the horizontality of the theoretical practice of anthropotechnics, where moral perspective articulates itself with the ontological ethics or ethical ontology born in Ephesus, outside of history.

a strange and sublime imperative

You must change your life, this sentence which Rilke wrote once is repeated over and over by Sloterdijk, each time with a more or less different emphasis, depending on the context where it is heard. And the light is so often Kantian that we tend no longer to distinguish between a grammatical imperative and moral or practical one. It is nevertheless, if you listen to it attentively, a strange imperative, which may explain why Sloterdijk calls it absolute or sublime rather than categorical. To express the imperative other than through a mode, one can use an auxiliary verb, namely, *sollen*, as Kant himself indicates. Rilke however writes, and Sloterdijk repeats without noticing: *Du mußt* (instead of *Du sollst*) *dein Leben ändern. You Must Change Your Life*, then, says the voice, instead of You *Ought* to Change Your Life. Now if you must, it means you do not have the moral obligation to do so, in fact you have no choice and there is no question of will: you will eventually change your life, you simply have to, whether you wish it or not. It is almost like saying: you will die, all humans must die, there is no question about it, it is a fact, even a fact of life, a fact of *physis*, a natural thing. The verticality of the order seems to have again disappeared.

But not its authority – and Sloterdijk is desperately in search of an authority, of something that will give authority to his discourse. That is the main reason why he chose such a seemingly dogmatic or arrogant title and why he begins with Rilke, that is, with a poem or a work of art. His ontologico-ethical and ascetological discourse requires the aesthetic and the artistic dimensions, for it is paradoxically the aesthetic that frees us from the threat and domination of the ethical. "Beginning with a poetic text seems apposite [*günstig* – *Gunst* being one of the fundamental concepts of Kant's aesthetics]," he writes, because "the powerless superiority of the works can affect observers who otherwise take pains to ensure that they have no lord, old or new, above them" (Sloterdijk, *You Must Change* 19). Even though Sloterdijk almost constantly uses the Kantian term imperative, the command does not in fact come from reason or Being, but from a stone, a work of art, a poem, which no longer imposes, but exposes itself; hence its sublime effect.

Yet this effect cannot last forever, it is vanishing, it can already no longer be heard today in art, religion, or wisdom.

> The only authority that is still in a position to say "You must change your life!" is the global crisis [...] Its authority is real because it is based on something unimaginable of which it is the harbinger: the global catastrophe [...] the Great Catastrophe [with capital initials ...] the goddess of the century [...] the monstrous [...] much like the God of monotheism [...] (Sloterdijk, *You Must Change* 444)

The Enlightenment-conservative tone adopted at the beginning has now taken, at the end of the book, such an apocalyptic turn that a detailed analysis of its stakes and implications would require at least another study; for it would inevitably have to take into account Derrida's analysis of the apocalyptic tone, which was itself already a deconstructive reading of Kant's opuscule *Of an Overlordly Tone Recently Adopted in Philosophy*, while being at the same time a defense and illustration of deconstruction as a continuation of *Aufklärung*.[10]

Kant's three questions about knowledge, morals, and religion become in Sloterdijk three questions about saying, hearing, and doing what the imperative prescribes: *Who may say it? Who can hear it?* and *Who will do it?* It prescribes everything and nothing, is everywhere and nowhere at the same time, is pronounced by or (rather) from a stone, but heard by indifferent spectators trying to deconstruct its warnings. It demands that:

> [at] every moment, I am to estimate the effects of my actions on the ecology of the global society [...] I am meant to stand my ground as a citizen of the world, even if I barely know my neighbours and neglect my friends. (Sloterdijk, *You Must Change* 448–49)

No wonder that such an imperative, if there is one, is not quite ready to be put into practice. Hardly postmodern and barely aesthetic, it maintains the delusion of a global conservative curator, whose task and claim is to preserve in one fell swoop the Enlightenment, the Renaissance, and Antiquity.

disclosure statement

No potential conflict of interest was reported by the author.

notes

1 This essay is based on a reading of two books by Peter Sloterdijk: *You Must Change Your Life*, trans. Wieland Hoban (Cambridge: Polity, 2013) and its extension *The Art of Philosophy. Wisdom as a Practice*, trans. Karen Margolis (New York: Columbia UP, 2012). It was first presented at the International Philosophical Seminar on July 3, 2017 in Castelrotto, Italy.

2 The French ed. is: Peter Sloterdijk, *Tu dois changer ta vie: de l'anthropotechnique*, trans. Olivier Mannoni (Paris: Libella-Maren Sell, 2011). Hereafter referenced as FE.

3 In the English translation *word* appears as *world*: cf. Sloterdijk, *You Must Change* 6 (FE 18).

4 Not *une entreprise de conservation éclairée*, as in FE 18.

5 Cf. FE 18: *l'éducation*, which unfortunately erases all direct reference to *Aufklärung*.

6 Sloterdijk, *You Must Change* 6 (German ed.: Peter Sloterdijk, *Du mußt dein Leben ändern: über Anthropotechnik* (Frankfurt: Suhrkamp, 2009) 17. Hereafter referenced as GE).

7 Sloterdijk, *You Must Change* 1. Thus, begins the book.

8 Cf. Sloterdijk, *You Must Change* 451, even though the imperative has ultimately become a mere directive: "protectionism of the whole becomes the directive of immunity reason [...] General Immunology is the legitimate successor of metaphysics and the real theory of 'religions.'"

9 Kant, *Critique of Pure Reason* 677 (A805/B833).

10 Cf. Kant, *Von einem neuerdings erhobenen vornehmen Ton in der Philosophie*; Derrida; and Trottein.

Trottein, Serge. "D'un autre ton adopté naguère en déconstruction." *Perspectives on Contemporary Literature: Vol. 12. Self and Other*. Lexington: UP of Kentucky, 1986. 57–64. Print.

bibliography

Derrida, Jacques. "Of an Apocalyptic Tone Recently Adopted in Philosophy." *Oxford Literary Review* 6.2 (1984): 3–37. Print.

Kant, Immanuel. *Critique of Pure Reason*. Ed. and trans. Paul Guyer and Allen W. Wood. Cambridge: Cambridge UP, 1998. Print.

Kant, Immanuel. *Von einem neuerdings erhobenen vornehmen Ton in der Philosophie*. 1796. Print.

Sloterdijk, Peter. *The Art of Philosophy. Wisdom as a Practice*. Trans. Karen Margolis. New York: Columbia UP, 2012. Print.

Sloterdijk, Peter. *Du mußt dein Leben ändern: über Anthropotechnik*. Frankfurt: Suhrkamp, 2009 (German original ed., referenced as GE). Print.

Sloterdijk, Peter. *Tu dois changer ta vie: de l'anthropotechnique*. Trans. Olivier Mannoni. Paris: Libella-Maren Sell, 2011 (French ed., referenced as FE). Print.

Sloterdijk, Peter. *You Must Change Your Life*. Trans. Wieland Hoban. Cambridge: Polity, 2013 (English ed.). Print.

Philosophy is its place comprehended in thoughts.

spheres: the grand narrative

The epigraph above is from Peter Sloterdijk's *In the World Interior of Capital*, a book that serves as a coda, of sorts, to his three-volume *Spheres* project, in which he undertakes a rather massive explication of a single concept. In Volume 1, he states that "being-in-spheres constitutes the basic human relationship" (Sloterdijk, *Bubbles* 45), where a sphere is an interior that is affected by an "outside" against which it must protect and expand itself. This holds for the earliest, prenatal bubble of a fetus and its placental enclosure, as well as a conscious subject existing in its surrounding world. It also holds for the earthly and heavenly globes of traditional cosmology and theology, as well as the modern earth of marine exploration and circumnavigation. And finally, it holds for the modern/post-modern plurality of spheres (foams) produced by late twentieth-century capitalism, technology, and telecommunication.

Sloterdijk's account is, by his own description, a grand narrative consisting of various lines of explication, which is a process of bringing an undisclosed background into an illuminated foreground. For him, explication is an unfolding of what Heidegger calls the *Lichtung*, the clearing in which humans encounter their world. But this openness is not, as in Heidegger, a *Geschick* (a sending) of being: it is technically constructed by humans themselves. Hence, when he states that philosophy is its place comprehended in thoughts, he not only

gary e. aylesworth

SPECTERS OF RELIGION
sloterdijk, immunology, and the crisis of immanence

re-words Hegel's famous statement in *The Philosophy of Right* ("philosophy is its own time apprehended in thoughts"), he puts the emphasis upon space as the primary dimension of philosophical orientation. Unlike Heidegger, who describes humans as fundamentally temporal-historical, the backdrop of our being-in-the-world is an ever-expanding exteriorization, where an outside is brought into the inside of the spaces we inhabit. This means there are no epochal (or revolutionary) breaks between historical periods. There are, instead, phases in the exteriorization of inhabited spaces, leading, finally, to our contemporary condition, where the *entire* outside is inside. The crisis of modernity is that we live in the midst of a monstrous immanence without any protecting dome, vault, or sky above us. Thus, Sloterdijk states, "being-in means: inhabiting the monstrous" (*das Ungeheuer*) (*Bubbles* 630).

This constitutes a crisis for the immunological function that spheres have provided since human beings first appeared: "the immunological catastrophe of the Modern Age is not the 'loss of the center,' but the loss of the periphery. The final boundaries are no longer what they once seemed; the support they offered was an illusion" (Sloterdijk, *Globes* 788). There is (at least) a twofold loss that humans must now cope with. On the one hand, there is a loss of transcendent meaning or value for the life of individuals, and, on the other hand, there is a loss of solidarity that came with bounded ethnic and territorial identities. Each person must now undertake the production of meaning and identity for themselves, through their own practices and activities. But this is not the old *engagement* of existentialism: our existence is not factically "given," but is a technical production to begin with, and selfhood is never isolated from the intimacy of being-with-another that is already present in pre-natal life.

religion and immunology

In his publications after *Spheres*, particularly in *You Must Change Your Life* and *Nach Gott* (*After God*), Sloterdijk takes up religion, or its current status, as a major theme. In *Spheres*, religious iconography and concepts figure prominently as features of symbolic immune systems, which, in the past, provided humans with meaning and solidarity. But, as he shows, the internal logic of these systems generates their exposure to an outside, leaving them non-functional when the outside comes inside. The expanding process of this interiorization–exteriorization provides the main line of Sloterdijk's narrative, which is itself a performative enactment of this process at a symbolic level. When he takes up religion again, he means the concept of religion that is conventionally modern. Here, he rejects the notion that, in the wake of contemporary crises, religion is re-emerging as a reactionary force threatening modernity itself. But, he says, "A spectre is haunting the Western world, the spectre of religion" (Sloterdijk, *You Must Change* 1).

Aside from the allusion to *The Communist Manifesto*, the statement speaks to the aftershock of an apparent resurgence, as if, having been driven from the field, religion is waging a comeback. But where Marx and Engels sought to replace the specter of an imaginary communism with the real thing, Sloterdijk sets out to show that the reality of religion is illusory. As he says: "I will show that a return *to* religion is as impossible as a return *of* religion – for the simple reason that no 'religion' or 'religions' exist, only misunderstood spiritual regimens" (Sloterdijk, *You Must Change* 3). In this regard, he turns to another side of immunology, the need for humans to set goals beyond themselves in order to give sense to their existence. What is returning instead, he says, is an awareness of this need, which is part of "the immunitary constitution of human beings" (3).

Immunology thus includes what Sloterdijk calls a general "ascetology" – a description of *repetitive practices* by which humans create new abilities, spaces, and values. Religions have shaped and protected human life through training in repeatable performances, and we have now reached a critical, or second-order, awareness that such is the case. As he declares: "It is time to reveal humans as the beings who result from repetition" (Sloterdijk, *You Must Change* 4). This explication is strategically aimed to render the conventional concept of religion non-functional by exposing it an illusion generated by an unilluminated background. As he declares:

> Our enterprise is no less than the introduction of an alternative language, and with the language an altered perspective, for a group of phenomena that tradition tended to refer to with such words as "spirituality," "piety," "morality," "ethics," and "asceticism." If the maneuver succeeds, the conventional concept of religion, that ill-fated bugbear from the prop studios of modern

Europe, will emerge from these investigations as the great loser. (4)

On his own account, Sloterdijk's alternative perspective on religion is not a break or rupture with an existing order, but an increase and expansion of its complexity. It is, in other words, an intervention in the symbolic system of the West that remains immanent within the system itself.

This feature can be illustrated through Sloterdijk's affinity with Niklas Luhmann, whose *Theory of Society* (*Gesellschaft der Gesellschaft*) also embraces the immanence of theory, or the description of the system, within the system. As he says:

> It can obviously be argued that society is immensely complex, and that a practicable methodology for dealing with highly complex and differentiated systems (so-called organized complexity) is lacking. This argument is all the more weighty if we point out that the description of the system is part of the system, and that there can be a plurality of such descriptions. (Luhmann, *Theory of Society, Vol. 1* 5)

The theory of society is a description of the system that expands its own complexity, but never objectifies society as a whole. Any observation of society still takes place within society, and it cannot observe itself. The description of society thus remains necessarily and perpetually incomplete. While he rejects Luhmann's formalism, Sloterdijk applies the logic of system theory to the development of spheres and their immunological functions.

Because of the immanence of description, Sloterdijk takes human beings to be irreducibly complex and disbarred from complete self-understanding. Humans live within no less than three immune systems: the biological, the social, and the symbolic-psychic, all of which are layered upon one another and provide positions for observation and description. The key for Sloterdijk, however, lies at the symbolic level, for that is where literary, philosophical, scientific, artistic, and indeed, religious, interventions take place. Following Luhmann, he adopts the concept that the environment of each system is the multiplicity of other systems, and that irritations and threats from the environment produce responses or repetitions that increase the system's complexity. As he says, "immune systems [...] can be defined *a priori* as embodied expectations of injury and the corresponding programmes of protection and repair" (Sloterdijk, *You Must Change* 8).

In addition to these system-theoretical notions, Sloterdijk credits Nietzsche for having discovered in humans another immunological function: a drive to surpass themselves by taking on "impossible" tasks. In *Human, All Too Human*, Nietzsche says: "Man takes delight in oppressing himself with excessive demands and afterwards deifying this tyrannically demanding something in his soul" (74; translation slightly altered). In recognition of this insight, Sloterdijk declares that "Nietzsche is no more or less than the Schliemann of asceticisms" (*You Must Change* 34). But where Nietzsche tends to emphasize the reactive side of asceticism as a denial of life, Sloterdijk uses the term *askesis* more generally to mean "training," "practice," or "discipline." And although he credits Nietzsche for developing "ascetology" as a method of cultural analysis, he resists Nietzsche's more shattering pronouncements, as when he prophesies an event of the "new" that will leap over the history of humanity up to now and open the time of the overman. Instead, Sloterdijk includes the notion of ascetic practices in his general immunology to emphasize *askesis* as systemic operation rather than a break with the system itself. As Sloterdijk says in *The Aesthetic Imperative*: "Community and immunity are basically expressions for the same thing. Both words derive from *munus*, which means something like social task or collective work that must be accomplished" (168). This holds for all cultural achievements, including philosophy, art, science, and religion.

As to the latter, Sloterdijk offers an example in his reading of Rilke's poem "Archaic Torso of Apollo." Here, the drive to surpass, which he refers to as "vertical tension," surfaces as a command from a piece of stone. As he remarks, "Rilke's 'Torso' is particularly suited to posing the question of authority, as it constitutes an experiment about allowing oneself to be told something" (Sloterdijk, *You Must Change* 19). He reminds us that Rilke had previously assisted Rodin in his workshop, when the sculptor pivoted away from *art nouveau* stylization to prioritize the materiality of objects. In his poetry, Rilke himself privileges human artifacts and living organisms as things that can demand our full gaze. The torso of Apollo, on display in the Louvre, embodies both senses of "thing-ness": it is a piece of stone that suggests the physical and sexual power of a youthful male form. Rilke's response is not a paean to the lost glories of Greek art; the torso's fragmentary state does not call for a retrieval, however imaginary, of its lost completeness. Rather, the fragment speaks from its own corporeal presence. Rilke's sense of this power, the re-affirmation of sexuality in particular, is at work here.

In this regard, he is part of the movement begun by Nietzsche and extended by Freud, i.e., the somatization of "higher values" as a step away from Christian renunciation. The poem is an instance of what Sloterdijk calls the de-spiritualization of religion: the stone torso speaks, not the god Apollo, and certainly not the God of Abraham. Its message is enigmatically stated in the last lines: "for there is no place / that does not see you. You must change your life." Sloterdijk sees in these lines Rilke's talent for religiosity, which is the ability to accept that the torso sees him as he sees it, and, in fact, that its gaze is more intense than his own. Such talent, Sloterdijk argues, is an *askesis*, an ability that can be developed through practice, and was, no doubt, developed during Rilke's apprenticeship in the atelier of Rodin. It is an inner gesture that reverses the subject/object relationship, so that things look upon us with commanding authority. As Sloterdijk remarks: "I receive the reward for my willingness to participate in the subject–object reversal in the form of a private illumination – in the present case, as an aesthetic movedness" (*You Must Change* 24).

"You must change your life" is an unchallengeable command that cannot be relativized as a command to perform this or that particular action. It is, instead, an impulse to break away from the ordinary and the familiar, to live differently. Sloterdijk concludes that Rilke

> discovered a stone that embodies the torso of "religion," ethics, and asceticism as such: a construct that exudes a call from above, reduced to the pure command, the unconditioned instruction, the illuminated utterance of being that can be understood – and which only speaks in the imperative. (*You Must Change* 25)

This having been said, Sloterdijk is skeptical that such an aesthetic experience would be possible today, because the complexification of the symbolic system has taken another turn. Rilke's talent for religiosity, rare enough for his time, is no longer contemporary with what unfolded in the later twentieth century.

Indeed, art no longer has the authority it still enjoyed in Rilke's time due to the expansion of aesthetic experience via telecommunication and mediatized images. Where everything is available and familiar, the struggle to introduce the unfamiliar (as authoritative) has reached its limit. This also has ramifications for religion, since religion is particularly dependent upon maintaining a sense of the transcendent, and that sense begins to fade as soon as religion becomes a matter for theoretical reflection or explication.

Sloterdijk points out that thematizing religion means, paradoxically, it can no longer serve the function it has lost simply by virtue of the fact that it can be indicated. As Luhmann states, observation is the operation of "making a distinction and indicating one side and not the other side of the distinction" (*Theories of Distinction* 85). There is always the unobserved "other side" that remains unmarked and indefinite, but which can be indicated in another distinction. The act of making a distinction, however, is invisible to itself and can never be included in what is indicated. Self-reflection is simply a "reentry" of the first distinction back into the system itself. Transcendence is therefore provisional and momentary, but the vacillation between transcendence and immanence can create illusions of an indicatable "higher power." According to Luhmann, this is where religion comes on the scene: "Religion comes into being as a first attempt to provide a place for the unfamiliar in the familiar" (*Theory of Society, Vol. 2* 33), and further, "we can also describe religion as 'reentry' of the distinction between the familiar and the unfamiliar in the familiar" (34).

This principle applies to all observing, hence modernity cannot understand itself from a transcendent position, for no such position can be maintained. Its relationship with other "times" is not so much a break from them as a complexification of their relations to one another; they can always be described and re-described in multiple instances. For the purpose of illuminating modernity's relation to religion, however, Sloterdijk chooses the following: "Modern is whoever believes you can, to the greatest extent, do otherwise than submit to God and to higher powers. A modern human wants to be, not endure, the higher power" [*Modern ist, wer glaubt, man könne bis ins Äußerste etwas anderes tun, als sich an Gott und höhere Gewalten hinzugeben. Der moderne Mensch will die höhere Gewalt nicht erleiden, sondern sein*] (*Nach Gott* 333). This does not mean that humans want to be God, it means, in fact, something more radical.

the monstrous: nietzsche and james

In the later nineteenth century, two philosophers of particular importance addressed this phenomenon: Friedrich Nietzsche and William James. Sloterdijk takes up their relationship in the later pages of *Nach Gott*, where he describes them as philosophers of "the monstrous" (*das Ungeheuer*), or the world bereft of transcendent meaning. The monstrous is "the necessarily true name for an exit-less world-totality transcending only in itself" [*der notwendige wahre Name für ein außenloses, nur in sich selbst transzendierendes Weltganzes*] (Sloterdijk, *Nach Gott* 343). This word has a long history in German letters, but for Sloterdijk, it announces the modern project of philosophy and science. While science investigates the world without thematizing its monstrousness, "the authentic philosophy of modernity," he says, "is a hermeneutic of the monstrous as a theory of the world existing solely in itself" [*Authentische Philosophie der Moderne ist die Hermeneutik des Ungeheren als Theorie der alleinigen Welt*] (343).

Both Nietzsche and James are aware of the systematicity of this world and its monstrous immanence. In *Human, All Too Human*, Nietzsche writes:

> With respect to the *past* we have enjoyment of all the cultures there have ever been and of their productions [...] In respect to the *future* there opens out before us, for the first time in history, the tremendous far-flung prospect of human-ecumenical goals embracing the entire inhabited earth. At the same time we feel conscious of possessing the strength to be allowed without presumption to take this new task in hand ourselves without requiring supernatural assistance. (257)

And in *Pragmatism* we have the following from James:

> Human efforts are daily unifying the world more and more in definite systematic ways. We found colonial, postal, consular, commercial systems, all parts of which obey definite influences that propagate themselves within the system but not to facts outside of it. The result is innumerable little hangings-together of the world's parts within the larger hangings-together, little worlds, not only of discourse but operation, within the wider universe. (64)

These statements describe a world that is rapidly complexifying through its own operations, and without access to an external standpoint from which a complete world-description could be given.

For Nietzsche, these developments have come about because the Christian "will to truth" has become reflexive, and has exposed itself as an endless unveiling of interpretations from which there is no exit to an absolute standpoint. As Nietzsche says in *The Gay Science*, "Rather has the world become 'infinite' for us all over again, inasmuch as we cannot reject the possibility that *it may include infinite interpretations*" (330). And as Nietzsche remarks in *The Genealogy of Morals*:

> All great things bring about their own destruction through an act of self-overcoming [...] the law-giver himself eventually receives the call: "*patere legem, quam ipse tulisti*" [*submit to the law you yourself have proposed*]. In this way Christianity *as a dogma* was destroyed by its own morality; in the same way Christianity *as morality* must now perish too: we stand on the threshold of *this* event. (161)

All of this is summed up by Nietzsche in the famous pronouncement of the Madman in *The Gay Science*: "God is dead [...] and we have killed him" (181). This pronouncement does not mean there are no longer humans who believe in God, but the notion of God as a transcendent eye that views, unifies, judges, and directs the world is no longer in effect. In this regard, believers and non-believers alike participate in the atheism of the world. But this is an atheism *in practice*. There can be no theoretical judgment "God does not exist," for such a judgment would presume to take a position that sees God's non-existence as a "fact," in other words, it would appropriate God's position for itself. Nietzsche's point is precisely the untenability of this presumption, either for God or for the judgment that asserts His existence or non-existence. Therefore, "we have killed him" means we have made God's transcendent position operationally impossible, for ourselves as well as for God.

For Sloterdijk, the pronouncements of Nietzsche's madman are an acknowledgement of events that occurred centuries earlier with the advent of modern cosmology:

> It is no coincidence that there are two reminders of the light from distant stars, for the true scene of God's murder is none other than the outermost shell of the ancient ethereal heaven, the sphere of fixed stars that had collapsed beneath the knife thrusts of the conspirators Digges, Bruno, Galilei, Descartes, and numerous others. (*Globes* 561–62)

Modern cosmology shatters the dome of heaven with its infinitely open universe, and de-centers the earth, then the sun, then any notion that there is a cosmic "center" at all. Nietzsche's message is not only that "we" murdered God with our science, but we are now called to take the *burden* of this catastrophe upon ourselves. The notion that the madman has come "too early" indicates humans are still blind and deaf to the enormity of what has happened. Nevertheless, on Sloterdijk's account, the later twentieth century is the time in which this task is carried out: the globes heaven and earth are shattered and humans now dwell in concatenated micro-spheres, or foams.

In the meantime, both Nietzsche and James carry out what Sloterdijk refers to as a somatization of the spiritual, where the psychic sphere interiorizes its material conditions. Somatization is a symbolic experiment in the application of bodily concepts to the life of the soul, where the soul becomes a scene of forces and relations that opens its self-containment to the world. As Sloterdijk says, for Nietzsche and James the psyche is "the adventurous heart of existence" [*das abenteuerliche Herz der Existenz*] (*Nach Gott* 346), and its concept drives them "toward an ethics of experimental life" [*zu einer Ethik des experimentierenden Lebens*] (346). Experimentation is the practice of theorizing the world *in* the world, and the production of effects that cannot be calculated in advance. This having been said, their styles of interpretation are distinctive.

On Sloterdijk's account, Nietzsche's experiments are illuminated through aesthetic-political concepts such as dream creation and will to power, while for James they are moral-religious experiences that put living hypotheses to the test. Nietzsche aims at an aristocratic-critical surpassing of modern humanity in the name of that which is higher, the "overman," whereas James is democratic, conciliatory, and open-minded (Sloterdijk, *Nach Gott* 347). Hence, Sloterdijk characterizes their interpretations of the monstrous as an alternative between "height" (*Höhe*) and "variety" (*Vielfalt*) (347).

For Nietzsche, the death of God opens the possibility of a higher human being, since "equality before God" has de-spiritualized itself as the levelling equality of the masses, with their demands for increased consumption and freedom from vertical tensions. In *Zarathustra*, Nietzsche writes:

> You higher men, learn this from me: in the marketplace nobody believes in higher men. And if you want to speak there, very well! But the mob blinks: "We are all equal."
> "You higher men" – thus blinks the mob – "there are no higher men, we are all equal, man is man; before God we are all equal."
> Before God! But now this God has died. And before the mob we do not want to be equal. You higher men, go away from the marketplace! (286)

For James, on the other hand, the issue is variety, and variety is democratic but not necessarily levelling. In *The Varieties of Religious Experience*, he professes a radical empiricism that does not reduce the multiplicity of religious experience to a general concept. Instead, he allows experiences that might otherwise be dismissed as excessive or pathological to speak for themselves. Their empirical particularities are allowed to stand and count "equally" in accordance with their effects. As Sloterdijk remarks: "We could say that James's empiricism was an American way into phenomenology" [*Man könnte sagen, daß James' Empirismus ein amerikansicher Weg in die Phänomenologie gewesen sei*] (*Nach Gott* 349) as well as an Americanization of the religious as a practical means to living successfully [*direkt an die Suche nach Lebenserfolg angeschlossen*] (352). In this regard, the variety of religious experience in America may not lend itself so easily to the equalizing and levelling *decadence* of religion that Nietzsche denounces in Europe. Nevertheless, Sloterdijk argues that James's psychological investigations are, in their fashion, as de-spiritualizing as Nietzsche's.

Like Nietzsche, James applies objective concepts to the soul without reducing it to the concepts themselves. His radical empiricism is an attack on intellectualism: the presumption that what is excluded from the definition of a concept is excluded from the things the concept applies to. There is always an excessiveness to experience that no concept can capture. "The actual universe is a thing wide open," says James, "but rationalism makes systems, and systems must be closed" (*Pragmatism* 16). In light of the impossibility of a conceptual system that captures the openness of the world, philosophy must be pragmatic, that is, experimental in testing ideas and concepts as hypotheses for living. In this regard, Sloterdijk finds that James's Americanism in religion is an acknowledgement of its connection to a technological age.

James describes religious experiences in terms of their fruitfulness for individual lives, without explaining them away as *mere* effects of physiological causes. Indeed, he submits the scientific non-believer to the same *patere legem* called for by Nietzsche:

> According to the general postulate of psychology just referred to, there is not a single one of our states of mind, high or low, healthy or morbid, that has not some organic process as its condition. Scientific theories are organically conditioned just as much as religious emotions are. (James, *Varieties* 14)

The grounds for accepting scientific explanations are the same as for religious beliefs, says James – "It is either because we take immediate delight in them; or else it is because we believe them to bring us good consequential fruits for life" (15). In other words, there is nothing intrinsically true about beliefs, either scientific or religious, other than the fact that we act them out and find the results to be pleasing and beneficial.

As to the specific nature of religious beliefs, James notes that "the word 'religion' cannot stand for any single principle or essence, but is rather a collective name" (*Varieties* 26). There are, in fact, many sentiments, objects, and practices that are considered "religious," a term for which no exact definition can be given. For methodological purposes James proposes the following: "Religion, therefore [...] shall mean for us the *feelings, acts, and experiences of individual men in their solitude, so far as they apprehend themselves to stand in relation to whatever they consider to be divine*" (31). Theologies and religious institutions are secondary and the practices that establish and maintain them come to the fore. For James, the reality of religion comes down to acting in accordance with things not objectively known to exist, but which nonetheless exert power through our capacity to act *as if* they existed. As Kant would say, we can act as if there were a God, an immortal soul, or a free will, and that is, for us, their only mode of being. But where Kant insists we are rationally obligated to act in these ways, James says we simply find such suppositions to be effective in living our lives.

James's lectures on religious experience are an attempt at an empirical science of religion, a science whose concepts and conclusions are themselves hypotheses to be tested in experience, which is always an individual matter. On this point he is clear: "Individuality is founded in feeling; and the recesses of feeling, the darker, blinder strata of character, are the only places in the world in which we catch real fact in the making" (James, *Varieties* 501). This having been said, he offers a conclusion about religious feeling in general. It consists in "a sense that there is *something wrong about us* as we naturally stand," along with "a sense that *we are saved from the wrongness* by making proper connections with the higher powers" (508). This feeling of wrongness would be James's version of Rilke's "You must change your life," and has the capacity to supply the vertical tension that Sloterdijk and Nietzsche find to be fundamental for human self-surpassing.

Despite his rather cursory and dismissive remarks about Nietzsche (*Varieties* 371–73), James's notion of "the darker, blinder strata of character" is virtually the same as Nietzsche's view of the self as a largely unconscious multiplicity of forces, impulses, and processes. For example, in *Zarathustra* Nietzsche writes: "soul is only a word for something about the body. The body is a great reason, a plurality with one sense, a war and a peace, a heard and a shepherd" (34). In a similar vein, James declares that "Apart from all religious considerations, there is actually and literally more life in our total soul than we are at any time aware of" (*Varieties* 511), and that "*the conscious person is continuous with a wider self through which saving experiences come*" (515). Quoting Frederic Myers, it is clear he takes this wider self to be an organic reserve that is never fully conscious. This, he says, is the source of religious feelings, indeed of all feelings, and hence it is a matter for science and philosophy, but also confirms the religious person's sense of a power greater than themselves.

These similarities between Nietzsche and James notwithstanding, Sloterdijk believes James is more in line with the way modernity actually unfolded, that is, as a transformation of mass culture rather than the achievement of an elite few. As Sloterdijk remarks: "Nietzsche was himself an actor in a genuine renaissance, and the reason he did not identify himself accordingly is that his notion of renaissance was too dependent on art-historical conventions" (*You Must Change* 30). He proposes, instead, to read Nietzsche from the standpoint of system theory and its notion of the complexification of society. The art-historical approach understands renaissance to mean the rebirth of classical models in the work of a few great artists. This attitude may have inspired the young Nietzsche to see Wagner's music as a rebirth of Greek tragedy in the midst of nineteenth-century decadence. On Sloterdijk's account, however, the real renaissance, that is, the real blossoming of modernity, is a movement away from great individuals and the elite classes. From a systemic standpoint, the forms of ancient art are a secondary to art's social function, and in that regard, art is for the entire community and not just for a cultivated few. "In order to separate from the few to the many," says Sloterdijk, "the renaissance had to discard its humanistic exterior and reveal itself as the return of ancient mass culture" (*You Must Change* 30). This requires, in turn, a re-definition of "renaissance" as a repetition of the past.

On Sloterdijk's reading, Nietzsche, whether he realized it or not, was envisioning not so much a step beyond modernity but a repetition of antiquity within modernity itself, a radical "allochrony" or other-timeliness in the present. Nietzsche's historicality is therefore a complexification of temporality: antiquity is a form of the non-historical, which is to say, a moment alongside the linear time of modernity. Nietzsche himself suggests the necessity of repeating this non-historical moment when he writes: "*the unhistorical and the historical are necessary in equal measure for the health of an individual, a people and of a culture*" (*Untimely Meditations* 63). This means the present must remain an open horizon, without pre-ordination from the past or future, and without a fixed periodization. It also opens temporal events to the possibilities of chance. Quoting Grillparzer, he declares:

> All human beings have at the same time their own individual necessity, so that millions of courses run parallel beside one another in straight or crooked lines, frustrate or advance one another, strive forwards or backwards, and thus assume for one another the character of chance, and so, quite apart from the influences of the occurrences of nature, make it impossible to establish any all-embracing necessity prevailing throughout all events. (Nietzsche, *Untimely Meditations* 89–90)

The question for Sloterdijk is whether the creative incalculability of chance offers individuals an exit beyond the history of humanity up to now, or whether, in system-theoretical fashion, it complexifies this history on a social scale. For him, the idea of an exit over man, over the mob and the marketplace, smacks too much of Old Europe and its romantic-aristocratic longings.

For him, modernity begins in the Baroque period, with the consolidation of nation-states and their policies for administration and improvement, including programs for the increase of population and public welfare. As he says, "In this situation, improving the world meant improving humans *en masse*" (Sloterdijk, *You Must Change* 347). The push to expand literacy on a mass scale, resulted in the establishment and expansion of schools, which then developed their own culture of "*Bildung*" (i.e., the development of individual personalities and the cultivation of cultural elites). We need not be reminded that those who introduced the term "renaissance" into historical discourse were products of this system, as was the brilliant student from *Schulpforta*, Friedrich Nietzsche. But this subjectification of a supposedly universal, orienting standpoint is an attempt to save what is already lost: a common ground in the present between the present and the past.

As Luhmann points out, this common ground does not hold when we experience time in time, that is, when the present is nothing but the difference between past and future. This difference does not have the stability of a thing, or a self, but pluralizes time in its operation. In his *Pragmatism* essay, James says much the same thing:

> Cosmic space and cosmic time, so far from being the intuitions that Kant said they were, are constructions as patently artificial as any that science can show. The great majority of the human race never use these notions, but live in plural times and spaces, interpenetrant and *durcheinander*. (82)

And in *A Pluralistic Universe* James remarks:

> Past and future, for example, conceptually separated by the cut to which we give the name present, and defined as being the opposite sides of that cut, are to some extent, however brief, co-present with each other throughout experience. The literally present moment is a purely verbal supposition, not a position. (746)

This statement is in almost perfect accord with Luhmann's description of temporality in

Theory of Society. There he says the renaissance is not only a period in history, but the advent of history itself, a time when humans began to orient themselves to the future, which was no longer seen as a repetition or fulfillment of the past, but an open horizon that allowed the possibility for novelty: "The future was the construction – generated in time, running and shifting with time – of still unknown meanings, and was in this sense, not only *different* from what was past, but also *new*" (Luhmann, *Theory of Society*, Vol. 2 256).

Since the past was now seen as the other side of its difference with the future, it took on the meaning of something lost and bygone. The present is the unity of this difference, nothing more; it is not time "but the blind spot that has to be presupposed if time is to be observed at all" (Luhmann, *Theory of Society*, Vol. 2 258). The repetition of this blind spot produces a sense of the future as "free" in relation to the past. As Luhmann puts it, "If we understand time as the continuous reproduction of a difference between past and future, this gradually undermines the notion of a causal determination of future states by past states" (260). Or in the words of William James, "Free will pragmatically means *novelty in the world*, the right to expect that in its deepest elements as well as its surface phenomena, the future may not identically repeat and imitate the past" (*Pragmatism* 55).

Now, it is one thing to say that the future is free in relation to the past, but it is another to say, as Nietzsche does, that Zarathustra "says Yes to the point of justifying, of redeeming even all of the past" (*Ecce Homo* 308). This is to project an "outside" from which *all* of the past can be viewed and assembled into one. (Such a "one" is precisely what redemption is supposed to mean.) For Sloterdijk, however, this still speaks from a standpoint of heroic individualism, a standpoint of one looking down upon all of history from a great height without seeing the blind spot that makes such a vision possible. For this reason, he prefers James's more modest project of risking hypotheses in the midst of the world, and whose pluralism extends to the irreducible variety of standpoints toward the past, a variety that cannot be viewed whole because we are always embedded in them.

a new solidarity?

While humans are always embedded in their interiors, Sloterdijk insists that we are compelled to surpass ourselves by interiorizing what is "outside" and exteriorizing what is "inside." As he put forth in his *Spheres* project, we now confront a world in which this process has reached a maximal outcome: the periphery that differentiated the interior from its exterior has dissolved into a monstrous immanence that calls for a new interpretation. This is the situation that Sloterdijk calls "the world interior of capital." To the extent that there is a common interior for human beings, it is a system of markets, credits, and commodities: everything is offered for sale, consumption, and disposal. As Sloterdijk remarks: "the basic fact of the Modern Age is not that the earth travels around the sun; it is that money goes around the earth" (*Globes* 54). Furthermore, by the turn of the twenty-first century, money has become a virtual totality: "The most effective totalization, the unification of the world through money in all of its transformations – as commodity, text, number, image and celebrity – took place through its own momentum" (Sloterdijk, *World Interior* 7). In this regard, "money has long since proved itself as an operatively successful alternative to God" (209). But this is not an ethical *co-munus*; the system generates innumerable inequities and conflicts, but no "universal" solidarity.

In the past, religion provided the immunological cover for a common "we" in spite of inequities and differences among individuals. But this is no longer possible under the reign of capital. As Sloterdijk remarks: "none of the so-called world religions can qualify as the Great Vehicle for all factions of humanity" (*Globes* 946; *World Interior* 146). Instead, he suggests that "the only fact of universal ethical significance in the current world is the diffusely and ubiquitously growing realization that things cannot continue in this way" (Sloterdijk, *You Must Change* 442). There is, then, something like an affective basis for a new solidarity, albeit one without the guarantee of a transcendent God. Nor can art speak any longer with sublime authority, as it did to Rilke. Nevertheless, notes Sloterdijk, there is a sense of foreboding about the so-called "global crisis" that is registering around the world. "Its authority is real," he says, "because it is based on something unimaginable of which it is the harbinger: the global catastrophe" (444).

The sublimity of the imperative "you must change your life!" arises from the monstrous immanence of the world and the inescapability of human overtaxing that Nietzsche discovered behind asceticism. On Sloterdijk's account, an effect of the modern Enlightenment was a shift in the experience of the sublime away from the ethical authority of God to the domain of aesthetics, where the subject could enjoy its affective agitations in contemplative serenity. But now the monstrousness of the world, which is sublime in its boundlessness, calls upon us to act. Quoting Hans Jonas, Sloterdijk formulates the contemporary imperative thus: "'Act in such a way that the effects of your actions can be reconciled with the permanence of true human life on earth'" (*You Must Change* 448). The imperative is sublimely absolute because it calls upon me, as an individual agent, to take responsibility for effects that I cannot completely foresee or calculate, as a member of a human race I cannot, as such, present to myself. This is indeed an "impossible" task. The question is how to bridge the gap between the absolute demand and any concrete human action.

Sloterdijk's answer is to do so through immunology. This requires an expansion of "solidaristic" and symbolic systems such that the self-concept extends beyond historically limited identities into the widest sense of co-immunity. What is needed is the co-operative creation of a genuinely common sphere: "every act of solidarity," says Sloterdijk, "is an act of sphere formation, that is to say the creation of an interior" (*Bubbles* 12). This would be an interior whose limit is the earth itself as the shared site of human action, and in this regard, he maintains that "Global immunitary reason is one step higher than all those things that its anticipations in philosophical idealism and religious monotheism were capable of attaining" (Sloterdijk, *You Must Change* 451). In terms of his *Spheres* project, the earth is to become the new "With" that accompanies and completes the human being since its placental surroundings *in utero*. "As far as the With is concerned," Sloterdijk says, "its quality of presence is neither that of a person nor that of a subject, but rather a living and life-giving *It* that remains yonder-close-by" (*Bubbles* 356). And in silent homage to Heidegger he declares "The With is the first thing that gives and lets things be" (357).

The earth is to be "a pre-objective something floating around me" whose purpose is "to let me be and support me" (Sloterdijk, *Bubbles* 478), except that it must now let be and support all of humanity. On the one hand, then, Sloterdijk's symbolic intervention is an attempt to begin the construction of this ultimate interior, while, at the same time, he could say he is explicating what was already there, folded invisibly into the background. Interestingly, his notion that humans are intimately involved with their spheres, and that the self is never separable from its completing "something," brings him near to James, who writes:

> From a pragmatic point of view the difference between living against a background of foreignness and one of intimacy means the difference between a general habit of wariness and one of trust. One might call it a social difference, for after all, the common *socius* of us all is the great universe whose children we are. (*A Pluralistic Universe* 644)

For both thinkers the envisioned "socius" could never be conceived as a globe, or an orb viewed from outside, but must be experienced as a relation of deepest intimacy, whether to the "great universe" as James puts it, or to the earth as the common site for human dwelling. That Sloterdijk opts to think this fundamental relation in terms of spherical interiors invites comparison with other models.

latour and actor–network theory

Sloterdijk and Latour often cite and refer to one another approvingly. In *Foams*, for instance, Sloterdijk credits Latour for bringing nonhuman and human agents together in a common ontological space (201) and goes so far as to say: "Latour's concept of articulation comes very close to what has here been termed explication. Like this, it straddles the threshold between science-theoretical and ontological meanings" (203). And in "Spheres and Networks: Two Ways to Reinterpret Globalization," Latour declares: "I was born a Sloterdijkian" and "Without knowing it, I had always been a 'spherologist'" (*Harvard Design Magazine, No. 30*). But these statements notwithstanding, their theoretical models are actually quite different. Latour, in fact, is critical of three-dimensional models of space, including spheres, and prefers to speak of "networks" instead, while Sloterdijk says "the image of the network suggests the notion of inextended points joined as intersections of lines – a universe for data fishers and anorexics" (*Foams* 237). Despite their common-cause alliance against "globalism," the differences between their concepts of space are worth noting.

Latour is an exponent of actor–network theory (ANT), which challenges traditional philosophy and sociology by not taking "agents" or "society" as *given*. Instead, he defines "actor" as "the moving target of a vast array of entities swarming around it" (Latour, *Reassembling the Social* 46) and the "social" as "a type of momentary association which is characterized by the way it gathers together into new shapes" (66). Society is not an already constituted space within which action occurs, but is always in the making, or assembling, as are agents, including humans and nonhumans. Concerning traditional theorists, Latour remarks: "they make such an inordinate consumption of three-dimensional images: spheres, pyramids, monuments, systems, organisms, organizations. To resist this temptation, I am going to offer a 2-D projection" (171–72). In other words, Latour proposes to flatten out the topography of any *socius* by tracing its networks.

Networks are "articulations," that is, the assembling of actions associated with humans and nonhumans such that the collective comes to "speak" (see *Politics of Nature* 86), and, as Latour declares, "There is nothing more political than this activity" (89). Society, then, is an assembling of human and nonhuman actors, who participate in shaping the world. As he remarks, "Society is not the whole 'in which' everything is embedded, but what travels 'through' everything" (Latour, *Reassembling the Social* 241). This is a performative process: there is no collective prior to its articulation, and articulation has no predetermined spaces or boundaries. In addition, articulation distributes places and localities into one another, and their points of convergence are "articulators." As Latour explains: "'local interaction' is the assemblage of all the *other* local interactions distributed elsewhere in time and space [...] It is the transported presence of places into other ones that I call *articulators* or *localizers*" (194). This means actor networks are de-centered and non-totalizable.

Furthermore, what remains between the meshes of the network is neither an "inside" nor an "outside," but a space of potential connections. "Contrary to substance, surface, domain, and spheres that fill every centimeter of what they bind and delineate," says Latour, "nets, networks, and 'work nets' leave everything they don't connect simply unconnected" (*Reassembling the Social* 242). He calls this background space "plasma" to indicate it is not empty, but is "that which is not yet formulated, not yet measured, not yet socialized" (244). These notions gain deeper importance in Latour's later work on the ecological crisis, which he designates as "the new climate regime."

In *Facing Gaia*, Latour addresses the crisis as a matter of eco-politics: the formation of a collective without any divide between the human and the nonhuman, i.e., without "nature" and "society" as collectives already constituted. Here, we see a specific point of convergence, but also a difference, between ANT and Sloterdijk's spherology. Latour is struck by Sloterdijk's explication of the non-commensurable spaces of the metaphysical and cosmological globes – between God as the center of being and the earth as the center of the cosmos. But the point for Latour is not so much that God's being and the cosmos are conceived as spheres; it is that they represent incommensurable spaces. One is a "universal" center, and the other is the "local," cosmological center of human experience, but at a distance from God's presence beyond the heavenly vault. As Latour remarks:

> The two images of the world in Christian theology are just as irreconcilable as the images that would be represented, for example, by the physics of the electron that is present *everywhere* in the world even as it is safely housed *in* J.J. Thomson's Cavendish Laboratory. (*Facing Gaia* 127)

In other words, a universal center is not located anywhere, and therefore is not really a "center," and a local center is necessarily at a distance from universality. The history of science repeats this problematic, and that is what interests Latour.

In this regard, Latour presents the prospect of political ecology in terms of negotiating the immanence of the world's existents and their localities. As he says: "We have to remain open to the dizzying otherness of existents [...] It is this opening to otherness that William James proposed to call the *pluriverse*" (Latour, *Facing Gaia* 36). Against this background, Latour proposes to think the immanence of this opening as "Gaia," in accordance with the work of James Lovelock. "Gaia," he says "is not an organism, and [...] we cannot apply to it any technological or religious model. It may have an order, but it has no hierarchy; it is not ordered by levels; it is not disordered either" (106). Nor, we should note, is Gaia a sphere.

Gaia, in this conception, is Earth (capitalized), but not the earth as a globe that we view from an imaginary-transcendent position, and not "nature" as an ontological block standing opposite "man," or "society." Latour finds a representation of Gaia in Caspar David Friedrich's painting *Das grosse Gehege bei Dresden* (The Great Enclosure near Dresden), a curious landscape depicting a scene on the banks of the Elbe. The canvas is divided horizontally between a globe-like mass in the foreground, appearing to curve beneath the opposite bank of the river, and a skyline bending upward at the edges, suggesting another curved space hovering over, and reflected in, the watery land mass below. Latour comments:

> What is brilliant about this painting is the way it marks the instability of every point of view [...] With the Great Enclosure, the great impossibility is not being imprisoned on Earth, it is believing that Earth can be grasped as a reasonable and coherent Whole. (*Facing Gaia* 223)

The painting, in fact, does not allow viewing from an established position, but pulls the viewer into its not-quite-reconcilable dimensions. In a striking parallel with Sloterdijk's reading of Rilke's *Archaic Torso*, Latour describes the experience thus:

> In the Great Enclosure where we are now confined, an eye is fixed on us, but it is not the eye of God fixed on Cain crouching down in the tomb; it is the eye of Gaia looking straight at us, in broad day light. Impossible, from now on, to remain indifferent. From now on, *everything is looking at us*. (*Facing Gaia* 254)

Following Carl Schmitt, who defines politics in terms of war, and war as a condition of enemies facing each other without a neutral "third party" (an established order of law), Latour states that Gaia is essentially political because it isn't "nature": it isn't an established order and it isn't neutral.

"If Gaia has such a powerful effect as a political lever," he says, "it is because it raises anew the now familiar question: in the name of what supreme authority have we agreed to give our lives – or, more often, to take those of others?" (Latour, *Facing Gaia* 226). Disputes over climate change force us to confront this question with ever-increasing urgency, especially since "others" include those who are human and those who are nonhuman, and even Gaia itself. Gaia is not only the Earth, the enclosure where existents, their spaces, and their actions impinge upon one another, Gaia is subjectivized as an actor who can also be an enemy. As Latour remarks in *Down to Earth*: "If the Terrestrial is no longer the framework for human action, it is because it *participates* in that action [...] Space has become an agitated history in which we are participants among others" (42). Gaia is the indeterminate space of action and an agent itself, the non-neutral third party to all of our doings. Hence, we find ourselves in an irreducibly political moment because, as Latour says, "the Dome of Nature, under which all the old conflicts took place, has disappeared" (*Facing Gaia* 237).

This condition echoes the loss of periphery that Sloterdijk explicates in *Spheres*. However, unlike spherology, political ecology is not anthropo-morphic. The spaces and agents Latour is concerned with are open to one another in contested lines of association, so much so that any "commons" would be produced by action among all parties in the absence of an established order. Nor would such an assemblage constitute a shared interior. Political ecology is not immunological, indeed, it is necessitated by the radical exposure of existents to *other* existents, perhaps to the point of death, without a protecting membrane between them or a sheltering sphere around them. Instead, it must come about through negotiation, the only way to achieve peace in a Schmittian condition of war. Nevertheless, as Latour clarifies, there must be an authority under whose name the warring parties are called together in the first place, and this calling is an essentially religious act.

Gaia is to be the authority recognized and respected by all that Latour proposes not to call "God" but "Out-of-Which-We-Are-All-Born" (*Facing Gaia* 159). In this regard, he says:

"religion" does no more than designate that to which one clings, what one protects carefully, what one this is careful not to neglect [...] to be religious is first of all to become attentive to that to which others cling. It is thus, in part, to learn to behave as a diplomat. (152)

Being religious, then, is the first condition for negotiating peace, and it means, above of all, not neglecting Gaia as that from which all are born.

This concept of religious action has a different quality from Sloterdijk's declaration that "none of the so-called world religions will ever qualify as the Great Vehicle," etc. For Latour, to act religiously is not to institute a religion, but to call together a collective, and his linguistic interventions are examples of this. They are, in essence, political gestures in the sense he borrows from Carl Schmitt. Sloterdijk, on the other hand, is a thinker of the absolute imperative: a command addressed to humans in their individual activities, a command no longer speaking in religious form. As he says: "What people called 'religion' was only ever significant as a vehicle of the absolute imperative in its different place-and-time-based versions. The rest is the chatter of which Wittgenstein rightly said that it should be brought to an end" (Sloterdijk, *You Must Change* 445). Instead, the command registers ethically, from a general unease about the "global crisis": "Act in such a way that the effects of your actions can be reconciled with the permanence of true human life on earth." It speaks only of human life, without reference to nonhuman others whose "life" may also be at stake. On this point, spherology and political ecology do not speak from or to the same place, despite their apparent proximity.

If, as Sloterdijk says, philosophy is its place comprehended in thoughts, the beginning of comprehension may be the problematization of place itself, for no figure of place firmly localizes philosophy or gives shape to the immanence of thought. The place of thinking remains open.

disclosure statement

No potential conflict of interest was reported by the author.

bibliography

James, William. "A Pluralistic Universe." *William James Writings: 1902–1910.* Ed. Bruce Kucklick. New York: Library of America, 1987. Print.

James, William. *Pragmatism.* Ed. Bruce Kucklick. Indianapolis: Hackett, 1981. Print.

James, William. *The Varieties of Religious Experience.* Harrisonburg: Penguin, 1982. Print.

Latour, Bruno. *Down to Earth: Politics in the New Climate Regime.* Trans. Catherine Porter. Cambridge: Polity, 2018. Print.

Latour, Bruno. *Facing Gaia: Eight Lectures on the New Climate Regime.* Trans. Catherine Porter. Cambridge: Polity, 2017. Print.

Latour, Bruno. *Politics of Nature: How to Bring the Sciences into Democracy.* Cambridge, MA: Harvard UP, 2004. Print.

Latour, Bruno. *Reassembling the Social: An Introduction to Actor–Network Theory.* Oxford: Oxford UP, 2005. Print.

Latour, Bruno. "Spheres and Networks: Two Ways to Reinterpret Globalization." *Harvard Design Magazine No. 30, (Sustainability) + Pleasure, Vol. I: Culture and Architecture*, Spring/Summer 2009. Web. <www.harvarddesignmagazine.org/issues/30/spheres-and-networks-two-ways-to-interpret-globalization.html>.

Luhmann, Niklas. *Theories of Distinction: Redescriptions of Modernity.* Trans. Joseph O'Neil, Elliott Schreiber, Kerstin Behnke, and William Whobrey. Stanford: Stanford UP, 2002. Print.

Luhmann, Niklas. *Theory of Society, Vol. 1.* Trans. Rhodes Barrett. Stanford: Stanford UP, 2012. Print.

Luhmann, Niklas. *Theory of Society, Vol. 2.* Trans. Rhodes Barrett. Stanford: Stanford UP, 2013. Print.

Nietzsche, Friedrich. *Ecce Homo.* Trans. Walter Kaufmann. New York: Vintage, 1989. Print.

Nietzsche, Friedrich. *The Gay Science.* Trans. Walter Kaufmann. New York: Vintage, 1974. Print.

Nietzsche, Friedrich. *Human, All Too Human.* Trans. R.J. Hollingdale. Cambridge: Cambridge UP, 1986. Print.

Nietzsche, Friedrich. *On the Genealogy of Morals.* Trans. Walter Kaufmann. New York: Vintage, 1989. Print.

Nietzsche, Friedrich. *Thus Spoke Zarathustra.* Trans. Walter Kaufmann. New York: Penguin, 1966. Print.

Nietzsche, Friedrich. *Untimely Meditations.* Trans. R.J. Hollingdale. Cambridge: Cambridge UP, 1983. Print.

Sloterdijk, Peter. *The Aesthetic Imperative: Writings on Art.* Trans. Karen Margolis. Cambridge: Polity, 2017. Print.

Sloterdijk, Peter. *In the World Interior of Capital.* Trans. Wieland Hoban. Cambridge: Polity, 2013. Print.

Sloterdijk, Peter. *Nach Gott.* Berlin: Suhrkamp, 2018. Print.

Sloterdijk, Peter. *Spheres, Vol. 1: Bubbles.* Trans. Wieland Hoban. Cambridge, MA: MIT P, 2011. Print.

Sloterdijk, Peter. *Spheres, Vol. 2: Globes.* Trans. Wieland Hoban. Cambridge, MA: MIT P, 2014. Print.

Sloterdijk, Peter. *Spheres, Vol. 3: Foams.* Trans. Wieland Hoban. Cambridge, MA: MIT P, 2016. Print.

Sloterdijk, Peter. *You Must Change Your Life.* Trans. Wieland Hoban. Cambridge: Polity, 2013. Print.

Archaic Torso of Apollo

We never knew his head and all the light
that ripened in his fabled eyes. But
his torso still burns like a streetlamp
   dimmed
in which his gaze, lit long ago,

holds fast and shines. Otherwise the surge
of the breast could not blind you, nor a
   smile
run through the slight twist of the loins
toward that center where procreation flared.

Otherwise this stone would stand cut off
and cold under the shoulders' transparent
   drop
and not glisten like a wild beast's fur;

and not break forth from all its contours
like a star: for there is no place
that does not see you. You must change
   your life.[1]

christina howells

SARTRE AND SLOTERDIJK
the ethical imperative. you must change your life

I seem to be haunted – happily haunted – by the Belvedere Torso. Having chosen it for the front cover of my book *Mortal Subjects* in 2011, it then featured in the International Philosophical Seminar (IPS) of 2014 on Rancière's *Aisthesis* where it was the subject of Rancière's first chapter on "Divided Beauty"; and later, in 2017, in the IPS on Sloterdijk's *You Must Change Your Life: On Anthropotechnics*, it was, once again, the subject of Chapter 1. This feels like something more than a lucky coincidence: Rilke believed that the Torso was addressing us directly in what Sloterdijk calls "The command from the stone"; it certainly seems to be addressing me.[2]

There are several translations of Rilke's poem "Archaïscher Torso Apollos": Archaic Torso of Apollo (in the translation by Edward Snow); Torso of an Archaic Apollo, in another (by C.F. MacIntyre); Apollo's Archaic Torso in a third (by Sarah Stutt). Almost all of them translate the last phrase in the same way: Du mußt dein Leben ändern, You must change your life. But there are innumerable variations on the translation of the poem as a whole, and even of the last two lines:

> [...] denn da ist keine Stelle, / die dich nicht sieht. Du mußt dein Leben ändern.
> [...] for there is no place / that does not see you. You must change your life. [MacIntyre and Snow]
> [...] for there is no angle from which / it cannot see you. You have to change your life. [Sarah Stutt, who also produced the following looser version]:
> [...] for its searing gaze / penetrates your soul, the way you live.

You must change your life. It is not possible to discuss moral imperatives without mentioning Kant and we will come back to him later. But it is worth noting straight away that there are many puzzles surrounding Kant's own comments on the language of imperatives. In *Foundations of the Metaphysics of Morals*, Kant writes: "Alle Imperativen werden durch ein *Sollen* ausgedrückt [...]," translated by Lewis White Beck as "All imperatives are expressed by an ought."[3] In fact, despite what Kant himself claims, none of his three major formulations of the categorical imperative uses *Sollen*, any more than the English translations use Ought, Should, Have to, Will, or Must. They use rather a simple, direct imperative: "Always act in such a way that [...] etc."

You must change your life. The Belvedere Apollo – or possibly Hercules or Ajax – a torso, headless and legless, is watching you. Indeed, it is addressing you directly, bursting forth from its marble contours like a star, blinding you. The positions of common sense are reversed: it is the ancient and headless statue that sees and smiles and glows, while the living, breathing reader is reduced to the status of object, silent and blind in the face of the "pure command" (Sloterdijk, *You Must Change* 25). We cannot determine the precise source of this "unconditional instruction"; it comes out of the blue, whether from below or above or indeed, as Sloterdijk suggests – though without any great certainty – from the statue itself. In Sloterdijk's view, the command, the "illuminated utterance," summarises and concentrates

> All the teachings of the papyrus religions, the parchment religions, the stylus and quill religions, the calligraphic and typographical, all order rules and sect programmes, all instructions for meditation and doctrines of stages, and all training programmes and dietologies. (25)

This is certainly a tall order, one might call it hyperbolic. Indeed, "*You must change your life*" is described by Sloterdijk as the "absolute imperative," "the imperative that exceeds the options of hypothetical and categorical" (25). Sloterdijk does not explain exactly how it exceeds the Kantian imperatives but his general meaning is crystal clear. This is the imperative to end all imperatives, "the quintessential metanoetic command." It is an unchallengeable call for personal revolution and it tells me that "I am not living properly."

> This authority touches on a subtle insufficiency within me that is older and freer than sin; it is my innermost not-yet. In my most conscious moment, I am affected by the absolute objection to my status quo: my change is the one thing that is necessary. (26)

On occasions Sloterdijk does give versions of his imperative formulated in Kantian style as part of a discussion of different instantiations of the metanoetic command: "Always behave in such a way that the account of your development could serve as the schema for a generalizable history of completion" (253), for example; or again, "You must act at all times in such a way that within your person, you anticipate a better world in the worse" (323); and finally, in ecological mode, "Act in such a way that the effects of your actions can be reconciled with the permanence of true human life on earth" (448). However, these are clearly partial when compared with the absolute command coming from the stone. *You must change your life* leaves us nowhere to hide: "There is no place that does not see you"; it is a necessary condition and consequence of our finitude. The one thing we know for certain is that we must strive for an improbable, even impossible, self-transcendence, "my innermost not-yet." We will leave Rilke and the Belvedere Torso for the moment, but we will return to them later.

Both the texts which form the main focus of this essay are ethical. *The Art of Philosophy: Wisdom as a Practice* (despite the title's radical difference from the German *Scheintod im Denken*) focuses on the role of detachment from the world in philosophical reflection, and on the role of "practice" in the formation of the (philosophical) self. *You Must Change Your Life: On Anthropotechnics* is even more clearly concerned with ethical issues. Sloterdijk's aim is to determine the potential extent and limits of human self-formation in the world – and to exhort us to accept the challenge to change. And despite his occasionally expressed reservations, Sartre is one of his most frequent reference points, along with Nietzsche and Heidegger, as Sloterdijk explains in his collection *Philosophical Temperaments*:

> As for Sartre, he remained true to leading a life of boundless freedom. For him, the void of subjectivity was not an abyss that pulls us down. Instead, it was a spring, gushing upwards and resisting all forms of enclosure. (91)

The "spring, gushing upwards" reflects Sloterdijk's adoption of the (Nietzschean) thrust towards verticality and away from the downward pull of gravity and mediocrity. His understanding of anthropotechnics and autopoiesis is of course primarily of self-fashioning but he is also clearly attracted by theories of self-liberation, and his notion of self-transcendence is arguably part of an attempt to bring the two together. This essay will use Sartre to help illuminate where Sloterdijk stands on a variety of interrelated ethical and potentially political issues including freedom, commitment, practice, habit, and, ultimately, the self or subject.

Before I get into the heart of my essay, I must sound a word of warning. Sloterdijk is a "difficult" writer, difficult in a relatively unusual way: his irony, playfulness, exaggerations, and provocations often *conceal* his views, sometimes to the point where critics may inadvertently attribute to him positions which are the polar opposite of those he really holds. He seems full of contradictions: not just the clever paradoxes of the postmodern writer (though there are plenty of those); nor just the teasing and provocative style of the orator and rhetorician; not even just the unclarities produced by reading him in often inaccurate and always cumbersome translations; but more fundamental and troubling inconsistencies that might arguably seem to cast doubt on him as a philosopher (and indeed, there are many philosophers who would deny him that title). In particular, it is difficult to disentangle his apparently shifting views on freedom, on being-in-the-world and the epoche, and, perhaps most tricky of all, on commitment. My purpose in this essay is to clarify his position on some of these issues and to analyse the complexities of his texts rather than judge him on the basis of his wilful provocations and self-confessed exaggerations (Sloterdijk, *Exaggerations* xviii).

In first place, the **epoche**. *The Art of Philosophy* traces the history of the philosophical *epoche*, that is to say philosophical detachment. It starts from Socrates's trancelike states when he seemed to have somehow left the human world for another realm (this is of course the *Scheintod*, the appearance of death, the suspended animation of the German title), and moves through the Roman Cicero (Sloterdijk, *Art of Philosophy* 68), the Christian Middle Ages with its contemplative mystics and saints (69), through Fichte (72), Valéry's almost inhuman Monsieur Teste (76), Buddhism (81), and eventually back to Husserl. Now this extended focus on the *epoche*, its origins and development, as well as its role in philosophical thinking, might lead us to think that it was being commended by Sloterdijk as the right path for would-be philosophers to follow in their "quest for truth and wisdom" (2). He describes it in his Introduction as inseparable from the ancient European culture of rationality (3) in which thinkers strive to become disinterested "pure intellects," and spends a lengthy section on Husserl's advice that theory needs to "suspend its agent's fixation on real existence" (17). The reflective life, or the *bios theoretikos*, is described as highly improbable in evolutionary terms and Sloterdijk devotes the third section of the book to an examination of "the formation or self-generation of the disinterested person" (2). But anyone who reads fast or carelessly and imagines that Sloterdijk is recommending the philosophical disinterestedness that he portrays would be gravely mistaken. On the contrary, Sloterdijk describes it as "life-stultifying asceticism" (7) and asks, rhetorically, whether it is "necessary to emphasize the disastrous effects on the history of the Western culture of rationality caused by the way knowledge has been made artificial through the reductionist idealism of the ancient Academy" (64–65).

So what is going on here? How can attentive readers find themselves so uncertain about Sloterdijk's attitude to an issue that is indisputably fundamental in his work? My first suggestion is to understand Sloterdijk's technique by analogy with Foucault's in *La Volonté de savoir* where the French philosopher lures the reader into an unthinking acceptance of what he calls the "repressive hypothesis," that is to say the familiar view that the Victorians were a repressive society in matters of sexuality. Once we have been drawn into this position Foucault takes pleasure in shocking us out of it – the real attraction of our view that Victorian society was sexually repressive, he claims, is that it makes us feel good about our contemporary sexual liberation. But in fact, neither the Victorians, nor their eighteenth-century predecessors, were any more sexually repressive than we are today, they simply had different targets for their repression or liberation. Foucault's trick, if we can call it a trick, lies in his syntax. He initially uses the conditional perfect tense and tells us what the Victorians "auraient fait," would have done, or "allegedly did." But quite soon, right from the second paragraph in fact, the conditional tense disappears and is replaced by the present so that, if we are not on our guard, we may unwittingly forget that this is merely a hypothesis. This device works particularly well in French.[4] Sloterdijk's approach is different and does not depend on syntactical slippage, but the end result is very similar. Although we have been warned early on that the ascetic path is stultifying (*Art of Philosophy* 7), we quickly lose sight of this warning as we start to follow the path in its many historical meanderings. Is this part of Sloterdijk's project, a way of forcing us to keep our wits about us, or simply a matter of careless drafting? My own, consciously disrespectful, view would be rather that it is in part a question of Sloterdijk's becoming caught up in his own narration so that he himself forgets quite where he is going, though he always seems to find his way again eventually.

The other side of the *epochal* coin is the question of **commitment**. Described by Sloterdijk as a "shining blemish" (or a "glittering flaw") in the twentieth century, and by Julien Benda (in 1927) as the "trahison des clercs," commitment looks initially like a false path taken by writers and artists who have forgotten their role as detached observers (*Art of Philosophy* 26). But then, we have just seen this very detachment described as "disastrous." So where does that leave us in our attempts to disentangle Sloterdijk's position from his complex and parenthetical prose? His short text on *Stress and Freedom*, published in English by Polity Press in 2016, may help clarify some of these issues. In it Sloterdijk traces the changing senses of the notion of **freedom** from the Ancient Greek *eleutheria* (*Stress and Freedom* 45), freedom from external despotic rule (13), right through to eighteenth-century Republican ideas of freedom (15) and ultimately the twentieth-century understanding of individual freedom arising from a chosen liberation from the ties of the empirical world and objective self (23). This, then, is the famous detachment, described in *The Art of Philosophy* and epitomised in the Husserlian *epoche*, towards which Sloterdijk seems so ambivalent. *Stress and Freedom* helps explain this apparent ambivalence as Sloterdijk makes clear that detachment is an essential phase in the human attempt to understand the self and the world, but it is not the end point. Individual free detached subjectivity does not, cannot, and indeed should not last, it must always re-enter the world:

> The released subject never maintains the stance of inaccessibility to the real in the long term. As soon as it discovers its freedom, it simultaneously discovers a virtually boundless accessibility within itself to calls from the real. Because of its availability [...] it independently finds its way back into the objective. (Sloterdijk, *Stress and Freedom* 53)

This text also helps clarify Sloterdijk's sometimes bewildering comments on commitment and his claim that "the model of committed literature does not apply" to him (*Exaggerations* viii). Reading *The Art of Philosophy*, it may initially seem almost impossible to reconcile Sloterdijk's critique of commitment (26) with his own political and philosophical interventions. One simple solution to the dilemma would be to conclude that the target of his attack must be something closer to propaganda than what we would understand by commitment proper, at least in its Sartrean sense. In fact, however, the answer may be rather more complex. As Carl Raschke, of the University of Denver, convincingly argues, what Sloterdijk condemns is the *illusion* of involvement that intellectual commitment can confer without any of the real, concomitant responsibility or political action. This kind of abstract commitment seduces the intellectual because it allows him to assuage his guilt about living in an ivory tower without ever actually having to get his hands dirty. As Raschke explains:

> Even though the philosopher may apologize for totalitarian ideologies, he never has to get his hands bloody in executing them. Thus commitment philosophy is tantamount to a philosophy without real commitment, a grand hypocrisy of the already defective moral imagination. (3)

Stress and Freedom further suggests that commitment, properly understood, is arrived at *after* the experience of freedom and detachment. Detachment is not the answer or end point, but conversely commitment cannot be genuine unless it follows a process or period of detachment. Sloterdijk uses Sartre to help explain this:

> I think this turn towards self-burdening is what Jean-Paul Sartre meant by the term "commitment" [...] The free subject does not only expect it; it goes towards it. Its commitment comes neither from a need for expression nor a lack; it is a consequence of the experience of freedom. (*Stress and Freedom* 53)

The idea that commitment arises from the experience of freedom is profoundly Sartrean, though Sartre stresses the way in which commitment not only originates in freedom but is also a call to freedom. For example, in the case of literature, commitment depends on a free writer making an appeal to the freedom of the reader to bring the work of art into being. Freedom is both the source and aim of committed literature. And for Sartre, furthermore, all literature is in a sense inevitably committed insofar as the writer, like all of us, is *embarqué*, that is to say, always already situated in the world, unable, even if s/he wished it, to avoid taking up a position. So the writer is committed, willy-nilly, just as we are free, like it or not: condemned to be free, and condemned to be committed. Then for Sartre there is a second level of commitment that corresponds to the way in which the novel, for instance, represents a certain world view which thereby passes from a merely implicit awareness in its readers to explicit consciousness. In this sense even the apparently uncommitted French drama of the seventeenth century, for example, is committed insofar as it makes its spectators see the world through a different lens (Sartre, *Situations* 141–42). And finally, at a third level, literature can be consciously committed to making its readers reflect on certain significant issues, it can pose important questions, and it can disrupt comfortable assumptions. "Poser des problèmes et non pas les résoudre" [Pose problems rather than resolve them] is the aim of Sartre's committed literature (*Théâtre* 247). Nothing could be further from propaganda, or indeed from the "shining blemish" Sloterdijk refers to in *The Art of Philosophy*.

Sloterdijk himself is arguably a profoundly committed writer, whatever his expressed reservations about the term. At the very least, his work is openly partial and this explicit partiality would certainly come into Sartre's third category of conscious commitment to disrupting facile assumptions. However, and again like Sartre, Sloterdijk takes no prisoners: for example, his now infamous conference paper, "Rules for the Human Park" (also tendentially translated as "Rules for the Human Zoo"), first presented in Basel in 1997, caused outrage, stoked by the German press and encouraged by no less a figure than Habermas, for its apparent promotion of selection and "breeding." To an anglophone reader, less sensitive to the terminology used by the Nazis in their drive for racial purification, the political row is easily comprehensible but probably does not trigger the same visceral horror. It was in fact in this same essay that Sloterdijk first made use of the term *anthropotechnics* which of course constitutes the subtitle of *You Must Change Your Life* and covers such a wide variety of techniques of self-creation and self-transcendence. As he explains:

> Anyone who speaks of human self-production without addressing the formation of human beings in the practising life has missed the point from the outset. Consequently, we must suspend virtually everything that has been said about humans as working beings in order to translate it into the language of practising, or self-forming and self-enhancing behaviour. (Sloterdijk, *You Must Change* 4)

This later text, however, did not elicit a similar reaction of outrage, presumably because its emphasis is almost entirely on individual self-creation rather than social selection, though its "elitism" was criticised by some more egalitarian thinkers and in fact Sloterdijk does still use occasionally the term "breeding": "Changing one's life now means breeding, through inner activations, a practice subject that will eventually be superior to its life of passions, habitus and notions" (195). Of course, Sloterdijk is not one to hide behind the pseudo-objective conventions of academic discourse and he willingly accepts his own investment and self-implication in what he is describing. In his "Introduction" to the work he explains how impartiality is both impossible and undesirable:

> The following investigations take their own result as the point of departure: they testify to the realization that there are objects which do not permit their commentator a complete *epoche*, no withdrawal into disinterestedness, even if the project is theory — which presupposes an abstinence from prejudices, caprices and zealous obsessions. We are dealing here with an object that does not leave its analyst alone [...] An anthropology of the practising life is infected by its subject. Dealing with practices, asceticisms and exercises, whether or not they are declared as such, the theorist inevitably encounters his own inner constitution, beyond affirmation and denial. (14)

I referred earlier to Sloterdijk's ambivalence with respect to detachment, to the *epoche*. Perhaps, however, this judgement (that Sloterdijk is "ambivalent," a term he uses himself (*Art of Philosophy* 4)) says more about our own binary expectations than it does about Sloterdijk. Sloterdijk refuses to adopt the conventional oppositional value judgements that make for an easy life. The *epoche* is both impossible and necessary, disastrous and essential. In more familiar terms, the *epoche* can be put to both good and bad uses, just as its moral companion, asceticism, can be both productive and damaging. Described in this way, Sloterdijk probably sounds more like a moderate than a radical, but this too is a measure of the extent to which he redraws the familiar categories rather than slipping easily into them.

The theorist, and *a fortiori* the theorist of **practice**, is in the world, not outside it, and his difference from the "mere" practitioner lies in his reflexive self-consciousness. For theory and practice are not, for Sloterdijk, opposed, indeed his Introduction to *The Art of Philosophy* is subtitled "Theory as a Form of the Life of Practice." By his own account, his analyses attempt "to restore the high status of practice" (Sloterdijk, *Art of Philosophy* 6), rejecting the traditional distinction between the *vita activa* and the *vita contemplativa*, between active and passive, and focusing on "a substantial complex of human behaviour" that is "a mixed domain," that is to say the "life of practice" (6). What I would like to do in the rest of this essay is to explore further the notion of practice and, in particular, to try to assess its originality and usefulness. I propose to do this once more with reference to Sartre whom Sloterdijk so frequently takes as sounding board, opponent, and sometimes even guide.

What then is *practice*, and how does the notion differ from other ways of trying to understand human life in the world? Why is it not a term which we recognise readily from other moral philosophers? Practice has many meanings, many ramifications and implications. I was reading Sloterdijk while the Olympics were on in Rio in 2016 and I almost felt that the athletes had been studying our texts, so focused were they on incremental improvement through practice. The ascetic life of a young would-be Olympic swimmer, getting up day after day at 5 a.m. to practise before school, sounded like a model Sloterdijkian discipline. And of course, in his view the same applies to philosophy and the arts as to swimming: we become good philosophers by constant philosophising, good artists by painting, good writers by writing. In practice we learn to overcome the inertia of our instinctive habitual behaviour and set ourselves free. This may remind some of us of Saint Paul to the Romans (6.20): when we imagine we are free to indulge our desires we are in fact slaves to sin, and it is the Law that frees us. This kind of paradox is very familiar, and is part of the *qui perd gagne*, loser wins, pattern which underpins much of Christianity (he who wishes to save his life shall lose it – and vice versa, the last shall be first, etc.) and, of course, Existentialism (where our inability to attain self-identity is what saves us from sclerosis, and where the absence of objective values is what frees us to create our own). So the use of paradox is certainly not new, but the emphasis on practice has considerably less of a history. Pascal's "mets-toi à genoux et tu croiras," kneel and you will believe, is one of the notable exceptions, in which we are encouraged to bring our bodies into line if we want our souls to be free to embrace the demands of Christianity.

C'est en faisant tout comme s'ils croyoient, en prenant de l'eau bénite, en faisant dire des messes, etc. Naturellement même cela vous fera croire et vous abêtira. / Mais c'est ce que je crains. / Et pourquoi? Qu'avez-vous à perdre? [...] cela diminue les passions qui sont vos grands obstacles. (Pascal 233)
[It is by acting as if they believed, taking holy water, going to mass, etc. Naturally that will make you believe and will make you stupid. / But that's what I'm afraid of. / Why? What have you to lose? [...] It will diminish the passions which are your major obstacles.]

Pascal, like Montaigne before him, is using *abêtir* [to make stupid, bestial, animal] with full awareness of its shock effect. It is part of the two thinkers' refusal to see humans as primarily spirit, as close to angels, and part of their insistence on the bodily nature of the human. We may be reminded of the old saying: the spirit is willing but the flesh is weak. If we cannot accomplish what we choose because our bodies refuse to obey us, in what sense can we claim to be truly free?

It is time now to tackle this issue directly. Sloterdijk considers that one of the purposes of practice is to overcome the inertia of the habits we have unconsciously drifted into and replace them by a life that we have chosen. Practice helps us to "change our life." But there is more: failure or refusal to practise will not simply leave things the same, on the contrary we will deteriorate rather than merely stagnate if we do not strive to improve. Sloterdijk makes clear that in his view most people refuse to accept this uncomfortable truth, and hesitate "before breaking out of a well-rehearsed and accepted misery" (*You Must Change* 416). Indeed, he maintains, "People have always recoiled from the inconvenient realisation that nothing happens unless one brings it about oneself" (416). It is not, *pace* Heidegger, a god who will save us: only we can and must save ourselves. Sloterdijk, like Sartre, believes that we make ourselves who we are, but unlike Sartre – and this is a crucial difference – he sees this in terms not so much of self-creation from nothing(ness) but rather as breaking away from what we have already become and creating new habits. He refers to this as *depassivization*, and it lies at the heart of his ethical project and at the heart of what it means to be human. Indeed, it is the key to subjectivation:

> Anyone who takes part in a programme for de-passivizing themselves, and crosses from the side of the merely formed to that of the forming, becomes a subject. (Sloterdijk, *You Must Change* 195)

This is clearly not just a matter of physical habits, or superficial and trivial ways of being: "Anyone with style will even see happiness as the good habit of being happy. Even genius is simply a group of good habits whose collision makes sparks fly" (322).

Sartre, Sloterdijk claims in a footnote, would disagree: "Sartre contradicts this with his thesis that there are no good habits because habits are inertias and thus bad *per se*" (*You Must Change* 474fn20). It is true that Sartre does indeed write this at the start of his posthumously published *Cahiers pour une morale*: "Morality: permanent conversion. In Trotsky's sense: permanent evolution. *Good* habits; they are never good, because they are habits" (12). Sloterdijk does not agree that morality can be a matter of "permanent revolution" (*You Must Change* 375). Indeed, he considers the idea potentially disastrous:

> If self-realization is presented as a rejection of passivity that must constantly take place anew, the ghost light of permanent revolution takes hold of the individual's self-relationship – and Sartre, referring to Trotsky, in fact spoke of true morality as a *conversion permanente*. This approach could only produce one result: the simultaneous destruction of politics *and* morals. (375)

We must of course remember that the *Cahiers* are simply notes from the late 1940s which Sartre never thought publishable, but putting this aside for the moment (though we will return to it shortly) it is still evident that there seems to be a serious point of disagreement between Sartre and Sloterdijk on the issue of habits and one that needs to be explored. Where Sartre and Sloterdijk are clearly in agreement is over the question of *bad* habits. Bad habits create a moral, personal, and physical inertia which becomes increasingly difficult to overcome. An example that illustrates this clearly comes from *L'Etre et le néant* (EN) and concerns some friends on a hike. One of them stops before the end, claiming he is too tired. Assuming he is not ill, Sartre asks, what does it mean to be "too tired." His stopping before the hike is over is interpreted as a matter of choice, related to his fundamental project, and part of a selfhood he has created gradually and which binds him to itself. "J'aurais pu faire autrement, soit, mais à quel prix?" I could have acted differently, of course, but at what cost? (EN 531). The cost would have been a "radical conversion," a "sudden metamorphosis" (542), always possible but involving a significant modification of my fundamental project. Furthermore, if we look more closely at this section of *Being and Nothingness* we will see that Sloterdijk's qualms about Sartre's notion of morality as permanent conversion may be misplaced. In his published text at least (that is to say, in *L'Etre et le néant* rather than the *Cahiers*) Sartre is far more circumspect:

> Moreover, we must not understand the original choice as "producing itself from one moment to the next"; this would be to come back to the instantaneist conception of consciousness in which Husserl was trapped. (EN 543)

Sartre then, like Sloterdijk, clearly acknowledges passivity and inertia and recognises their power over the individual. Where the two philosophers differ is over the issue of creating new habits to replace the old. What does Sartre really mean when he says that all habits are bad? Surely habits of kindness and honesty must be good? The opening pages of the *Cahiers* provide part of the answer to this question. Here, in the very first paragraph, Sartre explains his position. Morality is a matter of doing not of being. A religious view, he claims, would permit us to *do* Good in order to *be* moral. But a non-religious view requires something else: we must undertake acts of charity in order to serve our fellow men, not in order to *be* charitable. The aim of morality lies outside itself, in the action undertaken, its purpose is not to ensure that I am moral. I give water to the thirsty man to alleviate his thirst, not in order to be a good person. "La moralité se supprime en se posant, elle se pose en se supprimant" (Sartre, *Cahiers* 11). Morality is assumed by the moral act and disappears with it. It cannot be its own end and purpose. Sloterdijk, on the other hand, emphasises precisely self-making through practice and habit; practice is both active and passive, active as it is carried through, passive in the traces it leaves in the practising subject. There is a potential analogy to be drawn here with Sartre's later discussions of *praxis* and the *practico-inert* in the *Critique of Dialectical Reason*, not least because of recent debate amongst Sartre scholars concerning the possible benefits of the *practico-inert*, without which institutions and other functioning organisations would arguably be impossible. But we will remain in this essay with the early Sartre and the question of individual character or selfhood rather than with later social and political developments.

We have come now to the nub of one of the most significant differences between Sartre and Sloterdijk and that is the question of subjectivation and selfhood. For Sloterdijk, the autopoietic and anthropotechnic nature of the human necessarily means that self-formation lies at the heart of his vision. As we have seen, this self-formation involves self-transcendence rather than anything resembling identity or stasis but is none the less explicitly concerned to create human beings who strive to go beyond their own possibilities. This is indeed one of the major aims of practice. For Sartre, on the contrary, action – including not only single acts but also repeated actions aimed at some kind of enhancement, be it in sport or painting or music or any other domain – has as its aim improvement in the world or in the execution of the sport or the art being practised. Its aim is not seen in terms of self-formation or character. Of course, all our actions make us, create us, form us as people, but this formation is only ever a by-product for Sartre. It is our situation that gives us our apparent permanence and it is part of the *en soi*. In the eyes of others we may have a certain character, and indeed we may at times identify ourselves with it, to the detriment of our freedom to change. "In a sense," Sartre writes, "there is no character – there is only the project of one's self" (EN 637/551). And this difference is not just a matter of emphasis, it marks a deep ontological and moral divide between Sartre and Sloterdijk. I have discussed many times elsewhere[5] Sartre's accounts of subjectivity and selfhood – be it in the *Transcendence of the Ego* where he refuses any notion of an inner or transcendental self and argues that, rather than innate, our "self" is an imaginary construct, out in the world just like the egos of other people; or in *Being and Nothingness* where he explores the reflexivity of consciousness, and the *circuit d'ipséité* which personalises the *pour soi* and creates our riven human subjectivity: "S'il est présent à soi, c'est qu'il n'est pas tout à fait soi" [If it is present to itself, that is because it is not entirely itself] (EN 120). This philosophical analysis is very far from any notion of self-formation through practice and habit and is, indeed, ontologically at odds with it.

Of course, Sloterdijk's slogan, taken from the Rilke poem with which I started this essay, is not concerned with self-formation but with changing one's life. Perhaps then this is an area where we might find Sartre and Sloterdijk in closer accord? Indeed, this was my initial starting point, but the more I reflected the further away I found myself from any notion of agreement between the two thinkers. *You must change your life.* I referred briefly to Kant at the beginning of this discussion, and Sartre's objections to Kantian ethics are equally applicable to those of Sloterdijk. Sartre rejects outright the Kantian view of duty and imperative (despite flirting briefly with it in his 1946 lecture, *Existentialism and Humanism*). Even the notion of the will freely legislating to itself is, for Sartre, no more than an internalised alienation masquerading with a dangerous power of conviction as a self-given command.[6] "Duty," he writes, "is the Other at the heart of the Will" (Sartre, *Cahiers* 485, 147). And again, "Duty [...] is an order given by someone else, which retains for the agent its character of alterity" ("Détermination" 740).[7] By this token "You must change your life," though it too "exceeds" the Kantian imperative, is the paradigm of an ethics of heteronomy, and even were we to argue that the command comes, despite appearances, from within, it would still be liable to the same Sartrean accusation of internalised alienation. And Sloterdijk's conclusion is one of the places where his moralism becomes perhaps inadvertently explicit:

> Even without God or the *Übermensch*, it is sufficient to note that every individual, even the most successful, the most creative and the most generous, must, if they examine themselves in earnest, admit that they have become less than their potentiality of being would have required. (*You Must Change* 443)

For me then, the comparison with Sartre has certainly helped illuminate the mysteries of Sloterdijk's ethics. All the domains where I was initially tempted to see similarities between the two thinkers have withered into dust. Practice sounded promisingly active but on closer inspection proved to have too large a dose of inertia to be considered remotely Sartrean. Even the exhilarating exhortation *You must change your life*, with its apparent moral optimism, has been revealed as at least in part alienation rather than liberation insofar as it involves a negative comparison with what our "potentiality of being" would have "required" of us. Perhaps this should not come as a surprise. After all, in Sartre's view, all attempts to construct a positive ethics, including his own, are doomed to failure as a form of mystification. This was his considered view of his *Cahiers pour une morale*[8] which is why he never published the text in his lifetime. The *Cahiers* did constitute an early attempt to follow up on the suggestion tentatively sketched in the last pages of *Being and Nothingness* to construct an ethics of freedom where liberty would be taken as the source of all values, but even this was deemed too prescriptive, and ultimately a source of alienation. The posthumous publication of the unfinished and ethically experimental text was certainly not in accordance with Sartre's own wishes. No wonder then that the moralism of Sloterdijk, for all its provocations, paradoxes, and perversity, should be, in the last analysis, a failure when judged in Sartre's terms. But as Beckett famously said, this should not deter us, or indeed Sloterdijk: *Fail. Fail again. Fail better.*

disclosure statement

No potential conflict of interest was reported by the author.

notes

1 "Archaic Torso of Apollo" in *The Poetry of Rilke*, trans. and ed. Edward Snow 223.

2 Of course, Rancière and Sloterdijk make very different uses of the Torso: for Rancière it helps illustrate his idea of a new regime of sensibility, the aesthetic regime, whereas for Sloterdijk, as we shall see, it is used to explain the aesthetic imperative.

3 See an interesting discussion by Ronald Cordero 117–24.

4 It is a form of ventriloquism common to many modern French philosophers including Derrida but is probably most clearly illustrated by Foucault.

5 See, e.g., Howells, *Sartre: The Necessity of Freedom*, ch. 1.

6 Ibid. 32.

7 Sloterdijk too is, of course, aware of these dangers (see, e.g., "The Inner Witness" in *You Must Change* 237–39) though he is not always able to steer clear of them himself.

8 See the film by Astruc.

bibliography

Contat, M., and M. Rybalka. *Les Ecrits de Sartre*. Paris: Gallimard, 1970. Print.

Cordero, R. "Kant and the Expression of Imperatives." *Sorites (Σωρίτης)* 20 (Mar. 2008): 117–24. Print.

Foucault, M. *La Volonté de savoir*. Paris: Gallimard, 1976. Print.

Howells, C. *Mortal Subjects: Passions of the Soul in Late Twentieth-Century French Thought*. Cambridge: Polity, 2011. Print.

Howells, C. *Sartre: The Necessity of Freedom*. Cambridge: Cambridge UP, 1988. Print.

Kant, I. *Foundations of the Metaphysics of Morals*. Trans. Lewis White Beck. Indianapolis: Library of Liberal Arts, Pearson, 1989. Print.

Pascal, B. *Pensées*, first published 1670. Print.

Rancière, J. *Aisthesis: Scenes from the Aesthetic Regime of Art*. Trans. Paul Zakir. London: Verso, 2013. Print.

Raschke, C. "Peter Sloterdijk as 'First Philosopher' of Globalization." *Journal for Cultural and Religious Theory* 12.3 (Spring 2013): 1–19. Print.

Sartre, J.-P. *Cahiers pour une morale*. Paris: Gallimard, 1983. Print.

Sartre, J.-P. *Critique de la raison dialectique*. Paris: Gallimard, 1960. Print.

Sartre, J.-P. "Détermination et liberté." *Les Ecrits de Sartre*. Ed. M. Contat and M. Rybalka. Paris: Gallimard, 1970. Print.

Sartre, J.-P. *La Transcendance de l'Ego*. 1936. Paris: Vrin, 1965. Print.

Sartre, J.-P. *L'Etre et le néant*. Paris: Gallimard, 1943. Print.

Sartre, J.-P. *L'Existentialisme est un humanisme*. Paris: Nagel, 1946. Print.

Sartre, J.-P. *Sartre: un film réalisé par A. Astruc et M. Contat*. Paris: Gallimard, 1977. Print.

Sartre, J.-P. *Situations II: Qu'est-ce que la littérature?* Paris: Gallimard, 1948. Print.

Sartre, J.-P. *Un Théâtre de situations*. Ed. M. Contat and M. Rybalka. Paris: Gallimard/Idées, 1972. Print.

Sloterdijk, P. *The Art of Philosophy: Wisdom as a Practice*. Trans. Karen Margolis. New York: Columbia UP, 2012. Print.

Sloterdijk, P. *Philosophical Temperaments: From Plato to Foucault*. Trans. Thomas Dunlap. New York: Columbia UP, 2013. Print.

Sloterdijk, P. "Rules for the Human Park: A Response to Heidegger's *Letter on Humanism*." *Not Saved: Essays after Heidegger*. Trans. Ian Alexander Moore and Christopher Turner. Cambridge: Polity, 2017. Print.

Sloterdijk, P. *Selected Exaggerations: Conversations and Interviews 1993–2012*. Ed. Bernhard Klein. Trans. Karen Margolis. Cambridge: Polity, 2016. Print.

Sloterdijk, P. *Stress and Freedom*. Trans. Wieland Hoban. Cambridge: Polity, 2016. Print.

Sloterdijk, P. *You Must Change Your Life: On Anthropotechnics*. Trans. Wieland Hoban. Cambridge: Polity, 2013. Print.

Snow, E., trans. and ed. *The Poetry of Rilke*. New York: North Point, 2009. Print.

1 introduction

The change of the soul is the first politics.
Sloterdijk, Die schrecklichen 310

This essay builds on the hypothesis that the "labour of the self on itself" – as Michel Foucault named the practices which Peter Sloterdijk also refers to as ascesis (*askesis*), metanoia and anthropotechnics – is not only a matter of individual, existential, philosophical or psychological concerns. The questions raised by the care of the self are also in many ways political and are therefore inseparable from the political history of the West.

The essay explores these issues in the wake of Sloterdijk's philosophy of anthropotechnics – a task which is certainly not without challenges, as one would hardly find in his corpus anything like a systematic theory of politics and *askesis*. His thought may in fact be regarded, as some have done, and not entirely without reasons, as fundamentally solipsistic and politically unsophisticated and dubious (Lucci, this issue; Sutherland, "Ontological" and "Peter Sloterdijk").

As opposed to this, in what follows, I will argue that there are several textual moments, whose logic and connections I will attempt to reconstruct, which might suggest a rather different reading of Sloterdijk's oeuvre.[1] On their basis I will seek to outline – with and *after* Sloterdijk – a political genealogy of anthropotechnics, one that focuses in particular on the conditions of emergence of modern anthropotechnical regimes. More precisely, starting from a discussion of the birth of asceticism in the axial age (section 2) and its repercussions on classical politics (section 3), the horizon of concerns of this genealogy is the

andrea rossi

ASCETIC WORLDS
notes on politics and technologies of the self after peter sloterdijk

way a certain practice and understanding of self-mobilisation have come to saturate the political, economic and techno-scientific government of the self in the twenty-first century (section 4). As we shall see, this will entail asking, among other things, to what extent political action presupposes the subject's (ascetic) self-distancing from the world and, further, how anthropotechniques today tend to foreclose the possibility of this "estrangement" as the basis of our world in common.

2 the experiment of the world

[…] *primordial, thrown Being-in-the world as the "not-at-home."* (Heidegger 321)

The starting point of the genealogy I am attempting is a simple, if often overlooked, observation. Anthropotechnics is not an anthropological universal, but, as Sloterdijk suggests, a phenomenon that needs to be contextualised historically, as the correlative of determinate political, social and intellectual developments. Referring to the historical-philosophical periodisation proposed by Karl Jaspers in *The Origin and Goal of History*, Sloterdijk traces "the emergence of anthropotechnics [back to] the axial age of practice" (*You Must Change* 197; *Nach Gott* 41–54).[2] Roughly spanning the period between the second and the eighth century BCE – and marked by the appearance of world-historical figures such as Socrates, Christ, Confucius, Buddha and the Jewish prophets – Jaspers presents the axial age as a turning point within the history of advanced civilisations, one that allegedly lies at the roots of their common experience of being-human. In broad outline, axial cultures emerged out of the rejection of traditional modes of thought and cosmologies – "[r]ationality and rationally clarified experience launched a struggle against myth (*logos* against *mythos*)" (Jaspers 3) – and a concomitant "intellectualisation" of life, both at the individual and the collective level – albeit initially these transformations affected only a few individuals and then slowly their wider societies (4). For Jaspers, this process, however, was not only responsible for the emergence of objective knowledge or a scientific mindset. Rather, the latter were symptomatic of a wider development, which gave rise to a new type of *spirituality* and *consciousness*:

> In the past, spiritual conditions had been comparatively enduring [and] confined within the horizon of a still, very slowly spiritual movement that did not enter consciousness and was therefore not apprehended. Now, on the contrary, tension increases and causes a movement of torrential swiftness. This movement reaches consciousness. (4–5)

As a period of rapid and unprecedented changes in its existential horizon, the axial age produced in the subject a new critical awareness of its relation to itself, its history and place in the world. Needless to say, it would be impossible to render the exact meaning and scope of such transformations in a neat formula. The deliberately evocative nature of Jaspers' account – "[n]o one can adequately comprehend what occurred here and became the axis of world history" (18) – has in fact given rise to a manifold of diverse, sometimes diverging, interpretations. The axial age has variously been read as the historical phase in which humans first developed second-order thinking; a heightened capacity for reflexivity and critical thought; a sceptical view on institutions, society and the world; a new awareness of individuality, agency and historicity; and a transcendental view of divinity (Elkana; Momigliano 8–9; Wittrock; Eisenstadt, "Introduction"; Schwartz). Nevertheless, it seems clear – even though the literature does not always stress it as forcefully as it should – that the common basis of these diverse "positive" transformations was in fact a *shock*, one that proved to be irreversible within the history of advanced civilisations. The increasing clarification, rationalisation and enlightenment of thought characteristic of axial cultures grew out of a new sense of existential uncertainty and a loss of "tranquillity and self-evidence":

> man becomes conscious of Being as a whole, of himself and his limitations. He experiences the terror of the world and his own powerlessness [...] The unquestioned grasp on life is loosened, the calm of polarities becomes the disquiet of opposites and antinomies. Man is no longer enclosed within himself. He becomes uncertain of himself and thereby open to new and boundless possibilities [...] The unheard-of becomes manifest. Together with his world and his own self, Being becomes sensible to man, but not with finality: the question remains. (Jaspers 2–3)

The axial breakthrough introduced a certain opaqueness and fragility into the subject's relation to the world, where the latter is to be understood as both a political form and a cosmic unity. The development of critical, self-reflective and transcendental modes of thought was in a sense inseparable from the fact that, hitherto, being-in-the-world would no longer be experienced as a "fact," but as terror, anxiety or, in Sloterdijk's terms, the monstrous.[3]

This historically determined fracture between the human and the world[4] formed the basic framework of anthropotechnical practices. As the world ceased to be given stably and unproblematically – and as the conditions of its existential security began to shift ever more rapidly – man realised that he had "to reach out beyond himself by growing aware of himself within the whole of Being," while discovering "within himself the origin from which to raise himself above his own self and the world" (Jaspers 3). Self-experimentation, therefore, began not only as *experimentum suitatis*, but, first and foremost, as *experimentum mundi*:[5] as exercise and practice to come to a world in which humans were no longer at home.

As historian of religion Robert Bellah has shown, these developments were inseparable from the progressive weakening of sovereign institutions' capacity to mediate the subject's relation to the cosmos and the divine. What earlier civilisations experienced as a given and self-evident condition (the ontological continuity between the self, society and the universe) became after the axial breakthrough the object of increasing scepticism and discomfort. Whereas in tribal and archaic societies, "super-nature, nature, and society were all fused in a single cosmos," axial civilisations witnessed the appearance of "second-order thinking about cosmology, which for societies just emerging from the archaic age meant thinking about the religio-political premises of society itself" (Bellah 266, 275; see also Eisenstadt, "The Axial Conundrum" and "Cultural Traditions"). The axial age dissolved the unity between political order and the order of the cosmos which used to secure, in a relatively stable manner, man's standing vis-à-vis the Whole, thus producing a short-circuit that exposed the subject, in its singularity, to the "abyss" of the world, while depriving it of the "filter" of fixed collective norms and local allegiances.

In different places, Sloterdijk proposes a strikingly similar interpretation of these developments. Whereas the horde (as he refers to archaic and "paleo-political" societies) instantiated "a total psychosocial institution" in which "existence and belonging together are still almost indistinguishable dimensions" (Sloterdijk, *Im selben Boot* 17, 21), after the axial breakthrough, to become a subject – and, as we shall see, a political subject too – meant facing up to, and learning to inhabit, "the totality of facts, inside as well as outside" (*You Must Change* 193). To-*be*-in-the-world was translated into an effort to *come*-to-the-world (*Zur Welt Kommen*) and therefore to establish a new intimacy with its monstrosity. The life of practice, the exercise (*askesis*) to give life a new form and meaning, would here amount to introducing oneself into the "default of world" produced by the axial revolution. The care of the self is the effort to construe a world and uphold it: "the subject is all that which tries to become and to be one's own world [...] as the principle of an attitude deployed against the indolent, amorphous and diminishing outside world" (*Eurotaoismus* 183).

The endeavour to "auto-natality," as world-forming, should be thought of, more precisely, as the double articulation of the subject's *withdrawal from* and *ecstatic opening* to the world. The subject of practice is, in the first place, the "agent that cuts itself out," "the knife that makes the cut in the continuum" of the norms and customs of its social milieu (Sloterdijk, *You Must Change* 225, 220). To work on oneself is to detach oneself from "the first cultural community" (193) and, therefore, to resist the authority of social codes – the morality of customs, in Nietzsche's terms (Sloterdijk, *Die schrecklichen* 237–42) – so as to redefine the self and its place within the common. This is, in a way, the inaugural moment – the *krisis* – underlying any anthropotechnical practice: "Only the recessive self-insulation can give rise to the behavioural complex that Foucault, following on from the Stoic principle of *cura sui*, calls 'concern for oneself'" (Sloterdijk, *You Must Change* 227).

The subject's withdrawal from the world should not be seen, however, as only the effect of its arbitrary will to change or a mere desire for "more." By dissolving the continuity between being and political order, the axial age made the *possibility* of de-automatising common habits and frames of thoughts into, as it were, a *necessity*. As the world in common became incapable of sheltering the "I," fleeing from it became for the subject the precondition to find – by "contrasting himself inwardly with the entire universe," as Jaspers put it (3) – another world to inhabit. The secession from the world (*Weltfremdheit*) is, in a sense, the principle of a necessary self-overcoming, which is also the basis of the *upward movement* of *askesis*: an anti-gravitational attraction to the surreal, the unheard-of and the unrepeatable, aimed at replacing the common, yet uninhabitable, world of men and women with a different space of respiration and new mythologies.[6]

A traditional interpretation of ascesis – one that Nietzsche and Weber also partially contributed to propagate – would portray this exodus as the ultimate goal of the ancient, and above all Christian life of practice. Especially in its radical (and most notably Gnostic) expressions, the conversion of the self has often been thought of and theorised as an irreversible break with "this" world. As Sloterdijk suggests, this interpretation, however, would conceal the positive, world-forming dimensions of *askesis* (Sloterdijk, *You Must Change* 37; see also Ware). Withdrawal is only one facet of a twofold process, one that is at the same time propaedeutic to the subject's *ecstatic opening* to the world. To engage in the life of practice is to set up the symbolic, moral and ritual filters which, while sheltering the self from its surroundings, simultaneously expose it ec-statically to them. As it has been noted, this is the basic function of any immunity system:

> sphere-building is not aimed at withdrawing from the world [...] The therapeutic effect of sphere-building therefore depends on its capacity to produce the "good type of distantiation" which will allow connections to be established and thinking to thrive.[7] (Duclos 52–53)

The etymological resonance between "the Greek *ekstasis* and the Latin *existentia*" implies that:

> existing does not mean arising in unambiguous localization but being in a state of tension from here to there and from now to earlier or later [...] anybody who exists is called for at his "place" from elsewhere. (Sloterdijk, *Art of Philosophy* 31)

The call from "somewhere else" – which is arguably only another name for the "vertical pull" which inspires the subject's defection from the world, as analysed at length by Sloterdijk in *You Must Change Your Life* – is the distance that opens up and sustains inhabitable spheres. Withdrawal is the "underground levitation work" necessary to create "breathing spaces," for "without the greenhouse gases of frivolity, no inhabitable (sur-)reality bubble can be curved and kept in shape" (Sloterdijk, *Foams* 688, 690). With the axial breakthrough, a sense of suffocation came to suffuse the totality of the real. Here, accordingly, coming-to-the-world would amount to fashioning, on the horizontal plane of the common, a vertical depth capable of producing a "de-asphyxiated," breathable atmosphere.

To free oneself *from* the world is a way, perhaps the only way, to be *in* the terror and monstrosity of the world. This is precisely how Sloterdijk interprets Socrates – who, significantly, is also one of the inspiring figures of the axial revolution in Jaspers' account – and his break with the *doxa* of Athenian society. As the paradigm of any critical endeavour, his "secession" is "a form of not-being-in-this-world which is totally of this world, a non-transcending transcendence [...] an ontological difference, without metaphysics" (Sloterdijk, *Zur Welt Kommen* 96).[8] The recessive "I" does not efface its world, as though to secure itself within a sphere of absolute subjectivity. Its aim is in a way the opposite. After the axial breakthrough, and, therefore, after having foregone the "foetal" immunity of the horde, man is "no longer enclosed within himself" (Jaspers 3), but, in order to *ex-ist*, he must open himself up "as a door onto the unprecedented" (Sloterdijk, *Zur Welt Kommen* 120). His journey to the improbable is the effort to inhabit the improbability of its *kosmos*. Even in its most reclusive and solitary expressions, therefore, "[s]ecession produces real spaces" and "heterotopias" (Sloterdijk, *You Must Change* 220, 221; see also Macho, this issue) – provided, however, that the latter are not thought of as absolute "beyonds," but as passages that open into this world while suspending its facticity. As a Foucauldian heterotopy, ascetic withdrawal is a mirror that:

> exerts a sort of counteraction on the position that I occupy. From the standpoint of the mirror I discover my absence from the place where I am since I see myself over there. Starting from this gaze that is, as it were, directed toward me, from the ground of this virtual space that is on the other side of the glass, I come back toward myself; I begin again to direct my eyes toward myself and to reconstitute myself there where I am. (Foucault 24)

The subject who leaves the world returns to it ("there where I am") through an ecstatic projection which, like a de-forming mirror, casts a new light on it. To the withdrawing self, being-in-the-world would now appear, to use Heidegger's terminology, as "potentiality-for-Being-in-the-world" [*Sein-können-in-der-Welt*] (184). As the world lost its self-evidence, the subject could only ex-ist by taking charge, and therefore taking care, of its natality: for "without a beginning of your own, there is no world" (Sloterdijk, *Zur Welt Kommen* 119).

3 ascesis as first politics

Exercise yourself first, my wonderful friend, in learning what you ought to know before entering on politics. (Plato, *Alcibiades* 132b)

As anticipated, the birth of anthropotechnics did not only affect a few individuals and their relation to the world, but it also reverberated on, and transformed the political sphere at large and its conditions of possibility. The ascetics' *experimentum mundi* – which, to repeat, was not only an escape from the world, but an endeavour to inhabit its monstrosity too – also changed the *koinon* from which they defected. As Jaspers remarked, although the achievements of the first ascetics were "by no means passed on to all [...] what the individual becomes indirectly changes all. The whole of humanity took a leap forward" (4; see also Sloterdijk, *You Must Change* 192–93). The life of practice did not point, in this sense, to a possibility among others, but to the *exemplum* of what anyone could and should become. Anthropotechnics began to define the general horizon of existence, both for the individual (even for the many who never had the chance or the courage to enter the field of "acrobatics") and for the community (regardless of whether or not social norms were effectively transformed by it). To face up to these new circumstances, advanced civilisations fashioned new immunity, and therefore political, mechanisms. Whereas institutionally these changes were only intermittent and susceptible to setbacks, suspensions and reversals – and therefore by no means achieved once and for all, still to our days – the birth of the ascetic life nevertheless made clear and pressing demands on the public sphere.

Once the world as a whole entered a prism of systematic reflections, spurred by the perception that its current form was inadequate, men began to "feel the *desire to help* through insight, education and reform," while devoting their thoughts to "the manner in which human beings may best live together, may best be governed and administered" (Jaspers 5; emphasis in the original).[9] The common world of men now presented itself as a space of co-eccentricities and co-isolations, in need of new forms of organisation capable of taking into account the increasing improbability, for its subjects, to "just" be-in-the-world. As Sloterdijk remarks,

[a] world from which the ethically best flee can no longer be a maternal container for all life forms. Owing to the exodus of the ascetics, meditators and thinkers, it becomes the site of a drama that fundamentally questions its ability to house ethically aroused inhabitants sufficiently: what is this world if the strongest statement about it is a withdrawal from it? (*You Must Change* 221)

By impelling men to live in common with those with whom they "have nothing in common" (Sloterdijk, *Im selben Boot* 11), the axial age prompted a substantial rethinking of politics. To put it schematically, axial societies began to be confronted by the question of how to create a public space – a stage, an arena, a "theatre" – which could make room for the ec-centricity of its players, without letting it degenerate into alienation, political disengagement or anomy. Just like the individuals venturing into the life of practice, institutions had to tread the line which at once separates and connects the possibility of fleeing and having a world. This question, as we shall see, transpires most clearly in two of the central *problematiques* of classical politics,[10] namely, *political agonism* and *metaphysics* (as a geometric theory of political order).

3.1 agonism

To examine the connection between asceticism and political agonism in its inaugural (Greek) form, we shall briefly turn to Jean-Pierre Vernant's seminal study on *The Origins of Greek Thought*. In broad outline, the latter shows how Western philosophy emerged in the process which – from the political order of the Mycenaean civilisation centred on the *anax* (the divine king), his palace and a closed elite of intellectuals and functionaries – led to the creation of the *agora* as the central institution of the Greek *polis*. The latter's ideals of political equality, rational argumentation and logical contest provided theoretical rationality with its basic problems and standard forms. Importantly, according to Vernant, the nascent forms of political organisation and philosophical reflection also defined *the specific Western path to the axial age*.[11] Whereas in China, India, Palestine and Iran, the axial age induced changes primarily in the religious sphere – Confucianism, Buddhism, Jewish propheticism, Zorahastrism – in Greece, it was

> on the side and outside of religion [...] that a form of thought is instituted whose ambition is the access to truth through a personal search [...] in which everyone refuses its predecessors, opposing them with arguments that might also lend themselves to discussion by virtue of their rational nature. (Vernant, *Le Origini* 20)

Whereas elsewhere the axial revolution resulted in an increasing "intellectualisation" and "transcendentalisation" of religion, the Greek *polis* elected the *political realm* as the venue where the world and its extant order could be questioned. This did not only result in an institutional displacement, but also in a peculiar articulation of the basic *problematique* of the axial spirit. Differently from other axial religions, the *agora* did not rest on a set of stable and overarching truths. It rather delineated a space that could remain structurally open to the "personal search" and the "permanent reversibility" of truth. In this sense, democratic agonism accentuated the individualistic tendencies of axial cultures. The unwalled space of the *agora* instituted the virtually inexhaustible possibility to question the world of traditions, as an "affirmation of [one's] originality" (13), while at the same time making individual self-assertion into a collective good.[12]

Even though Vernant did not frame these questions specifically in terms of *askesis*,[13] the parallels with the themes explored so far are striking. What Vernant refers to as the assertion of subjectivity vis-à-vis the world of traditions resonates in particular with Sloterdijk's remarks on world-withdrawal. In a passage that touches directly on the ascetic conditions of possibility of political agonism, Sloterdijk writes:

> The change of the soul is the first politics. After it, all human beings have an incontestable pretence to be in the wrong vis-à-vis the

vast majority of those who belong to the same group. No one must approve the customs, opinions and the lies of his people of origin, just because the predecessors did not know anything else. (*Die schrecklichen* 310)

Metanoia – the conversion of the soul to a new figure of truth and mode of being-in-the-world – appears here as the force which, by suspending the giveness of the world, re-centres the political scene on the individual possibility to make a new beginning in the world. Bringing one's world into being, within and against the world as it stands, is the principle of animation of the *agora*, in as far as it embodies "the consciousness of the arena and [...] the belief that men are beings capable of completely coming to the world in order to be a part of it" (Sloterdijk, *Zur Welt Kommen* 134).

At the level of its basic spatial-ontological structures, the *agora* mirrored and redoubled the ascetic "games" that it staged and made possible. As seen, in *The Origins of Greek Thought* Vernant retraced the historical-political processes which moved the centre of power away from the closed palace of the Mycenaean *anax* towards the open space of the *agora*. The latter's openness was therefore one of its central features. The *agora* brought *es to meson*, in the middle – and therefore rendered manifest, visible and publicly accessible – what was previously hidden, centralised and in the hands of a closed elite (Vernant, *The Origins* 47). Its openness, however, did not only enlarge and illuminate the basis of power, one might add, but also transformed its nature. Whereas the Mycenaean palace enshrined an *arche*, a foundation spreading its light to the rest of the city, the *agora* formalised a lack of origins and originary lights. The *agora* did not bring to light the centre of a world. Rather, it organised and gave an institutional form to the constitutive dissonance between the world and its subjects. Its openness was the wound – the *munus*, default, lack, absence – out of which the subjects' coming-to-the-world, and therefore the com-munity itself, could come into being (cf. Esposito). More than an open ground, the public square was the ungrounded opening – the *Lichtung* or clearing – that let other openings happen. More than a beginning, the cut that makes new beginnings possible.

It is precisely along these lines that Sloterdijk proposes an "onto-topological definition of the public sphere [*öffentlichkeit*] as non-uterus, that is to say, as a space of natal unveilings and as the ontological glacis of that which is capable of coming" (*Eurotaoismus* 155). If coming-to-the-world implies a withdrawal from the *koinon* as the precondition of the care of the self, it should already be clear to what extent asceticism could be said to infuse the spatiality of the *agora*. The latter's openness is the lack of origins that makes possible the individuals' self-origination in a world which is not given, but only forms through the defection from the common. The public disclosure of their withdrawal, as an *experimentum* and *exemplum* worth looking up to, animated the agonic spirit of the city, as the space where men could "break through the commonly accepted and reach into the extraordinary" and thus "do permanently [...] what otherwise had been possible only as an extraordinary and infrequent enterprise" (Arendt 205, 197).

3.2 metaphysics

To conceive of the political *agon* as the opening which makes the subjects' secession from the world and ecstatic return to it possible only indicates one of the basic questions, i.e., a spatial-ontological one, underlying the constitution of the Greek *agora*. Empirically, the latter was not, and perhaps could never have been, a pure, unconstrained opening. It goes without saying that the game of dissonances, conflicts, separations and betrayals staged in the public arena needed at the same time a whole set of rules, values, measures, categories (*kata-agoreuein*) and ways of judging capable of giving form to a relatively stable "in-between." Without them, no political form – no *Lichtung* – could ever be established or preserved.

According to Vernant, Western philosophy emerged precisely with such aim in view, as knowledge of the *metron* and the right proportions to be applied to a world that was no longer ruled by traditional mythologies and quasi-divine authorities. Ultimately, this is what determined the isomorphism between Greek democracy and philosophy. The *agora* could multiply the opportunities to secede from and speak against the world (the world of traditions, customs and existing powers) only on condition of making a certain understanding of *logos*, reason, moderation, equality, virtue, justice, etc.[14] into the general framework of life- and truth-experiments. From Anaximander onwards, this transpired in the philosophical attempt to translate the laws of the democratic contest into a *geometrical interpretation of the cosmos*. Whereas archaic cosmogonies explained the emergence of order out of chaos as the result of the active intervention of an all-powerful God (Vernant, *The Origins*, ch. 7), philosophical *logos* worked to demonstrate how order was a property of *physis* itself. This signalled the passage from a mythology that was always already, in a way, myth of sovereignty, to a rational discourse according to which

> [i]ts geometrical structure gave the cosmos a kind of organization that was contrary to the one ascribed to it by myth [...] no longer was any physical power to be in the dominant position of a *basileus* exercising his *dynasteia* over all things [...] It was the equality and symmetry of the various powers that made up the cosmos that characterized the new natural order. Supremacy belonged exclusively to a law of equilibrium and continuous reciprocity. *Monarchia* was replaced, in nature as in the city, by a rule of *isonomia*. (Vernant, *The Origins* 121–22)

Leaving aside the historically ambivalent and conflictual relation between philosophy and political order (as well as the innumerable transformations undergone by both, in their mutual relation), here it is only necessary to stress how the latter did not just *translate* the topological problem concerning the rightful distance, tensions, symmetries and balance between the elements composing the democratic order into a discourse on the *logos* inherent to nature. At the same time, it provided a *model* and a *method* for the concrete organisation of the *polis*, starting from its institutional make-up down to the details of its urban configuration, as part of a "general effort to order and rationalize the human world" (125). It is precisely to the extent that it served to secure – geometrically, ethically and cosmologically – a new articulation of power and social order that philosophy, as Vernant remarked, was "in essence political" (130).

Anyone familiar with Sloterdijk's *Spheres* will recognise here some of the central preoccupations of his theory of classical immunity. Metaphysical globalisation, "began as the geometrization of the incommensurable," as an effort to "place [humans] within an intelligible, formal and constructive relation with the world-whole"; and in such a way that "the city order as a whole, as a harmonic joining of parts, [could share] by analogy in the divine-geometric order of the tiered and rounded universe" (Sloterdijk, *Globes* 46, 358). To be sure, in *Globes*, Sloterdijk's focus is chiefly on the interplay between the centre and the periphery of metaphysical spheres and, therefore, on the hierarchies between the high and the low, the inner and the outer, rather than on the symmetry that obtains, or should obtain, between equidistant points. Yet, similarly to Vernant, he also interprets ancient metaphysics as the organisation of logical spaces according to ideal principles of rationality. It was precisely their idealised form to enable classical spheres to immunise large-scale societies, as they came to integrate a multiplicity of hordes and tribes, while dis-integrating their prior networks of solidarities. Metaphysics staged a "logical counter-society" (18) in which the place of each point-citizen could be determined unambiguously on the basis of their relation to the Whole, irrespective of their tribal, familial and mythical allegiances (118; see also 301, 369 and *Im selben Boot* 36). The rarefied laws of universal order overlaid the density of local resonances, while, in the process, geometry became "the science of political theory" (*Globes* 368).

For Sloterdijk, this process was intimately connected to the birth of anthropotechnics. As he shows in *Globes*, the construction of metaphysical spheres did not simply aim at reconstituting the quasi-spontaneous intimacy of tribal bonds. This, strictly speaking, would have been impossible, given that globes emerged against the background of a world which, having been upset by the spirit of ascetic secession, could now only be inhabited as a non-given, non-factical *topos*: a "non-uterus" (Sloterdijk, *Eurotaoismus* 155). The search for a model of social cohesion in the abstraction of geometrical order ensued from the dissonance between the world and the subject produced by the axial age[15] – the very same dissonance, that is, which defined political relations in the *agora*. Metaphysics elaborated the symbolic shelters for a society of individuals who could only find in a world "beyond" the world – in "a new *koinon* over the old communes" (*You Must Change* 193) – their in-between. The orb served to integrate, on a noetic and cosmic plane, the centrifugal and self-isolating tendencies of recessive subjects: "The purpose of being-in-the-orb was precisely to separate the point-individuals from their egotistical self-referentiality and relate them to the universally shared center in a great moral and ontological extraversion."[16]

Metaphysical globes, however, were not only *ex post* attempts to direct and contain the potential dispersion of axial subjectivities. As though in a circular relation, they also delineated the horizon of possibility of *askesis*. The cosmic sphere – as representation of the One and the Whole, *logos*, rationality, *physis*, *metron*, etc. – simultaneously embodied the idea of the good, the best, the most beautiful and primal, *virtue itself*. To translate this into the language of *You Must Change Your Life*, the centre of the orb coincided with "the vertical pole" and "the absolute imperative" setting the direction and goal of the life of practice, as "the Great Other that makes [humans] possible through their intimate augmentation" (Sloterdijk, *Globes* 402; see also 17, 103, 121, 305; *You Must Change* 35, 64).

The "'[s]oul,' in the sense of a microcosmic or inner-world organ for doubling the existent as a whole" was born exactly at this point (Sloterdijk, *You Must Change* 274). By welding together the principle of universal order and the possibility of individual self-elevation, metaphysics brought "into resonant proximity [...] [t]he epicentre of the small ellipse [i.e., the individual] and the centre of the large order" (Sloterdijk, *Globes* 507), thus making possible to re-centre, as it were, the ex-centricity of *askesis*. This was the prime political task of metaphysics in the axial age: to ensure that "social synthesis would be adequately supported from above and within" (353).[17]

4 self-mobilisation

the nature of Power, is [...] like the motion of heavy bodies, which the further they go, make still the more hast. (Hobbes, ch. 10)

To clarify, political agonism and metaphysics, as I have framed them through a reinterpretation of Sloterdijk's thought, should be regarded neither as universals (since, as seen, they arose at a specific point in history), nor as the empirical determinants of the whole of classical politics, between the birth of the Greek *polis* and the dawn of modernity (it goes without saying, for one, that democratic and republican ideals only resurfaced sporadically throughout this period). The foregoing analysis only sought to identify some of the general features of political spheres in the axial age. A detailed account of their historical vicissitudes – which, no doubt, would also have to be an account of their alternate alliances, conflicts, reversals and antagonisms – would necessarily lie beyond the scope of this essay. To draw this genealogy closer to the present, so as to point to the role that anthropotechnics continues playing in our current political phase, in the following I will thus limit myself to a preliminary analysis of how modernity has tended to remodel the nexus between classical politics and *askesis* and, therefore, the structures that used to secure life – from within and above – in the metaphysical age.

As Sloterdijk argues, the death of God, as announced by Nietzsche, marked a turning point in this regard – with the caveat, however, that this is not interpreted only in terms of the self-devaluation of the Christian God, but as a symptom of the exhaustion of classical *global* immunity mechanisms more generally, of which Christian theology was only a late and specific manifestation. On this view, modern humanity did not only kill God, but also the possibility of any metaphysical shelter encompassing the cosmos, the self and the *polis* in their unity (Sloterdijk, *Globes* 553–63). As far as the history of anthropotechnics is concerned, this implies that, *in principle*, no Whole, no matter whether placed somewhere beyond or within this world, could still provide a common horizon or a vertical pole of attraction to ascetic subjectivities. No longer constrained within the perimeter of the One, the self became again – or, perhaps, indeed, for the first time – an object of limitless experimentation, conducted beyond traditional frames of spiritual training. What followed was a virtually unbounded proliferation and "deregulation" of the life of practice:

> schools and more schools, then artists' studios, theatres, concert halls, barracks, factories, clinics, prisons, speakers' pulpits, markets, places of assembly, stadiums and sport studios. What began in the Modern Age was no less than a new form of large-scale anthropotechnic regime, a fundamentally changed battle formation of disciplines. (Sloterdijk, *You Must Change* 323)

Politically, this (at once quantitative and qualitative) extension of *askesis* had several, far-reaching consequences. In the first place, it is easy to see how democratic ideals and a culture of political agonism could come again to the fore so prominently in the modern age. As the life of practice ceased to be a privilege of the few – as more and more individuals began to cultivate new abilities and lifestyles, away from established habits and modes of thought – the need naturally arose to remodel the public sphere accordingly. At risk of oversimplifying, one might regard modern theorisations of political freedom precisely as the correlative of this anthropotechnical shift. Modernity's democratic aspirations, along with its enlargement of the political *agon* and of political rights, could be seen as a response to the expanding chances for self-development and self-realisation made available by the breaking up of classical metaphysical spheres. As the One ceased to be the only attractor of the life of practice, a manifold of autonomous and irreconcilable life projects and political programmes came into being. As John Stuart Mill put it, modern liberalism emerged precisely out of a universal (and, in fact, one might add: ascetic) desire to break with the world:

> He who lets the world, or his own portion of it, choose his plan of life for him, has no need of any other faculty than the ape-like one of imitation. He who chooses his plan for himself, employs all his faculties. (124)

In passing, the history of several other ideologies and political programmes – from Marxism and anarchism up to contemporary anarcho-capitalism – might be re-read along similar lines.[18] Seen from this perspective, the modern political arena could be framed as a battlefield of life-experiments and projects for the transformation of the self and the world, as the *theatre for ascetic revolutions on a mass scale*.

Obviously, it would simply be wrong to interpret modern democracy as a revival of the ancient spirit of the *agora*. If nothing else, the *scale* of the transformations involved in the process witnesses to an essential difference between the two. Once *metanoia* became a collective task pursued by mass-based parties and ideologies, the affirmation of the subject's singularity *in* and *against* the world, as one of the original impulses of Greek democracy, inevitably got lost, to some degree at least. On the other hand, and perhaps more problematically, the death of God meant that universal spheres, such as those fashioned by classical metaphysics, became technically unsustainable in the modern age. While the end of the great orb produced an unprecedented proliferation of programmes for the reform of humans, it at the same time deprived the political *agon* of any all-comprehensive (ethical, metaphysical or cosmological) mechanisms of security. Hence, it became increasingly difficult to recompose the eccentric tendencies of (individual or collective) subjectivities into a totality, and thus to fabricate a Whole out of their dispersion. Among other things, this suggests that the failure of global ideologies to immunise post-metaphysical societies is somehow co-originary with the modern age, and not only the consequence of its end, the end of history and its "grand narratives."

Nonetheless, modern societies have not been stripped bare of any ontological shelter. Along with their reiterated attempts (and failures) at establishing logical, spiritual, national, humanitarian and ideological "absolute containers," they have sought, and have largely been able to articulate different (non-metaphysical) logics and practices of immunity. As Sloterdijk suggests in different places, their general tendency has been to replace geometrical globes with political, economic and technological mechanisms geared to the *permanent mobilisation of subjectivity*.[19] Having unchained the care of the self from the One as a vertical attractor – and, hence, no longer being able to centre the *agora* on some shared conception of the good, virtue, reason, justice, etc. – modern societies have their principle of stability in a law of compulsory and general mobility. This dynamism has provided a synthesis and, in a sense, the common ground to the kaleidoscope of life-experiments that makes up the modern political arena.

The heir of the "exercises of ascetic self-intensification" fashioned in the monastic milieus of the high Middle Ages, the "secret" of modern subjectivity, Sloterdijk contends, manifests itself as "self-movement towards movement." Anthropotechnics here aims at the progressive "accumulation of subjectivity," at extending the latter's potentials for action ideally *ad infinitum*. The life of practice has thus transmuted into pure kinetics, "self-movement *sans phrase*," indefinite search for the "ever more" (Sloterdijk, *Eurotaoismus* 64–66).

This tendency shows up more clearly, without a doubt, in the rationality of capitalist accumulation and, today, especially, in neoliberal discourses revolving on investments on the self, self-entrepreneurship, human capital, life-long learning, etc. and allied transhumanist ideologies of genetic and cognitive self-enhancement (cf. Schultz; Becker; Harris; Bostrom; Buchanan). Yet, the paradigm of self-mobilisation has marked not only the trajectory of modern economics and technology, but, more generally, the conditions of possibility of the labour on the self, thoroughly redefining this way the life of practice and its two main axes, i.e., withdrawal from and ecstatic return to the world. To put it schematically, in the age of mobilisation, to secede from the world is no longer to approach the centre of a sphere (the Good, the One, the Whole), but to project oneself onto the time to come as a promise of self-regenerating surplus – as an extension of what the subject already is but has not yet become. It is from this beyond – which in fact invariably lies ahead and onwards, on a horizontal plane, so to speak – that the self now introduces its difference into the world and opens itself (ec-statically) to it.

The modern imperatives to growth, innovation, development, progress, mobility and enhancement appear only as the surface effects of this ascetic scheme. In a world where global immunity mechanisms seem doomed to fail, self-mobilisation has provided the matrix (or perhaps the "axiomatic," to borrow this term from Deleuze and Guattari) to order and synthesise the proliferation of life-experiments in the modern *agora*. This has ensured that the infinite void which opened up before the "I" after the death of God could be given again a stable, univocal and, to some degree, predictable direction. Horizontal movements ahead, onwards and to the surplus have supplanted the vertical dimension that used to secure the political world in the metaphysical age (Sloterdijk, *You Must Change* 369–72). The enhancement of the subject's agency, rather than the conversion to a new figure of truth and form of life, now guides its efforts to assert its singularity *in* and *against* the world – in such a way, moreover, that its acceleration may still partake of a common world.[20]

The Earth itself, as remoulded by technoscientific and economic rationalities, is here made to appear as the universal *koinon* of humanity. The call from "ahead" which urges the "I" to break with the world discloses nature as a set of material constraints to be worked upon, displaced, disposed of and reprogrammed, in order to liberate the subject's potential for acceleration. The labour of the self translates this way into material production – the production of "a new world of mobile artefacts" (Sloterdijk, *Eurotaoismus* 64) and artificial prostheses, whose rationale is ultimately to expedite the (ethical, economic and ascetic) mobility of the "I." By so doing, contemporary anthropotechniques ensure that the "movement of our life becomes identical with the movement of the world," while making nature itself appear as "the execution of the project that we have for it" (23).

The unfolding of this *pro-ject* is in a way the general horizon – the world – of subjects in a permanent "productive" retreat. It is the point at which the quasi-automatic movement of the self merges with a world which is itself "movement *sans phrase*," or, in other words, where the euphoria of neoliberal and transhumanist self-enhancement carelessly calls for the total re-engineering of the Earth.[21] Hence, the surreal hope of our *askesis*: that we may mobilise ourselves and the world to the point of one day erasing their *distance* – the tear where the world itself forms.

disclosure statement

No potential conflict of interest was reported by the author.

notes

1 For other interpretations emphasising the political dimension of Sloterdijk's thought, see Van Tuinen; Consoli; Janicka.

2 This is not to say, however, that humans first began to "operate" on themselves in a conscious or systematic fashion starting from this period (roughly, the first millennium BCE). As Jaspers also emphasises (36–40), the *plasticity* of Homo sapiens has been present throughout, and has perhaps even set its history into motion. As we shall see, with the axial breakthrough, anthropotechnics nevertheless took on a very specific ontological, spiritual and cosmic dimension.

3 "[Humans] explicate themselves as beings that must secure themselves in the monstrous – in-the-world, Heidegger says" (Sloterdijk, *You Must Change* 333).

4 Cf., for example, Sloterdijk, *Weltfremdheit* 12: "The era of advanced civilisations [...] appears to us as the period in which an increasingly litigious process of divorce between man and the world began – an epoch of estrangement and disagreement."

5 Cf. Sloterdijk, *Not Saved* 122: "the care for enhousing and the care for self are not to be distinguished in the beginning." On philosophical ascesis as encounter with the world, see Pierre Hadot's classical *Exercices Spirituelles et Philosophie Antique*, and especially the section "Le Moi et le Monde" (323–92).

6 In the sphere of *vita contemplativa*, this is the "apparent death" which the "I" must undergo in order to convert itself into a subject of theory: its *epoche* is not only suspension of the belief in the world but also an "exchange of the local ego for the higher self" (Sloterdijk, *Art of Philosophy* 82).

7 Or, as Sloterdijk puts it, "to conceive finitude and opening simultaneously: that is the matter at hand" (qtd in Duclos 39).

8 See also Sloterdijk, *Stress and Freedom* 53: "The released subject never maintains the stance of inaccessibility to the real in the long term. As soon as it discovers its freedom, it simultaneously discovers a virtually boundless accessibility within itself to calls from the real."

9 Cf. Eisenstadt, "The Axial Conundrum" 207: "The zeal for reorganization and transformation of social formations [...] made the 'whole world' at least potentially subject to cultural-political reconstruction."

10 Following Sloterdijk (*Im selben Boot*) I employ this term to refer to politics after the axial breakthrough and before the dawn of modernity.

11 Vernant's comments on the axial age only appear in the preface to the second edition of *The Origins of Greek Thought*, which is not included in the English translation. See Vernant, *Le Origini* 11–22.

12 For a partially overlapping analysis of the political effects of the axial breakthrough, see Arnason et al. 2–3:

> The cultural mutations of the Axial Age generated a surplus of meaning, open to conflicting interpretations and capable of creative adaptation to new situations [...] The new horizons of meaning could serve to justify or transfigure, but also to question and contest existing institutions [...] the complex interplay of patterns and processes is conducive to more autonomous action by a broader spectrum of social actors and forces.

See also Eisenstadt, "Cultural Traditions" and "The Axial Conundrum."

13 Even though he hinted at how a certain form of *askesis* – entailing the discipline, education and training necessary to achieve *sophrosyne*, moderation, rejection of *hubris* and "the virtue of the happy medium" – was crucial to establishing a "political order that sets up an equilibrium between opposing forces, establishing an accord between rival groups" (Vernant, *The Origins* 85).

14 See n13 above.

15 Cf. Bellah 276:

> Transcendental breakthrough occurred when in the wake of second-order weighing of clashing alternatives there followed an almost unbearable tension threatening to break up the fabric of society, and the resolution of the tension was found by creating a transcendental realm and then finding a soteriological bridge between the mundane world and the transcendental.

16 Sloterdijk, *Globes* 120–21. See also 93 ("the whole, in its geometric euphoria can only last if it manages to keep the eccentric under control"), 103, 120, and *Foams* 243ff.

17 Plato's *Alcibiades* is exemplary in this respect, in as far as it presents possibly the first metaphysical scene in which the interweaving between the cosmic and the ascetic also appears as the ideal ground of political order. This theme, however, also transpires in other dialogues by Plato (cf. Carone).

18 Cf., for example – as a mere indication of where this investigation could set out from – Marx 807: the "development of human energy [...] is an end in itself, the true realm of freedom"; Kropotkin 234: "[...] Man would thus be enabled to obtain the full development of all his faculties, intellectual, artistic and moral"; Schultz 1–2: "the economic capabilities of man are predominantly *a produced means of production*."

19 This theme is developed by Sloterdijk especially in his early works (*Eurotaoismus*; *Zur Welt Kommen*; *Im selben Boot*). In different ways, yet, it resurfaces in more recent texts too (see, e.g., *In the World Interior*; *Die schrecklichen*).

20 In *The World Interior of Capital* (249), Sloterdijk describes this *world* as the last sphere, the "crystal palace": "in the crystallized world system, everything is subject to the compulsion of movement. Wherever one looks in the great comfort structure, one finds each and every inhabitant being urged to constant mobilization."

21 As exemplified today most notably by geoengineering projects aimed at remodelling the Earth and its atmosphere on a planetary level, as a remedy to climate change and other environmental disasters. For a critique, see, e.g., Altvater.

bibliography

Altvater, Elmar. "The Capitalocene, or, Geoengineering against Capitalism's Planetary Boundaries." *Anthropocene or Capitalocene? Nature, History, and the Crisis of Capitalism*. Ed. Jason Moore. Oakland, CA: PM, 2016. 138–52. Print.

Arendt, Hannah. *The Human Condition*. Chicago: U of Chicago P, 1998. Print.

Arnason, Johann P., et al. "General Introduction." *Axial Civilizations and World History*. Ed. Johann P. Arnason et al. Leiden: Brill, 2005. 1–14. Print.

Becker, Gary. *Human Capital: A Theoretical and Empirical Analysis, with Special Reference to Education*. Chicago: Chicago UP, 1994. Print.

Bellah, Robert N. *Religion in Human Evolution: From the Paleolithic to the Axial Age*. Cambridge, MA: Harvard UP, 2017. Print.

Bostrom, Nick. *Human Enhancement*. Oxford: Oxford UP, 2011. Print.

Buchanan, Allen. *Better than Human: The Promise and Perils of Biomedical Enhancement*. Oxford: Oxford UP, 2017. Print.

Carone, Gabriela Roxana. *Plato's Cosmology and its Ethical Dimensions*. Cambridge: Cambridge UP, 2011. Print.

Consoli, Dario. *Introduzione a Peter Sloterdijk. Il Mondo come Coesistenza*. Genoa: Il Melangolo, 2017. Print.

Duclos, Vincent. "Falling into Things: Peter Sloterdijk, Ontological Anthropology in the Monstrous." *New Formations* 95 (Jan. 2019): 37–53. Print.

Eisenstadt, S.N. "The Axial Conundrum: Between Transcendental Visions and Vicissitudes of their Institutionalizations: Constructive and Destructive Possibilities." *Análise Social* 46.199 (2011): 201–17. Print.

Eisenstadt, S.N. "Cultural Traditions and Political Dynamics: The Origins and Modes of Ideological Politics. Hobhouse Memorial Lecture." *The British Journal of Sociology* 32.2 (1981): 155–81. Print.

Eisenstadt, S.N. "Introduction: The Axial Age Breakthroughs – Their Characteristics and Origins." *The Origins and Diversity of Axial Age Civilizations*. Ed. S.N. Eisenstadt. New York: SUNY P, 1986. 1–28. Print.

Elkana, Yehuda. "The Emergence of Second-Order Thinking in Classical Greece." *The Origins and Diversity of Axial Age Civilizations*. Ed. S.N. Eisenstadt. New York: SUNY P, 1986. 40–64. Print.

Esposito, Roberto. *Communitas: The Origin and Destiny of Community*. Stanford: Stanford UP, 2009. Print.

Foucault, Michel. "Of Other Spaces." *Diacritics* 16.1 (1986): 22–27. Print.

Hadot, Pierre. *Exercices Spirituelles et Philosophie Antique*. Paris: Albin Michel, 2002. Print.

Harris, John. *Enhancing Evolution: The Ethical Case for Making Better People*. Princeton: Princeton UP, 2010. Print.

Heidegger, Martin. *Being and Time*. Oxford: Wiley-Blackwell, 1978. Print.

Hobbes, Thomas. *Leviathan*. Cambridge: Cambridge UP, 1996. Print.

Janicka, Iwona. "Are these Bubbles Anarchist? Peter Sloterdijk's Spherology and the Question of Anarchism." *Anarchist Studies* 24.1 (2016): 62–84. Print.

Jaspers, Karl. *The Origin and Goal of History*. London: Routledge, 2011. Print.

Kropotkin, Peter. *Kropotkin: "The Conquest of Bread" and Other Writings*. Cambridge: Cambridge UP, 1995. Print.

Marx, Karl. *Capital. Vol. III (Karl Marx/Frederick Engels. Collected Works, Vol. 36)*. London: Lawrence, 1998. Print.

Mill, John Stuart. *On Liberty*. New Haven, CT: Yale UP, 2003. Print.

Momigliano, Arnaldo. *Alien Wisdom: The Limits of Hellenization*. Cambridge: Cambridge UP, 1990. Print.

Schultz, Theodore W. "Reflections on Investment in Man." *Journal of Political Economy* 70.5, pt. 2 (Oct. 1962): 1–8. Print.

Schwartz, Benjamin I. "The Age of Transcendence." *Daedalus* 104.2 (1975): 1–7. Print.

Sloterdijk, Peter. *The Art of Philosophy: Wisdom as a Practice*. New York: Columbia UP, 2012. Print.

Sloterdijk, Peter. *Die schrecklichen Kinder der Neuzeit: Über das anti-genealogische Experiment der Moderne*. Frankfurt: Suhrkamp, 2015. Print.

Sloterdijk, Peter. *Eurotaoismus: Eine Kritik der politischen Kinetik*. Frankfurt: Suhrkamp, 1989. Print.

Sloterdijk, Peter. *Foams: Spheres Volume III: Plural Spherology*. Los Angeles: Semiotext(e), 2016. Print.

Sloterdijk, Peter. *Globes: Spheres Volume II: Macrospherology*. Los Angeles: Semiotext(e), 2014. Print.

Sloterdijk, Peter. *Im selben Boot*. Frankfurt: Suhrkamp, 1995. Print.

Sloterdijk, Peter. *In the World Interior of Capital: Towards a Philosophical Theory of Globalization*. Cambridge: Polity, 2013. Print.

Sloterdijk, Peter. *Nach Gott*. Frankfurt: Suhrkamp, 2017. Print.

Sloterdijk, Peter. *Not Saved. Essays after Heidegger*. Cambridge: Polity, 2017. Print.

Sloterdijk, Peter. *Stress and Freedom*. New York: Wiley, 2018. Print.

Sloterdijk, Peter. *Weltfremdheit*. Frankfurt: Suhrkamp, 1993. Print.

Sloterdijk, Peter. *You Must Change Your Life*. Cambridge: Polity, 2014. Print.

Sloterdijk, Peter. *Zur Welt Kommen. Zur Sprache Kommen*. Frankfurt: Suhrkamp, 1988. Print.

Sutherland, Thomas. "Ontological Co-belonging in Peter Sloterdijk's Spherological Philosophy of Mediation." *Paragraph* 40.2 (2017): 133–52. Print.

Sutherland, Thomas. "Peter Sloterdijk and the 'Security Architecture of Existence': Immunity, Autochthony, and Ontological Nativism." *Theory, Culture & Society* 36.7–8 (2019): 193–214. Print.

Van Tuinen, Sjoerd. "From Psychopolitics to Cosmopolitics: The Problem of *Ressentiment*." *Sloterdijk Now*. Ed. Stuart Elden. Cambridge: Polity, 2012. 37–57. Print.

Vernant, Jean-Pierre. *Le Origini del Pensiero Greco*. Milan: SE, 2015. Print.

Vernant, Jean-Pierre. *The Origins of Greek Thought*. Ithaca, NY: Cornell UP, 1984. Print.

Ware, Kallistos. "The Way of the Ascetics: Negative or Affirmative?" *Asceticism*. Ed. Vincent Wimbush and Richard Valantasis. Oxford: Oxford UP, 2002. 3–15. Print.

Wittrock, Björn. "The Meaning of the Axial Age." *Axial Civilizations and World History*. Ed. Johann P. Arnason et al. Leiden: Brill, 2012. 51–85. Print.

1 introduction

The present work has two main objectives: one genealogical-reconstructive[1] and the other critical-deconstructive.[2] On the one hand, it will offer a reconstruction of the origin and development of the concepts of "anthropotechnics" and "homeotechnics" in Peter Sloterdijk's thought (section 2), of the anthropological basis of his social philosophy (section 3), and of the question of subjectivity addressed in his book *You Must Change Your Life* (2009) (section 4). On the other hand, the objective of the present paper is to bring into focus, through this reconstruction, what I believe to be one of the most critical points in Sloterdijk's philosophy: what could be described as a "constitutive deficiency" with regard to the concept of "otherness" in his theory as a whole. As I will try to demonstrate below, the otherness that Sloterdijk brings into play has only a logical-operational, and therefore formal, character, and not an ethical-social, and therefore substantial, one: in his philosophical works Sloterdijk theorizes different forms of otherness, but these forms mostly turn out to be mere means, useful only to define and determinate the subject. Consequently, the other is never considered in his or her individuality and irreducibility, but only in an instrumentalized way.[3] I will analyze three central aspects of Sloterdijk's work, trying to show how a constitutive deficiency in the definition of otherness can be highlighted in relation to each of them. The first aspect that I will take into consideration will be the one related to the definition of the concept of "technique" in Sloterdijk:

antonio lucci

THE LIMITS OF THE SPHERES
otherness and solipsism in peter sloterdijk's philosophy

my aim will be, first of all, to reconstruct the different definitions of this concept in the Sloterdijkian corpus analytically, and then to investigate the concept of otherness that results from them. The second aspect that I will take into consideration is the one connected to Sloterdijk's social philosophy: his way of understanding communities and societies, their modes of formation, and the reasons that keep men together in suprapersonal formations. Finally, I will focus on the theory of the subject that Sloterdijk develops in *You Must Change Your Life* and on the possible solipsistic implications contained in this work.

2 technology, allotechnics, anthropotechnics, and homeotechnics

I believe that the best way to investigate the first problematic approach to otherness in Sloterdijk's work is a reconstruction of his concept of anthropotechnics, of which I will give a brief genealogy below. First of all, in order to understand the role, development, and functions of the concept of anthropotechnics in Sloterdijk, it is necessary to define it comparatively to the other definitions of the concept of "technique" that he provides.

It should first of all be noted that Sloterdijk defines what commonly falls under the label of "technology" by the term "allotechnology" [*Allotechnik*] (Sloterdijk and Heinrichs 135). The meaning assigned to this concept is mainly pejorative: allotechnics is a way of relating to the world and things based on their exploitation:[4]

> For this era it tended to be true that the subjectivist master, when he used tools, enslaved objects and was seldom or never just to their own nature, especially when these "instruments" were themselves human beings who should have been able to make a claim to subjectivity or freedom from masters. From this there arises an image of technology that is based on simple tools, classical machines, and traditional relations of domination between souls and materials: this complex remains determined by allotechnological means that serve to carry out violent and counternatural incisions into that which is discovered and to employ materials for ends that are indifferent or alien to them. (Sloterdijk, "The Domestication of Being" 143)

According to Sloterdijk, this way of understanding technique is the one that has most imposed itself in the Western world, making a form of logical dualism (i.e., that between true and false) effective, which in turn supports an ontology of the monistic sort (i.e., based on the clear division between the field of "Being" and that of all which is not "Being," and which is thus placed on the side of nothingness).[5] Sloterdijk sums up this kind of technical conception of the world in a pithy way: "The older technology shifts the world of things into a state of ontological slavery" ("The Domestication of Being" 143).

Despite his critical views of (allo)technology, Sloterdijk is well aware of the potential of this concept, and therefore proposes an alternative interpretation rather than a rejection of it.

Sloterdijk introduces a new concept, *homeotechnics* [*Homöotechnik*], which is a composite term that refers both to the new possibilities – opened up by biotechnologies – to act with nature through processes that are close to the ones used by nature itself, and to "old technologies" like breeding and farming (i.e., non-invasive technologies that operate "in consonance" with and not in opposition to natural processes):

> We become witnesses to the fact that with intelligent technologies a non-domineering form of operativity is emerging for which we propose the name "homeotechnics" [...] Homeotechnics only progresses on the path of the non-violation of what is present [...] A few prominent natural scientists of the present day express similar ideas with the metaphor of a "dialogue with nature." This expression only makes sense if one also keeps in mind that it is supposed to supersede the standard idea of a war with nature. ("The Domestication of Being" 144)

However, the horizon depicted by the concept of homeotechnics – the idea of an *imitatio naturae* by technological means – is not an unproblematic one, partly because Sloterdijk does not describe the concept systematically and extensively. For instance, merely mentioning monoculture farming or genetically modified vegetables can call into question the somewhat "Romantic" idea of homeotechnics as a non-invasive technology for nature. However, after the publication of "The Domestication of Being," Sloterdijk abandoned the concept of homeotechnics for a long time – he has recently returned to it, although not yet systematically – in favor of a third definition of technology: anthropotechnics. The theorization of this concept, expressed for the first time in the renowned essay "Rules for the Human Park," was anticipated in two previous works – *In the Same Boat* [*Im selben Boot*] and *Strangeness to the World* [*Weltfremdheit*] – in which Sloterdijk began to take an interest in the problem of anthropogenesis and the structure of human "collectives" [*Kollektiven*]. In *Im selben Boot*, Sloterdijk analyzes how the prehistoric horde – meaning the first social group – was shaped and developed, and how community living influenced hominization: "Hordes are groups of men who raise men, and who, along enormous stretches of time, entrust their progeny with ever more dangerous as well as valuable skills" (19; my translation). In this phase of his philosophical production, Sloterdijk focused on the social genesis of *Homo sapiens* by those autoplastic processes that produced a significant "cultural" deviation from natural evolution:

> One could also say that the content of the history of the most remote humanity is the secession from the Old Nature by the first beings belonging to the horde, and at the same time by the first essential hordes. (20; my translation)

In this passage, Sloterdijk encapsulates those characteristics that will later make up the term "anthropotechnics," which was originally the human "production" of that prehistoric "social womb" that he calls the horde. In these passages Sloterdijk uses a biological lexicon that conveys an idea of social groups that is not based on concepts such as "responsibility," "ethics," "decision," "contract," or (also) "conflict": the "human shaping" (19) is the result of passive-biological, and not of active-political, processes. The human beings Sloterdijk is talking about are not the active subjects of a process of becoming human through coexistence in tribal groups, but rather the passive objects of bio-social evolution.

In 1993, the same year when *Im selben Boot* was published, Sloterdijk published *Weltfremdheit*, a book that can be considered the logical prosecution of the analysis first found in the collection of ancient Gnostic writings he co-edited with Thomas Macho, *Weltrevolution der Seele* [*The World Revolution of the Soul*]. The eight essays on historical and cultural anthropology in *Weltfremdheit* constitute an analysis of the strategies employed by civilizations in antiquity and late antiquity to give meaning to the course of the world, to events such as sickness, healing, birth, and death, which in themselves escape the grasp of the intellect and expose humanity to existential questions regarding meaning and the lack thereof. Here, for the first time, Sloterdijk fully developed his idea of "immunology," which states that religion and philosophy are systems of thought with a common root that makes them ontologically equivalent (indeed, Sloterdijk will include both fields under the heading "metaphysics"). In the second essay of the collection – "Where Do Monks Go? On the Escape from the World from an Anthropological Point of View" ["Wohin gehen die Mönche? Über Weltflucht in anthropologischer Sicht"] (80–117) – some fundamental elements are present that will later reemerge with the concept of anthropotechnics. Sloterdijk writes that Christianity's (particularly Byzantine Christianity's) first solution to the problem of evil in the world was for people to become "athletes" of renunciation, keen creators of the desert of asceticism, which, while much heavier than the natural desert, is also more bearable because it is created and desired by humanity. In the third essay of the collection "What About Drugs? On the Dialectic of World-Flight and World-Addiction" ["Wozu Drogen? Zur Dialektik von Weltflucht und Weltsucht"][6] (118–60), Sloterdijk interprets the use of drugs and other disinhibiting means as one of humanity's most ancient attempts to escape from the burden of this world and reach other, artificial worlds that provide "ecstasy" (a word coming from the Greek "*ék-stasis*," literally "standing outside") against the pain of everyday life, however temporary. "Is the World Deniable? On the Spirit of India and Western Gnosis" ["Ist die Welt verneinbar? Über den Geist Indiens und die abendländische Gnosis"] (213–66) is the third and last essay that

I will analyze to understand the origin of the concept of anthropotechnics. According to Sloterdijk, what Gnosticism, Buddhism, and Brahmanism have in common is that they symbolically transpose explanations of nature and the origin of evil onto the transcendental plane. These three religious systems, the exercises of the ascetics, and the negation of the world practiced by drug addicts and alcoholics are all examples of anthropotechnics *ante litteram*: ways of engaging individual subjectivity and collective awareness in a cognitive battle against the pain inherent to existence. Also in this case, as previously pointed out in relation to *Im selben Boot*, the idea that a wide range of social dimensions (religion, metaphysics, even drug use) are to be attributed to immunological reasons paints an unsettling biological picture. According to Sloterdijk's immunological vision, cultures are protective walls that human subjects have erected over the centuries to defend themselves against an alterity considered threatening. The social element thus acquires a negative value, as a form of "protection against" something, losing its creative, positive potentialities (Sunderland, "Peter Sloterdijk" 207).

Sloterdijk will use these premises to elaborate upon the concept of anthropotechnics (between 1997 and 2001), and extensively propound his viewpoint in two essays: "Rules for the Human Park" (1997) and "The Domestication of Being" (2000).

Beginning with *Im selben Boot*, the process of anthropogenesis (the birth of the actual human being) emerges from the increasing cultural coexistence in the horde: cohabitation in micro-social entities in the prehistoric era crucially influenced the evolution of humans from members of the species *Homo sapiens* into actual human beings.

Sloterdijk primarily uses "anthropotechnics" to define these retroactive influences of culture on human biological evolution:

> In order to cope with the self-endangerments that increase for sapiens-beings from their unique biological position, they have produced an inventory of procedures for the formation of the self, which we discuss today under the general term "culture" [...] – all those ways of ordering, techniques, rituals, and customs with which human groups have taken their symbolic and disciplinary formation "into their own hands" – [...] It is these ways of ordering and formative powers that characterize anthropotechnics in the proper sense of the word. ("The Domestication of Being" 126–27)

In order to further define anthropotechnics, Sloterdijk introduces a distinction between primary and secondary anthropotechnics. He writes that "primary anthropotechnics [...] aims at shaping the human being directly through civilizing impressions" ("The Domestication of Being" 127), whereas about the definition of secondary anthropotechnics he writes:

> But whether long-term development will also lead to a genetic reform of attributes of the species – whether a future anthropotechnology will advance to an explicit planning of traits; whether humanity will be able to carry out, on the level of the species as a whole, a switch from the fatalism of births to optional birth and prenatal selection – these are questions with which the evolutionary horizon begins to clear before us, however indistinctly and frighteningly. ("Rules for the Human Park" 211)

At the time of their publication these reflections raised some concerns (Nennen; Couture 74–84). However, when they are interpreted within the theoretical coordinates that I have outlined, the accusations of extremism – even of eugenics – advanced by the Habermasians Mohr and Assheuer are unjustified. Indeed, Sloterdijk deliberately uses the adjectives "indistinctly" [*verschwommen*] and "frighteningly" [*geheuer*] to refer to the universe disclosed by anthropotechnics.

Regarding the sentence about optional birth and prenatal selection – "these are questions with which the evolutionary horizon begins to clear before us" – I am persuaded that it should not be read as a celebration of the transcending of human limits, but rather as a problematic reflection on anthropotechnics. "The evolutionary horizon," indeed, first emerged at the beginning of the anthropogenic process, when the horde (the first social group) was created and pushed humanity in the direction of exercising a cultural influence over human biological evolution. According to Sloterdijk, if human cultural evolution now faces the issue of the prenatal selection of genetic human traits,[7] this is only a consequence of the anthropotechnical constitution of the human being.

It is now possible to return to the concept of homeotechnics and integrate it with our new understanding of anthropotechnics:

> Even where it [homeotechnics] is initially employed as egotistically and regionally as any conventional technology it must draw on co-intelligent, co-informative strategies [...] One may even ask whether homeotechnological thought announced up to now by titles such as ecology and complexity science does not possess the potential to open up an ethics of relations that are free of enemies and domination [...] Advanced biotechnology and nootechnology groom a refined, cooperative subject who plays with himself, who is formed in association with complex texts and hyper-complex contexts. Here emerges the matrix of a humanism after humanism. (Sloterdijk, "The Domestication of Being" 144–46)

As we can see in the above passage, the distinction between secondary anthropotechnics and homeotechnics is a subtle one.

Despite the high hopes that Sloterdijk has for homeotechnics, it poses some serious questions regarding who would implement it and whether it would be regulated. In this sense, the lack of a proper distinction between secondary anthropotechnics and homeotechnics could be seen as conceptually suspicious: ensuring that homeotechnics does not turn into a secondary anthropotechnics[8] involves limiting homeotechnics to cooperation with nature but without direct experimentation on humans. Even though Sloterdijk does not employ this important distinction between secondary anthropotechnics and homeotechnics, it appears to be crucial. If secondary anthropotechnics were to become part of homeotechnics, it could mean that direct experimentation on living beings (including humans) could be considered legitimate if it helped to rescue the biosphere. Paradoxically, this would place both anthropotechnics and homeotechnics under the paradigm of allotechnics: if secondary anthropotechnics, based on genetic engineering, is not adequately distinguished from homeotechnics, it can – in principle – become a subcategory of it, as a set of techniques to produce, enhance, and modify human beings. If secondary anthropotechnics, however, becomes a subcategory of homeotechnics, since only the latter, according to Sloterdijk, can provide a technological development that is not destructive of natural otherness, it should be planned in such a way as to ensure cooperation with natural otherness and to safeguard the latter as an end in itself. In this case, then, anthropotechnical measures would be conceivable (such as, for example, the preventive sterilization of a certain number of individuals before birth to prevent overpopulation) which, in order to "cooperate" with Nature, fall into the technical error of favoring one part of the living beings (considered as "Being") over others (regarded as "not-Being"). Although these dystopian scenarios are not taken into consideration by Sloterdijk (nor should they necessarily be considered a direct consequence of his arguments), I believe it is necessary to stress the need for a more systematic definition and delimitation of his tripartition of techniques, in order to avoid dangerous theoretical drifts which could even partially justify ethical perplexities (like those following the publication of "Rules for the Human Park").

As I have mentioned, Sloterdijk has returned to the concept of homeotechnics after a prolonged silence in a recent essay dedicated to "The Anthropocene." He has reiterated the need to rethink the triadic relationship between humanity, nature, and technology:

> A completely different image of the interplay between environment and technology emerges with the conversion of the

technosphere to a homeotechnological and biomimetic standard. We would learn what the Earth, as terrestrial body, is capable of the moment human beings reorganize their handling of it from exploitation to coproduction. If we follow the path of sheer exploitation, the Earth will forever remain a finite monad. If we follow the path of co-production between nature and technology, a hybrid planet could result on which more would be possible than conservative geologists believe. (Sloterdijk, "The Anthropocene" 20)

Even in this late resumption of the division between anthropotechnics and homeotechnics, it seems that Sloterdijk missed an essential opportunity for conceptual clarification. In particular, although we do not necessarily apply the division between primary and secondary anthropotechnics to a text published more than twenty years after "The Domestication of Being" and "Rules for the Human Park," I believe that what is problematic here – as in these earlier texts – is still the question of otherness. Sloterdijk embarks on his argument by setting out from a "we" (the whole of humanity) faced with the otherness of Planet Earth, with respect to which homeotechnical strategies of cooperation should be developed in order to safeguard our common world. The otherness here, therefore, is that of the non-human, to which humanity must approach. Human otherness – the other woman and man, other human beings – is not mentioned, which seems to be done consciously and programmatically by Sloterdijk, since, in the same passage, he reduces the forms of technology to just two: allotechnics and homeotechnics, thereby totally excluding anthropotechnics.[9] If Sloterdijk, by this exclusion, intended to suggest that all human beings are to be viewed as subjects – subjects that must stop opposing the otherness of the planet, by reincluding it in the subjective sphere – we would have an effective theoretical turning point in the author's thought. This would also involve a decisive change in the focus of his analyses: from the analysis of the techniques that produce subjects to an analysis of those that cooperate with nature. Also in this case, however, an important point would remain unaddressed: the one related to the modalities of the constitution of that "we" which in the Sloterdijkian argument just reported seems to be given as an assumption. That this "we" cannot be assumed as a given, especially within the Sloterdijkian philosophical categories, is shown by most of the author's texts (above all, the *Spheres* trilogy), which have not only made the dynamics of the constitution of collectives their central theme but have also subjected them to radical criticism. Without a *pars construens*, following the criticism of the concept of society advanced by Sloterdijk with *Spheres*, the theorization of a "we" seems indistinct, if not devoid of actual content. If we also consider that, with the exception of the passage just mentioned, the concept of "homeotechnics," after its theorization in 2001, has practically disappeared from Sloterdijk's work in order to make way for an expanded idea of anthropotechnics (which I will analyze in section 4 of this essay), we may also argue that a possible "homeotechnic turn" does not represent the thematic center of his philosophical interests. The environmental otherness, therefore, however frequently evoked, claimed, or kept in the background, is not considered in its specificity, but only as a referent for an appeal which nonetheless remains indistinct.

In my opinion, the reasons for this are to be found in Sloterdijk's previous works and, in particular, in his deconstruction of the concept of society, which he began to lay out in writing at the end of the 1980s. However, in order to understand this crucial problem, a brief reconstruction of the main principles of Sloterdijk's social philosophy is necessary.

3 sloterdijk's deconstruction of the concept of society

Sloterdijk first inquired into the concept of subjectivity – both single and collective – at the end of the 1980s,[10] but he only achieved a true systematization with the publication of *Spheres*.

According to Sloterdijk, even before being born the subject *in fieri* (called the "Nobject," to indicate his or her irreducibility to the fields of subjectivity and objectivity) (*Spheres I* 291–321) has experiences that will play a fundamental role throughout his or her conscious life. The examples that Sloterdijk gives are inclusion in the maternal body which is shared with the placenta (the true and proper doppelgänger of the subject that is being formed, the origin of each opening to otherness), suspension in the amniotic fluid, and the fragments of acoustic communication shared with the mother. Using the concept of "the with" [*das Mit*], in the first volume of *Spheres* Sloterdijk defined the placenta as a real doppelgänger of the subject that formed in the mother's womb (356–59). Birth, which leads to the loss of this first double, is configured as the traumatic scene of the opening up to intersubjectivity; because the subject was left alone, he or she will always tend to create cultural (as well as intersubjective) supplements to make up for such solitude. As Thomas Sunderland points out: "What makes Sloterdijk's account somewhat problematic is the way that it tacitly treats the encounter with alterity that grounds our Being-in-the-world as an *unfortunate* (albeit necessary) consequence of our existential facticity" ("Ontological Co-belonging" 145–46). Sloterdijk highlights how the human being moves towards the other, but also, and above all, implements a "technical substitution" of the other, to make up for the trauma of the original loss of the "placental double" (*Spheres I* 382):

> the game of the individual's self-completion before the mirror (and other ego-technical media, especially the book, whether being written or read) would lose its attraction if it were not usable for the sublime fiction of independence [...] It is thus not far from "know thyself" to "complete thyself." (203–05)

By setting out from these few initial considerations, it is possible to start to understand how Sloterdijk's conception of the dual constitution of the subject, and consequently its openness to otherness, is based on an anthropo-biological construction and not on an ethical choice.

The point that I would like to underline, radicalizing the doubts developed in this sense by authors like Thomas Sunderland[11] and Vincent Duclos,[12] is how the relationship with otherness developed by Sloterdijk on the basis of his microspherological model is a relationship that has nothing to do with the other as a subject, with respect to which one can develop any relationship (and a wide range of feelings, both positive and negative) based on free choice. Rather, it is a relationship where the other is always a complement to the subject, which the subject is forced to seek because of the trauma of his or her birth. In particular, it should be pointed out here that the types of relationships that Sloterdijk describes – especially in the first volume of *Spheres* – are relationships that reproduce in the post-natal world the nobjectual stages that the fetus experienced before birth. These stages are the repetition of the original relationship not between the fetus and the mother,[13] but between the fetus and the pre-subjective (= nobjectual) realities. Indeed, the mother as such doesn't exist for the fetus, except in the form of anonymous medial traces (such as vocal traces) (cf. "La Musique retrouvée"): there is a type of relationship only with respect to these, not with respect to the maternal subject, which does not yet exist for the unborn child. In this vision of the other as a supplement and a complement sought by subjectivity to compensate for the trauma of an original loss, the other disappears as a free, irreducible individual: if the "other" is an (almost) physical need, he or she cannot really be an "other" (i.e., a person that is seen in his or her individuality and not only for the role that he or she can play in the process of subjectivation), and the openness towards alterity is not a choice, but a form of (pseudo-neurotic) repetition of an *Urszene*.

In Sloterdijk's narrative the entire history of civilization is the history of the titanic and pathetic human attempts to "air condition"[14] the disorienting post-natal exteriority by creating material, symbolic, architectural, cultural, and metaphysical systems of inclusiveness, the *spheres*: "The sphere is the interior, disclosed, shared realm inhabited by humans – in so far as they succeed in becoming humans [...] Spheres are immune-systemically effective space creations for ecstatic beings that are operated upon by the outside" (*Spheres I* 28). The sphere is, therefore, Sloterdijk's answer to the question about our "where." It is always articulated from the double point of view of the individual and the community: the history of civilization repeats the phases that the individual-in-formation has gone through before becoming a subject. Parallel to the anchoring of the cultural genesis of the human being in the legacy of his *bios*, in the 1990s Sloterdijk analyzed "social agglomerations" at an archaeological level (cf. *Der starke Grund zusammen zu sein*), performing a continuous criticism and deconstruction of society. Beginning with the work *The Nature of Cultures* by sociobiologist Heiner Mühlmann, Sloterdijk argues that what we call "society" does not exist in reality: human beings aggregate into precarious conglomerates owing to the propagation of what can be defined as a real "media infection," consisting in the diffusion of collective passions (mostly destructive-antagonistic ones, which bring human beings together against what is seen as the stranger, enemy, or threat) through the means of communication available in any given era.

These reflections will even lead Sloterdijk to abandon the term "society," which will be replaced by terms such as – in addition to "spheres" – "collectors" (*Spheres III* 584–602), "polycosmic agglomeration" (60), "network of actors" (272), and "self-vaulting autogenous containers" (285), which are aimed at emphasizing the precariousness and the illusory nature of the social construct. These reflections on the mechanisms of social formation will find their outlet in *Rage and Time* – the next book published by him after *Spheres* – and in some coeval minor texts on stress (cf. *Stress and Freedom*), which Sloterdijk views as a factor at play in social cohesion.

Here Sloterdijk expresses the idea that "rage" – or, better, its Greek equivalent, *thymos*, the collective and collectivizable passion par excellence – is the *primum movens* of every social conglomerate: rage is a monetizable psychic energy because it is susceptible to accumulation and deferral, qualities that are typical of, but not exclusive to, monetary capital.

We are thus faced with a further step in Sloterdijk's deconstruction of the concept of "society": in addition to being macro-constructs that regulate themselves on a continuous stressful-thymotic infection, societies could be described as giant "banks" for the instinctual energies of individuals who regulate and maintain themselves by storing negative passions, in order to "positivize" them through the constitution of social constructs such as the Catholic Church, the Communist Party, or the welfare state of contemporary nation-states. In 2010, Sloterdijk gathered a series of interviews about *thymos*, stress, and the global economic-financial crisis and published them along with a short theoretical essay in a volume entitled *The Taking Hand and the Giving Side* [*Die nehmende Hand und die gebende Seite*].[15] Here Sloterdijk provocatively argues that contemporary democratic nation-states are the greatest parasitic systems in history from an economic (that is, both monetary and psychic) point of view. Indeed, the mandatory taxation system has its historical basis in the hybridization of the collective systems of levies in feudal and later socialist states, which considered private property a privilege that was (at least partially) expropriated through the tax system. These historical-ideological foundations have lost all their validity with the disappearance of the political-social structures that generated them, but the tax system has remained in place; it is part of those social mechanisms that perpetuate great social and economic privileges, as well as an instrument of psychic disempowerment used by economic systems that have decided to annihilate the thymothic *côté* of individuals. On the one hand, the "normalization" of the tax and fiscal system which is common in modern Western state apparatuses tends to advocate a "miserabilistic" [*miserabilistisch*] anthropological model (championed by the illustrious founding fathers: Hobbes, Pascal, Proudhon, Marx, Girard, and Gehlen) (Sloterdijk, *Spheres III* 635; *Die nehmende Hand* 40, 47, 48). According to this model, the human being is able to donate his or her energy, attention, and (above all) money and goods only if forced to do so by a coercive power. On the other hand, the operation in question strips the individual act of giving of all its thymotic potential, turning it into something due, normalized, and devalued. Sloterdijk maintains that it will only be possible to overcome the global crisis through a recognition of the *gebende Seite*, the *giving side*, and that this can only happen through the removal of the obligatory tax contribution and its transmutation into a voluntary contribution. According to Sloterdijk – who here is inspired by ancient euergetism – one could reestablish a vision of the human being that is valued for its (Zarathustrian) "gift-giving virtues" [*schenkende Tugenden*]. This would shape an "ethic of giving" [*Ethik der Gabe*] (Sloterdijk, *Die nehmende Hand* 11) whose founding fathers would be Nietzsche, Mauss, Bataille, and Derrida:

> No one believes that this can happen automatically, overnight. The next century will be characterized by a titanic struggle between the reasonableness of generosity and the calculations of downwards thought. The ethics of generosity will only succeed if the growing pressure caused by the mutual dependence of global actors will act in that direction. The global society will be a patchwork of thymotic communities, or it will not be at all. (51; my translation)

In this text, after highlighting the two dominant directives in the interpretation of the tax system (miserabilism vs. generosity), Sloterdijk simply points out a third way, namely, "thymotics communities," yet without providing even a basic description of them: this proposal appears suddenly, without being substantiated by any kind of structural argument. The following questions then arise: what actors should constitute these communities? How could they emancipate themselves from existing systems? What kind of (economic and social) links would connect the individuals who are part of these communities? How can we envisage thymotic communities that are independent of the medial-stressing factors, which have had so much weight in the Sloterdijkian theorization of the social spheres? If we keep in mind the coordinates sketched out not only by this essay, but also by the texts previously taken into analysis, it is possible to understand how the indeterminacy of this concept is not random, but rather constitutive: the "patchwork of thymotic communities" *must* necessarily remain indeterminate, because Sloterdijk has pushed the limits of the impossibility of being together too far, destroying every form of non-performative or self-hallucinatory being-in-society (including the very possibility of it on a lexical level); and this has produced the consequent impossibility of reconstructing the foundations of a community that would not collapse under Sloterdijk's own prior criticisms.[16] The reference to a "patchwork of thymotic communities" is representative of a typically Sloterdijkian rhetorical gesture: after offering a long critical account, towards the end of his works he often provides a brief opening to a totally different reality, which is only mentioned and never discussed in detail.[17] This aim of being constructive and proposing solutions fails because of a lack of argumentation, which makes his theses appear insufficiently justified and somewhat weak.

4 *you must change your life*: a verticalistic anthropotechnical "turn"

I believe that the problems Sloterdijk encountered in founding a social philosophy after theorizing and describing its deconstruction led him to focus on the issue of the subject. As we have seen, this had already been the topic of a series of seminal works by the German thinker, who had analyzed it in its genesis through the concept of "anthropotechnics" in the essays contained in the 2001 volume *Not Saved*. Compared to "The Domestication of Being" and "Rules for the Human Park," in *You Must Change Your Life* the concept of anthropotechnics takes on a different substance and shape. Most importantly of all, it begins to have a strong normative value.

The conceptualization and placing of "practice" [*Übung*][18] at the core of anthropotechnics is the main difference that can be found between *You Must Change Your Life* and Sloterdijk's previous works on anthropotechnics: "Practice is defined here as any operation that provides or improves the actor's qualification for the next performance of the same operation, whether it is declared as practice or not" (*You Must Change* 4).[19]

This concept allows Sloterdijk to overcome the dichotomy between primary and secondary anthropotechnics by defining the latter into a specific case of what could be defined as "tertiary anthropotechnics" (Lucci 139–69). Sloterdijk employs this new kind of anthropotechnics in his work as a guiding thread to reconstruct the entire history of culture.[20] Indeed, *You Must Change Your Life* is an extensive phenomenology of exercise from the ancient to the modern world, focusing on several significant (individual and collective) "figures" that are glaring examples of the passage from one type of exercise to another. From the perspective of tertiary anthropotechnics, the other, understood as another human being, simply becomes a tool to improve the anthropotechnical self:

> The practicing life form is like an inner protectorate with a temporary government and an introspective supervisory authority. In practical terms, this modus vivendi can only be established through an ascetic pact with a teacher whom one supposes already to have achieved ethical reform. (229)

The "teacher" to whom Sloterdijk refers is only one of the forms of otherness mentioned in his text, and is accompanied by figures such as the Indian guru, the Greek sophist, the professor, and the sports coach (276–97). However, the ten kinds of "teachers" analyzed by Sloterdijk are not "real" others: they are nothing more than model figures that do not establish any kind of intersubjective relationship, recognition, or "opening" to the other; they merely serve as a mirror in which the scholar can recognize oneself, as a library from which to learn, and as a source to quench one's thirst without ever having a real "relationship" or human bond. The solipsism of the practicing subject appears to be definitive, since it even goes so far as to include the other without the necessity of having a function that extends beyond the instrumental role of a *trainer* for the anthropotechnical life of the subject. It is no coincidence that all the relationships analyzed by Sloterdijk in this chapter dedicated to otherness are "vertical" relationships, in which there is an exemplary model and someone whose goal is the imitation of this model. Sloterdijk does not mention the loved/lover relationship, friendship, the relationship between siblings, or that between parent and child.[21]

The first part of the book examines the anthropotechnics of the ancient world, bringing into play Christian monks, Indian gurus, and Zen masters (among others), without failing to mention more secular practices that are ubiquitous throughout history: education and sport, above all. Sloterdijk uses the term "religioid" (*You Must Change* 96) to refer to these practices, because he thinks that "no 'religion' or 'religions' exist, only misunderstood spiritual regimens" (3). With this surprising and provocative statement, Sloterdijk advances the hypothesis that religious (as well as philosophical) systems are immunological expedients that arose in the unbearable conditions of misery of the ancient world in order to make life more "human" and meaningful through theoretical and physical exercises.

The anthropotechnics of the ancient world end, according to Sloterdijk, with the externalization of ascetic practices: the modern – as opposed to the ancient – world is based on labor and production, which in anthropotechnical terms are nothing more than attempts to move the object of intervention from the self to the world. This intervention occurred according to two modalities: revolution and evolution. Historical events proved the revolutionary modality of doing politics in the twentieth century wrong, because after the totalitarian catastrophes of "the short twentieth century" revolution was superseded by slow, reformist change, which was guided by the invisible hand of the free market. According to Sloterdijk, this gradual change inarguably had the effect of sensibly improving the material conditions for part of humanity (the Western/Westernized section of the planet, which benefited from the capitalist economic system to the detriment of the rest of the world), but it did not make people happy. The unhappiness of this nevertheless privileged part of humanity can be seen in the number of cases of depression and burnout.[22] Furthermore, we must not overlook the fact that the increase in material wealth that capitalism has ensured for a section of humanity has brought the entire planet to the brink of environmental collapse. At this point Sloterdijk – introducing a normative turn into his argument, which up until now was largely phenomenological-descriptive in nature – advances his proposal to both overcome the unhappiness that characterizes modern Western society and to stop the race towards the abyss of ecological catastrophe: following Nietzsche, we need to "reverticalize" existence (*You Must Change* 443). The prospect of a gradual increase in well-being has neglected and humiliated the acrobatic, "vertical" tendency of human beings, or – in layman's terms – their impulse towards improvement and performative self-modification.

While the *Spheres* trilogy ended with a fictitious dialogue between various scholars waiting for Sloterdijk himself,[23] who was destined never to arrive – an emblem of the impossibility of bringing the narrative to a subjective close – he now actively takes on the task of defining the future goal of philosophy: to dismantle the anthropotechnical nucleus of different religions in order to re-orient them towards a being-in-the-world that will no longer aim to achieve the perfection or salvation of the individual, but rather a global salvation of human beings as a species and of the world as their "ecclesia."

The last part of *You Must Change Your Life* is dedicated to this perspective and articulated into three main questions: *Who is Allowed to Say It? Who Can Hear It? Who Will Do It?* (442–52). Only the philosopher (the one "who is allowed to say it") can understand that the imperative of the contemporary world is imposed by the economic crisis and the looming ecological catastrophe. For Sloterdijk the purpose of the future philosophy is to dismiss the "religioid" core of the old anthropotechnics and to reshape it through the conceptual tools of narrating, deconstructing, and designing.

The recipients of this philosophical call to acrobatics (those "who will hear it") are the contemporary "last men," who have already accepted to transfer their anguish for the future onto the "imaginary" side, incognizant of the fact that the ecological catastrophe is closer than the screens on which they watch the projection of their apocalyptic fears in the form of movies or video games.

Therefore, the answer to Sloterdijk's last question ("Who will do it?") is the community: all of us. As he writes, "at every moment, I am to estimate the effects of my actions on the ecology of the global society" (*You Must Change* 448). What Sloterdijk means is that we should project the transcendence that was once "God" onto a new entity called "World," and reason according to the laws of what will be – according to Sloterdijk – the philosophical science of the future: General Immunology. By following such a science, humanity will need to draw up the "monastic rules" of living together without destroying our biosphere:

> they [the monastic rules] will encode the forms of anthropotechnics that befit existence in the context of all contexts. Wanting to live by them would mean making a decision: to take on the good habits of shared survival in daily exercises. (452)

This *plaidoyer* for a global co-immunitarian anthropotechnics occupies the last, surprisingly short, pages of this monumental book. As in the two cases previously analyzed, the one relating to homeotechnics and the one relating to thymotic communities, here too Sloterdijk seems to remain imprisoned by his own critical force when he has to make a concrete proposal. After having destroyed, in *Spheres*, the possibility of a social philosophy, by reducing it to a phenomenology of post-spherical conglomerates functioning through imitative logic and stress "infections," and after having conceived an idea of autopoietic subjectivity, in *You Must Change Your Life* – where the subject is not really open to the other, but rather uses the other for the purpose of self-improvement – it seems difficult, if not impossible, to theorize the foundations of a global co-immunitarian anthropotechnics. What steps can push human beings – first – to form a homogeneous community, and – then – to include the world in the "personal sphere"? Which global media (which Sloterdijk never analyzes as dependent on concrete configurations of power and historical and political interests) should operate this synthesis? How is it possible, after the failure of the "exercises of the moderns" (Sloterdijk, *You Must Change* 313–435), the only ones who tried to collectivize exercises (but who ended up turning them into dictatorships) (426–28), to think of a common, collective, global form of exercise? And how is it possible to combine this necessity with the envisaging of a future society as a "patchwork of thymotic communities"?

5 conclusions: the limits of anthropotechnical solipsism

These questions are destined, at least in the post-*You Must Change Your Life* works of Sloterdijk, to remain unanswered.

As mentioned in the introduction to this paper, I believe that this lack of answers is constitutive of Sloterdijkian arguments, and – as I have tried to point out – always reflects a deficiency in the conception of otherness.

In the case of the anthropotechnical/homeotechnical dichotomy, the lack of clarity in establishing the limits between the lawful manipulation of nature (homeotechnics) through genetic engineering and the illicit manipulation of humans by the same means is based on the lack of basic anthropological definitions. Sloterdijk does not define the limits of the human or the constitutive characteristics of nature, leaving the two concepts undetermined. This would not be a problem in itself, were it not for the fact that the lack of indeterminacy creates dangerous grey areas, in which it seems even possible to fear the use of homeotechnics in relation to men.

In the case of Sloterdijk's social philosophy, it seems to me, the problem always concerns the concept of otherness: on the one hand, because of his or her nobjectual constitution (with the loss of the placentary "double" at the moment of birth), the subject is forced by his or her dual biological constitution to look for the other, in order to reconstruct the lost uterine pleromatic completeness. The other in this context is something we need, but not a being that interests us per se: it is a means, not an end in itself, to put it in Kantian terms. On the other hand, "social collectors" [*Kollektoren*] and classical conceptions of society (like contractualism or organicism) (*Spheres III* 243–85) are deconstructed by Sloterdijk, which makes them collectors of human beings who stay together because of "mimetic contagion" (240) and waves of collective stress. In this context it seems impossible to envisage any relationship with an other, an other that is free: the other is either sought because the subject needs a complement or is close to us because of supra-subjective dynamics related to stress and media propagation. Finally, the Sloterdijkian "tertiary" anthropotechnics, based on exercise, only strengthens the idea of a strong, autopoietic subject, who is faced with an alterity always exclusively conceived as a mirror in front of which to practice and to improve ourselves, or as someone to help us in this. However, he or she does not represent for us a figure through which to develop attention, love, care, or any (even negative) feeling.

Because of this, it is possible to find perhaps the most acute criticism of Sloterdijk's verticalist model in the writing of his friend Thomas Macho. Macho devoted the last chapter of his text on cultural models to Sloterdijk, adopting a critical perspective (431–59). In the last two pages of the book, Macho reports an anecdote about Jacques Cousteau narrated in the novel *Lowboy* by John Wray: Cousteau, already an old man, is immersed underwater, holding a special tablet that allows him to annotate data. To his great astonishment, at the depth of ninety-one meters Cousteau sees a man below him without any equipment. A sort of unspoken contest is established between the two, as both plunge lower and lower; but Cousteau is always behind, amazed and irritated. Finally, unable to restrain himself, he writes on his annotation tablet the question "How can you survive at such depths?," letting it fall into the hands of the man, who writes his answer on it and sends it back to Cousteau. The simple answer is: "I'm drowning, imbecile" (458–59).

Through this anecdote, Macho conveys a radical critique: when Sloterdijk's verticalist philosophy becomes a "one-to-one" confrontation in which the other is always only a model for his own self-overcoming, devoid of all interest except in relation to his own autopoietic dimension, it proves a deadly philosophy, which risks sinking the subject into the abyss of an endless exercise, at the end of which there is always a very high peak, yet one where we find ourselves alone and without oxygen.[24]

In conclusion, Sloterdijk rows too strongly in the direction of an isolated, Zarathustrian thymotic subject, who rises above the world and the self through autopoiesis. At the same time, he deconstructs the concept of society too deeply through a semantics of stress and *thymòs*, in order to finally advance a proposal for "being together" that is neither weak nor vague, as is instead his proposal for a *thymotischer Kommunen*.[25]

disclosure statement

No potential conflict of interest was reported by the author.

notes

1 This reconstruction will be confined to Sloterdijk's thought: it will not be a matter, therefore, of reconstructing which authors and theories have played a role, as sources, in the theorization of Sloterdijkian concepts, but rather of outlining the path of theoretical development that has led Sloterdijk, during its production, to determine the salient features of such concepts.

2 I will use the term "deconstruction" in the present paper not in a strictly Derridean sense, but following the interpretation of this concept that Sloterdijk himself provides in *Derrida, an Egyptian*: "Once multifocality is taken as a point of departure, all theory moves to the level of second-order observation: one no longer attempts a direct description of the world, but rather re-describes – and thus deconstructs – existing descriptions of the world" (7).

3 Iwona Janicka points out: "The relations between microspheres are based on imitation and contagion [...] Sloterdijk claims: 'in social foam there is no "communication" [...] but instead only interautistic and mimetic relations'" (76). This paper represents an interesting example of how, although the author is well aware of the most problematic points in Sloterdijk's philosophy, it is possible to use his "conceptual arsenal" to build a theory that allows us not only to analyze phenomena different from the ones the author has investigated, but also to envisage social and ethical models not to be found in Sloterdijk's work. I will come back to this point later. Cf. note 16.

4 In this particular sense, it is possible to identify some specific parallels between the concept of allotechnics in Sloterdijk and that of technique expounded by Martin Heidegger in his essay "The Question Concerning Technology." Cf., for example:

> The revealing that rules throughout modern technology has the character of a setting-upon, in the sense of a challenging-forth. That challenging happens in that the energy concealed in nature is unlocked, what is unlocked is transformed, what is transformed is stored up, what is stored up is, in turn, distributed, and what is distributed is switched about ever anew. (16)

5 Sloterdijk discusses these categories extensively in his *God's Zeal* (92–95) in relation to the internal logic of monotheistic discourse. However, as a subject that Sloterdijk applies both to the history of mentalities and to culture, the categories in question can be generalized: they could be understood as a way of interpreting all reality based on the (supposed) dichotomy that exists between entities placed on the side of the subject (= being) and entities placed on the side of the object (= non-being). The fact that (allo-)technique has been the dominant way of interpreting technique in the part of the world where monotheism is the dominant religious conception supports this thesis.

6 In the original German text, *Wozu Drogen? Zur Dialektik von Weltflucht und Weltsucht*, there is a play on words between "Weltflucht" and "Weltsucht," which are impossible to fully translate into English. "Weltsucht" evokes both the "search for the world" and "addiction to the world."

7 Sloterdijk carefully uses the expression "something that can be neither avoided nor mastered" to define its reach ("Rules for the Human Park" 211) ["das Unumgängliche, das zugleich das Nichtbewältigbare ist" ("Regeln für den Menschenpark" 330)].

8 The limits of the employment of these techniques on humans should be the subject of an in-depth bioethical analysis because the specter of eugenics and human enhancement always hovers over them. Jürgen Habermas's book *The Future of Human Nature*, immediately following the controversy with Sloterdijk, represents an attempt to reflect on the issues raised by the anthropotechnical debate (although there is no mention of it as such).

9 "A while ago, I suggested distinguishing between heterotechnics and homeotechnics – with the first based on violating and outwitting nature, and the second based on imitation nature and pursuing natural principles of production in artificial contexts" (Sloterdijk, "The Anthropocene" 20) (Sloterdijk uses here the variant "heterotechnics" to designate what prior was "allotechnics").

10 Sloterdijk had already analyzed this topic in his Ph.D. dissertation on autobiographical literature in the Weimar Republic *Literatur und Organisation von Lebenserfahrung: Autobiographien der Zwanziger Jahre.*

11 In other words, the spheres that humans construct for themselves – remembering that such spheres are always constructed "not according to free choice [...] but under preexisting, given and handed-down conditions" – are a form of de-severence, enabling access to that which is remote, allowing us to safely approach and internalize externalities, or to distance ourselves from those that we cannot. (Sunderland, "Ontological Co-belonging" 140)

12 "How can we remain attentive to the consistency involved in sphere-building without reducing it to mere attempts at adapting to, at enduring ambient pressure?" (Duclos 53).

13 I believe that this is a crucial point which distinguishes my interpretation from others, like the one presented in Dario Consoli's *Introduzione a Peter Sloterdijk* (e.g., 190–91). Consoli interprets the original spherological relationship as the mother–fetus relationship (i.e., an intersubjective one). As I have tried to point out above, the relationship occurring at the nobjectual level is between the fetus and the nobjects (because the mother can be present in this phase only through her nobjectual supplements): "a language of sharing, of solidarity, of going out of oneself and meeting the other" (190; my translation) can be given only as the result of an original relation with the other. If instead the other is only sought in order to compensate for the loss of nobjectual realities, and if the other is not yet given in the most crucial phase of subjectivation, then it seems difficult to conceive of such a "language of sharing."

14 "Spheres are air conditioning systems" (Sloterdijk, *Spheres I* 46).

15 There is no English translation of this work, but a good *resumé* of Sloterdijk's position can be found in the interview titled "What Does a Human Have that He can Give Away?"

16 Within a less critical framework, yet one still focused on the same issues, Henk Oosterling has pointed to the need to integrate Sloterdijk's ethic of gift-giving into a more intersubjective theory (365–76). Without referring to the idea of "thymotic communities," Iwona Janicka has put forward an interesting anarchist interpretation

of Sloterdijk's spherological project. For Janicka, with his theory of the Spheres, on the one hand, and with the emphasis on the concept of homeotechnics as cooperation with nature, on the other hand, Sloterdijk can be taken as a reference thinker for an anarchist thought that requires a philosophical-anthropological theory as its foundation (78). Janicka's hypothesis is particularly interesting in relation to Sloterdijk's expression "thymotics communities," which would fit well with an anarchist context. Probably, it is precisely the vagueness of this concept that ensures its productive potential, despite its intrinsic shortcomings: for it can be defined and reinterpreted from different perspectives precisely because of its lack of definition.

17 For example, Sloterdijk has ended the *Spheres* trilogy without a *pars construens*. Sloterdijk himself must be aware of this lack because at the end of *Spheres III* he has inserted a fictional dialogue in which readers await the author in the hope of asking him some questions about the book, but he never shows up (801–27). Another example is the end of the essay "The Plunge and the Turn": "Perhaps these two statements give us the code word for a maneuver yet to be attempted: follow the star, reach the earth" (48).

18 The German word "Übung" literally means "exercise." Following the official English translation, I will use the word "practice," but also ask the reader to keep in mind that the meaning "exercise" (mostly physical exercise) is even more appropriate.

19 On this topic, see Couture 45.

20 Despite his attempt to explain the anthropotechnical side of Indian (*You Must Change Your Life* 260–70 and 277–81) and Japanese philosophy (281–84), Sloterdijk's "big anthropotechnical narrative" remains a Eurocentric one: there is no mention, for example, of African or Pre-Colombian anthropotechnics, and the historical, geographical, and ethnic specificities of the cultures he discusses aren't taken into account. Also in the *Spheres* trilogy, traces could be found of "an unwitting but potent Eurocentrism": see Thrift 126.

21 The only mention of a parent–child relation in *You Must Change Your Life* leads to a sort of evolutionary-pedagogic foundation for human verticalism:

In its relationship with its mother, every infant experiences a pre-symbolic and supra-spatial Above to which it looks up before it learns to walk. Fathers and grandparents are likewise "up there," long before the child begins to build towers from blocks and place one piece on top of the others as the uppermost [...] The "looking up" of children to their parents and adults in general, especially to cultural heroes and transmitters of knowledge, gives rise to a psychosemantic system of co-ordinates with a pronounced vertical dimension. One could almost describe the world of the early psyche as monarchic. (113–14)

22 Cf. also on this topic Crary.

23 Sloterdijk has recently continued this dialogue in a new book: Sloterdijk, *Polyloquien*.

24 Eduardo Mendieta describes (in a positive way) this tendency of Sloterdijk's theory as "hyperhumanism" [*Überhumanismus*] (75–76).

25 Pier Aldo Rovatti, unlike myself, concluded his critical paper with a positive reflection on Sloterdijk's anthropotechnics (17–18). According to his viewpoint, Sloterdijk's theory of anthropotechnics should be appreciated for its ironic tone and linguistic innovations, because these serve as provocations to rethink the philosophical vocabulary. In a less critical way, but always highlighting the problems inherent to the political and social perspectives of Sloterdijkian theories, see Morin 69.

bibliography

Assheuer, Thomas. "Das Zarathustra-Projekt: Der Philosoph Peter Sloterdijk fordert eine gentechnische Revision der Menschheit." *Die Zeit* 2 Dec. 1999: 31–32. Print.

Consoli, Dario. *Introduzione a Peter Sloterdijk. Il mondo come co-esistenza*. Genova: Il Melangolo, 2017. Print.

Couture, Jean-Pierre. *Sloterdijk*. Cambridge: Polity, 2016. Print.

Crary, Johnathan. *24/7. Late Capitalism and the Ends of Sleep*. London: Verso, 2013. Print.

Duclos, Vincent. "Falling into Things: Peter Sloterdijk, Ontological Anthropology in the

Monstrous." *New Formations: A Journal of Culture/Theory/Politics* 95 (2019): 37–53. Print.

Habermas, Jürgen. *The Future of Human Nature.* Trans. Ella Beister, Max Pensky, and William Rehg. Cambridge: Polity, 2003. 1–23. Print.

Heidegger, Martin. "The Question Concerning Technology." *The Question Concerning Technology and Other Essays.* Trans. William Lovitt. New York: Garland, 1977. 3–49. Print.

Janicka, Iwona. "Are these Bubbles Anarchist? Peter Sloterdijk's Spherology and the Question of Anarchism." *Anarchist Studies* 24.1 (2016): 62–84. Print.

Lucci, Antonio. *Un'acrobatica del pensiero. La filosofia dell'esercizio di Peter Sloterdijk.* Rome: Aracne, 2014. Print.

Macho, Thomas. *Vorbilder.* Munich: Fink, 2011. Print.

Macho, Thomas, and Peter Sloterdijk, eds. *Weltrevolution der Seele. Ein Lese- und Arbeitsbuch der Gnosis von der Spätantike bis zur Gegenwart.* Zürich: Artemis, 1991. Print.

Mendieta, Eduardo. "A Letter on Überhumanismus: Beyond Posthumanism and Transhumanism." *Sloterdijk Now.* Ed. Stuart Elden. Cambridge: Polity, 2016. 58–76. Print.

Mohr, Reinhard. "Züchter des Übermenschen." *Der Spiegel* 6 Sep. 1999: 268–69. Print.

Morin, Marie-Eve. "Cohabitating in the Globalised World: Peter Sloterdijk's Global Foams and Bruno Latour's Cosmopolitics." *Environment and Planning D: Society and Space* 27.1 (2009): 58–72. Web. <https://doi.org/10.1068/d4908>.

Mühlmann, Heiner. *The Nature of Cultures: A Blueprint for a Theory of Culture Genetics.* Trans. Robert Payne. Vienna: Springer, 1996. Print.

Nennen, Heinz-Ulrich. *Philosophie in Echtzeit. Die Sloterdijk–Debatte: Chronik einer Inszenierung.* Würzburg: Königshausen, 2003. Print.

Oosterling, Henk. "Interest and Excess of Modern Man's Radical Mediocrity: Rescaling Sloterdijk's Grandiose Aesthetic Strategy." *Cultural Politics* 3 (2007): 357–80. Print.

Rovatti, Pier Aldo. "Esercizi, ma senza ascesi." *aut aut* 355 (2012): 7–18. Print.

Sloterdijk, Peter. "The Anthropocene – A Stage in the Process on the Margins of the Earth's History?" *What Happened in the 20th Century?* Trans. Christopher Turner. Cambridge: Polity, 2018. 1–23. Print.

Sloterdijk, Peter. *Der starke Grund zusammen zu sein.* Frankfurt: Suhrkamp, 1998. Print.

Sloterdijk, Peter. *Derrida, an Egyptian.* Trans. Wieland Hoban. Cambridge: Polity, 2009. Print.

Sloterdijk, Peter. *Die nehmende Hand und die gebende Seite.* Frankfurt: Suhrkamp, 2010. Print.

Sloterdijk, Peter. "The Domestication of Being." *Not Saved. Essays after Heidegger.* Trans. Ian Alexander Moore and Christopher Turner. Cambridge: Polity, 2017. 89–148. Print.

Sloterdijk, Peter. *God's Zeal. The Battle of the Three Monotheisms.* Trans. Wieland Hoban. Cambridge: Polity, 2009. Print.

Sloterdijk, Peter. *Im selben Boot. Versuch über die Hyperpolitik.* Frankfurt: Suhrkamp, 1993. Print.

Sloterdijk, Peter. "Ist die Welt verneinbar? Über den Geist Indiens und die abendländische Gnosis." *Weltfremdheit.* Frankfurt: Suhrkamp, 1993. 213–66. Print.

Sloterdijk, Peter. "La Musique Retrouvée." *The Aesthetic Imperative. Writings on Art.* Trans. Karen Margolis. Cambridge: Polity, 2017. 3–14. Print.

Sloterdijk, Peter. *Literatur und Organisation von Lebenserfahrung: Autobiographien der Zwanziger Jahre.* Munich: Hanser, 1979. Print.

Sloterdijk, Peter. "The Plunge and the Turn. Speech on Heidegger's Thinking in Motion." *Not Saved. Essays after Heidegger.* Trans. Ian Alexander Moore and Christopher Turner. Cambridge: Polity, 2017. 1–48. Print.

Sloterdijk, Peter. *Polyloquien. Ein Brevier von Peter Sloterdijk.* Frankfurt: Suhrkamp, 2018. Print.

Sloterdijk, Peter. *Rage and Time. A Psychopolitical Investigation.* Trans. Mario Wenning. New York: Columbia UP, 2008. Print.

Sloterdijk, Peter. "Regeln für den Menschenpark. Ein Antwortschreiben zu Heideggers Brief über den Humanismus." *Nicht gerettet. Versuche nach Heidegger.* Frankfurt: Suhrkamp, 2001. 302–37. Print.

Sloterdijk, Peter. "Rules for the Human Park." *Not Saved. Essays after Heidegger*. Trans. Ian Alexander Moore and Christopher Turner. Cambridge: Polity, 2017. 193–216. Print.

Sloterdijk, Peter. *Spheres I. Bubbles, Microspherology*. Trans. Wieland Hoban. Pasadena: Semiotext(e), 2011. Print.

Sloterdijk, Peter. *Spheres III. Foams, Plural Spherology*. Trans. Wieland Hoban. Pasadena: Semiotext(e), 2016. Print.

Sloterdijk, Peter. *Stress and Freedom*. Trans. Wieland Hoban. Cambridge: Polity, 2011. Print.

Sloterdijk, Peter. "What Does a Human Have that He can Give Away?" *Giving and Taking. Antidotes to a Culture of Greed*. Ed. Joke Brouwer and Sjoerd van Tuinen. Rotterdam: V2, 2014. 9–26. Print.

Sloterdijk, Peter. "Wohin gehen die Mönche? Über Weltflucht in anthropologischer Sicht." *Weltfremdheit*. Frankfurt: Suhrkamp, 1993. 80–117. Print.

Sloterdijk, Peter. "Wozu Drogen? Zur Dialektik von Weltflucht und Weltsucht." *Weltfremdheit*. Frankfurt: Suhrkamp, 1993. 118–60. Print.

Sloterdijk, Peter. *You Must Change Your Life. On Anthropotechnics*. Trans. Wieland Hoban. Cambridge: Polity, 2013. Print.

Sloterdijk, Peter, and Hans-Jürgen Heinrichs. *Neither Sun nor Death*. Trans. Steve Corcoran. New York: Semiotext(e), 2011. Print.

Sunderland, Thomas. "Ontological Co-belonging in Peter Sloterdijk's Spherological Philosophy of Mediation." *Paragraph* 40.2 (2017): 133–52. Print.

Sunderland, Thomas. "Peter Sloterdijk and the 'Security Architecture of Existence': Immunity, Autochthony, and Ontological Negativism." *Theory, Culture & Society* 36.7–8 (2019): 193–214. doi:10.1177/0263276419839119. Web.

Thrift, Nigel. "Different Atmospheres: Of Sloterdijk, China, and Site." *Environment and Planning D: Society and Space* 27.1 (2009): 119–38. Web. <https://doi.org/10.1068/d6808>.

In my movie I'm putting everything in.
Even a tap-dancing sailor.

Fellini, 8½

8½ begins with a dream sequence in which Fellini's creatively blocked screen alter-ego, Guido the director, sits trapped and asphyxiating in the hermetic capsule of a stationary car parked on the deck of a ferry that is nevertheless conveying him – and the gawping weekenders around him – slowly somewhere. When he escapes from the car it is to soar upward into the clouds before crashing down to an earthly awakening. Waking by self-suffocation from this nightmare of stymied enclosure followed by soaring weightlessness – in which he became unstuck only to come unstuck – the director's therapy is to breathe slowly and deeply. As he breathes he can begin to experiment with a superabundance of worldly ideas and things, drawing them into the uterine cavity of his creative mind until from all of this practising the film is made. Reversing the intersubjective dynamic on the ferry, as the director prolongs his experimenting, drawing ever more of the outside into the ever more capacious inside of the work – even a tap-dancing sailor – his entourage becomes progressively more exasperated and he gradually more serene. The directors cure themselves by pulling everything into the healing orbit of a work at once aesthetic and anthropotechnical. As the sphere of the work expands, those involved fret about their investment in it and the artist's sanity; as the work approaches completion they fear some sleight of hand, an impending final humiliation to repay their perhaps misplaced confidence.

oliver davis

ANTHROPOTECHNICAL PRACTISING IN THE FOAM-WORLD

I am also talking about Peter Sloterdijk, who similarly "writes a lot about a lot of things" (Thrift 136). Although it may be an exaggeration to say he has already "written about almost everything" (Ernste 273), the profusion of his existing body of work is such that, given time, one feels it might well expand to draw in even the tap-dancing sailor. The exorbitant "generosity" of his voluminous enterprise perturbs even Sloterdijk's most accomplished and long-suffering English translator, for whom its embrace of hyperbole sometimes also involves fact-dissolving generalizations (Hoban 117–18). Stuart Elden, who played a prominent role in the early dissemination of Sloterdijk's work in the English-speaking world, cautioned his own endeavour by also conveying nagging doubts about that work's scope and superficiality (3). So wide does Sloterdijk range, it is as though a kynical dog-philosopher were pissing on everything he encounters to mark out his territory or just for the fun of it.

Long before the fights with Jürgen Habermas and Axel Honneth, Sloterdijk poured scorn on professors: "fools of their own doctrinal structures," "vain babblers" who "complicate the simplest things to the point of unrecognizability" (*Critique* 181). Not unlike Jacques Rancière in *The Ignorant Schoolmaster*, he sneered at their stultifying curricula which organize the administering of knowledge as mere externality: "The more systematically education is planned, the more it is a matter of accident or luck whether education as initiation into conscious living takes place at all" (84). He held open the hope for teaching as a deviation from what was expected, whereas "The ordinary guides for children, teachers and others who also take money bring young people where they for the most part want to go anyway, to career stages and the orator's rostrum" (Sloterdijk, "The Plunge and the Turn" 37). On television, in the newspapers – flaunting his opinions as a philosopher "on the stage," engaged not reluctantly but fervently in public debate – in museums and architecture schools, as well as over the umpteen thousand pages of his books, he has fashioned himself into that rare object of envy: a scholar of stature who is also a charismatic teacher (5). To professors in their bubble he imagines his work spells *Sphärentod*: his mise-en-scène of three discipline-bound and dull-witted professors, who mull inconclusively over the significance of the *Spheres* trilogy at its close, is ironizing and Sloterdijk's irony is primarily not self-directed. One declares: "'It will not seize the masses; even academics feel unease'" (Sloterdijk, *Spheres 3: Foams* 808). *Especially* academics feel unease. More argumentative real professors could have pointed out that, in numerous respects, Sloterdijk is in step with a neoliberal university which overvalues quantitative production and slick performance. His polymathic project can all too readily be translated into a pallid managerialist "vision" of interdisciplinarity ready to be tossed down to subordinates (as by Thrift 146) and the way he urges philosophers "who remain hidden in the bosom of universities" to "leave their hiding place behind" in this time of "global crisis," to "take to the streets and plazas, to the *pages littéraires* and screens, to schools and popular festivals" and make their discipline "relevant" reeks of the public engagement "agenda" that is currently sweeping British universities and saturating the airwaves with professorial commentary, to the point of asphyxiation (Sloterdijk, *What Happened?* 105). His charismatic performances might be said to "set a new standard" for the ordinary lecturer, shaming them into enhancement like a TED talker's rehearsed and scripted passion. It is possible to take a more positive view of his transcendent relation to the university system he has so often denigrated, as Paul North does in his sharp-eyed encomium, "Absolute Teacher, Sloterdijk," or as Jean-Pierre Couture has done by seeing him as an inspirational rejoinder to the proletarianizing overspecialization of contemporary academia (*Sloterdijk* 95, 118). Yet it is worth noticing that many who work in it feel that the neoliberal university already views them with something very like Sloterdijk's scorn and shares his hectoring insistence that they enhance their performance and "raise their game": you especially, professor, must change your life!

Sloterdijk occupies a privileged and singular institutional position, as Rector of the Karlsruhe School of Design, an establishment situated to one side of the ordinary university system in Germany. For Bruno Latour, this setting is a clue that Sloterdijk's theoretical writing is on the side of "design," which Latour thinks betokens modesty by contrast with real construction and, perforce, "an attentiveness to *details*" (153). This attentiveness to details in their profusion has also been accounted for as a corollary of Sloterdijk's taking space seriously in philosophical terms, with "confidence in facing up to constant variation" (Thrift 139). Yet as North has discerned,

Sloterdijk's *Spheres* trilogy is rather more than an agglomerated manifold of spatial stuff: while the sphere has a spatial or ontological meaning, one which will in due course be a major concern of this article, it also has a more generalized and abstract crypto-Kantian sense as a "sphere schemata," the pure and empty form of all schematizing, "the horizon of all horizons" which "contains all antitheses" (North 45, 33, 34). The question of the "spheric" unity of Sloterdijk's work, beyond its antitheses, over and above the profusion of its local detail, has nevertheless been avoided by most of his scholarly readers: North and Couture are, to my knowledge, the only ones to have approached the entirety of his work and with a presumption that it might have this kind of overall integrity. Most of his readers prefer to focus instead on a particular moment of his thirty-year project. There are various reasons why this might be, among them the feeling that there is too much to tackle everything, or that Sloterdijk is not a systematic thinker who lends himself to a reading in terms of overall unity, or that such readings have no value. However, the rationale for restricting the scope of discussion is seldom made the subject of explicit comment by Sloterdijk's scholarly readers. His many detractors on the Left – those who can bring themselves to actually read him – have been complaining of a neoconservative, cynical, hawkish, *Kehre* since the publication of *Rage and Time* [2006] (Couture, *Sloterdijk* 89). My undertaking here will necessarily be more narrowly focused than North's and Couture's but it starts out with a similar eye to the overall coherence of his thought. In what follows, I explore a particularly vexed yet crucial juncture: the relationship between Sloterdijk's spheric general immunology, as the trilogy [1998–2004] envisages it operating in today's foam-world, and the general ascetology of *You Must Change Your Life* [2009]. I thus seek to probe and explicate the relationship between the *Spheres* trilogy and what Couture delineates as the second phase of Sloterdijk's anthropotechnics (Couture, *Sloterdijk* 45), works from either side of his alleged turn. This is a juncture which Sloterdijk has attempted to make himself, although his remarks in making this join raise more questions than they answer; even if, as readers, we do not generally think questions of systematic unity are of paramount importance, this particular moment of joining can still make some claim to our attention.

Introducing *You Must Change Your Life*, Sloterdijk signals its continuity with the *Spheres* trilogy by noting that human beings have realized that they "exist not only in 'material conditions,' but also in symbolic immune systems and ritual shells" (*You Must Change* 3); from the trilogy we know that "Spheres are immune-systemically effective space creations," though as has already been noted the sphere also has other meanings than simply the spatial (Sloterdijk, *Spheres 1: Bubbles* 28; North 33–36). In Sloterdijk's introduction to *You Must Change Your Life*, in addition to the human body's biological immune system, he identifies three types, levels or layers of cultural immune systems: (i) the socio-immunological (legal, "solidaristic" and military), for the resolution of confrontation with aggressors and harmful neighbours; (ii) the symbolic, or "psycho-immunological," practices designed to cope with human "vulnerability through fate, including mortality" by deploying "mental armour"; and (iii) the anthropotechnical, with which he asserts *You Must Change Your Life* is primarily concerned (9–10). While this may appear to situate his second anthropotechnics very neatly in relation to his spheric general immunology, grafting the later book cleanly on to the earlier trilogy, the picture is immediately complicated by the fact that all three layers of the human cultural immune system are also said to function "in close collaborative interaction and functional augmentation" (9). Anthropotechnics thus not only constitutes the third layer but can, it seems, encompass and functionally augment (or diminish) the other two layers in its concern with the way in which "humans from the most diverse cultures have attempted to optimize their cosmic and immunological status" (10). In so far as Sloterdijk is concerned in *You Must Change Your Life* with "the biography of *Homo immunologicus*" in its generality it is clear that he is concerned not just with this third layer but simultaneously with all three layers of the human cultural immune system as he understands it. Rather than a clean graft of the "general ascetology" of *You Must Change Your Life* on to the "general immunology" of *Spheres*, Sloterdijk's only superficially straightforward presentation of their relationship leaves open the possibility that *You Must Change Your Life* may even have been construed by its author as a tacit revision of, rather than simply an addition to, the immunological paradigm of *Spheres*, and regardless of how he construed it, it may nevertheless be such a revision: more dangerous supplement than simple sequel.

Put succinctly, the issue at stake here is individualism: on the face of it, the spheric general immunology is resolutely anti-individualist and the second anthropotechnics decidedly less so. Couture suggests that in *You Must Change Your Life* the "We" of the spheres seems to have been discarded "in favor of focusing exclusively on a 'You' imperative aimed at self-improvement through exercise" (*Sloterdijk* 45), with Sloterdijk himself subsequently suggesting that, today, "the search for identity and immunity must increasingly shift from collective to individual strategies" (*What Happened?* 53). Whether this individualist emphasis can be read as anything other than a flagrant contradiction, or undoing, of the trilogy's captivating account of originary intersubjectivity is to be established. My suggestion is that an accurate understanding of the (dis)junction between these two phases of his project is critical if a meaningful assessment is to be made of the political bearing of his anthropotechnical work, as perhaps of his entire body of work. The features of Sloterdijk's work I have surveyed in this lengthy preamble – its profusion and its capaciousness in accommodating flourish and detail, as well as its author's pugnacious pre-emptive strikes against scholarly critical interpreters – do tend to discourage analysis of the type I undertake here while, to my mind, making such scrutiny all the more imperative. Sloterdijk may be a gas giant, too engrossed in his own inspirational effulgence to tie up loose ends, an orbmaker rather than a carpet-weaver. His readers may be ants on the carpet of his work, scrambling around trying to discern its overall pattern. Yet it is that pattern, not to mention the structural integrity of the entire fabric, which concern me as antlike I now proceed.[1] My argument is that there are design flaws in both spheric general immunology and in practising general ascetology, flaws which are less apparent when each domain is approached separately but which become glaring and substantial when the two are conjoined. I will first identify these two sets of problems separately before discussing their combined effect.

spheric general immunology and the limitations of the foam model

In this section, I present an analytical reconstruction of the paradigm of general immunology in the *Spheres* trilogy, focused mainly on originary intersubjectivity and immunology in the foam-world of contemporary society, before moving on, in the next section, to anthropotechnical practising. In the trilogy Sloterdijk asserts that "What recent philosophers referred to as 'being-in-the-world' first of all, and in most cases, means being-in-spheres," that "living always means building spheres" and that spheres are "immune-systemically effective space creations" (*Spheres 1: Bubbles* 46, 28, 28). In other words, rather than being "thrown" into the world alone, as Heidegger suggested, humans as subjects and species are contained and nurtured in protected spheres, starting with the womb, the first sphere or "bubble." If Heidegger gives us "a lonely, weak, hysterical-heroic existential subject that thinks it is the first to die, and remains painfully uncertain of the more hidden aspects of its embeddedness in intimacies and solidarities" (*Spheres 1: Bubbles* 341), Sloterdijk's first volume develops Hannah Arendt's turn from death to birth in her discussion of "natality" with a rhapsodic gynaecological fantasia which similarly seeks "a *positive* theory of man's [*sic*] finitude" (Van Tuinen 49). Rather than an essentially lonely subject, Sloterdijk posits an originary human being-with which finds its first expression in the fetus's cohabitation of the womb with the placenta, the first companion which Sloterdijk, in a lyrical pastiche of existential-phenomenological style, names "the With" (*Spheres 1: Bubbles* 356), "the most intimate and general organ of relationships," which "disappears as soon as it has served its purpose" (358) but which, while it served that purpose, was "our private nymph fountain and our sworn genius" (360). He shows a very striking image of a pharaoh's procession headed by his "placental standards" (381) and tells of a German tradition honouring the placenta by burying it under a fruit tree (378), before male medical science in the latter part of the eighteenth century taught us all to abhor the afterbirth. He speculates about the connection between "the cultural excommunication of the placenta" and the birth of "modern individualism" (384):

> since people stopped burying the intimate With in the house or under the trees and roses, all individuals are latent traitors who have a guilt without a concept to deny; with their resolutely independent lives, they deny that they are constantly repeating the betrayal of their most intimate companion in their remorselessly autonomous being. (386)

He moves effortlessly from this phenomenological gynaecology to the theology of the Trinity, which he uses to develop his account of originary human being-with, or "being-in-relation": the three elements "produce, harbor and surround themselves in such close reciprocity that their intertwinement exceeds all external conditions" (614).

After birth, the counterpart of the evolutionary human characteristic of neoteny is the necessity that the infant be held in a protective sphere if it is to survive and flourish. Sloterdijk construes this environment of nurturing and all later cultural spheres as, in a fairly strong sense, uterine analogues or reconstructions, "amniotic communes" (*Spheres 2: Globes* 200): "peoples, empires, churches and, above all, modern nation states, are not least space-political attempts to recreate fantastic wombs for infantilized mass populations by imaginary and institutional means" (Sloterdijk, *Spheres 1: Bubbles* 67–68). To exist within a sphere is to live in an "inner, co-animated realm," to be protected and differentiated from externality with its overwhelming mass of "dead and outer things" (54). Sloterdijk's underlying conviction is that human beings can only live – and in evolutionary, historical and individual terms have only lived – by protecting themselves from complete exposure to the deathly coldness of radical or absolute externality: "Humans have never lived in a direct relationship with 'nature'" (46). Whether it be a couple forging the sphere of their household in the midst of a twenty-first-century global city, or a group of hunter-gatherers establishing the circle of their shared life in the Palaeolithic Age, or a Mesopotamian city with staggeringly thick walls, for Sloterdijk essentially the same sphere-building activity is in evidence: "among those who truly live together, inner relationships take absolute precedence over so-called environmental ones" – what is being asserted is "the primacy of the inner" (*Spheres 2: Globes* 192). These people could all be saying:

> Here, from the indifferent, immense space, we cut out an animated orb, the community that we are: this is the place we will inhabit as our cosmic quarters. Here we know what we mean when we say we are at home *in the world*. (195)

Being-in-spheres thus involves existing with others inside a nurturing, meaning-rich, bounded, "relational" space of interiority (Ernste 274), whereas – to skip quickly through the second volume – what "globalization" in the dominant economico-political sense of the term implies is "the indifference of a space in which no dwelling occurs" (Sloterdijk, *Spheres 2: Globes* 897). This dominant conception of globalization, which for Sloterdijk boils down to the global market, implies that "all suppliers and customers meet in a general externality," unprotected and infinitely exposed in a "homogeneous space" of radical externality characterized by the coldness of its "homogeneous indifference" (950, 947, 777). Alluding to Nietzsche and Heidegger, Sloterdijk suggests that under the sphere-shattering pressure of globalization "the last humans have become the external ones" as they are pulled "toward the general emptying of the inner world," drawn by comfort and self-objectifying science (in particular, technoscience and neuroscience), as much as by hardship and scarcity, to self-externalization as "the 'they'" [*das Man*] (*Spheres 1: Bubbles* 629). Though unprecedented in its intensity, the economic and scientific pressure of this general externality is nevertheless viewed by Sloterdijk as a pull or tendency, rather than an unavoidable destiny: he remains optimistic about the enduring power of the countervailing human tendency towards sphere-creation, if not about our capacity for awareness of it (627). According to his developmental narrative it is only after the grander spheres of cosmos, tribe, ecumene or nation have been shattered that they are replaced by the contemporary form of being-in-spheres, "being-in-foam" (Sloterdijk, *Spheres 3: Foams* 59).

Foam: "The term stands for systems or aggregates of spheric neighborhoods in which each individual 'cell' constitutes a self-augmenting context (more colloquially: a world, a place), an intimate space of meaning" (Sloterdijk, *Spheres 3: Foams* 52). Unlike the Mesopotamian cities Sloterdijk surveyed in the second volume, to give one of his many examples of hard-walled spheric constructions, foams and the cells comprising them, are said to be thin-walled and therefore fragile – moreover, each cell in the foam shares its thin boundary wall with several other surrounding cells, implying their "co-fragility" (Sloterdijk, *Spheres 3: Foams* 236; Borch 552). Foams "tend to be ungovernable structures" (Sloterdijk, *Spheres 1: Bubbles* 73) and Sloterdijk's theory – or descriptive-morphological metaphor – is intended to reflect his conviction that today "'life' unfolds multifocally, multiperspectivally and heterarchically" (*Spheres 3: Foams* 23). Foams are accordingly thought to be as resistant to totalizing description as they are to sovereign rule: "every cell and every association of cells, that is to say culture, is incorporated into a fluctuating variety of one-sided and reciprocal imitations, crossings and mixtures in which no homogeneous basic form can ever be identified" (463–64). Nevertheless, the fragility and shared character of the cell walls enable imitative-mimetic resonances to spread easily from one cell to another. Sloterdijk draws on sociologist Gabriel Tarde's *Laws of Imitation* [1890] to suggest that the primary relation between cells in the foam is imitative, a mimetic resonance which the mass media intensify and channel. It is not clear from Sloterdijk's account why such imitative-mimetic resonance is said to replace the "general magic of intersubjectivity," as he analysed its development from the fifteenth century in the first volume in waves including sympathetic magic, mesmerism and psychoanalysis, above all transference (*Spheres 1: Bubbles* 124), though he may simply consider this a matter of historical contingency: it may simply be that what we know as Modern individualism describes the replacement of earlier forms of rich intersubjective relationship by their degraded mass-mediatized descendent, imitative resonance – but if so then this constitutes a substantial, though tacit, retrospective historicizing qualification of the first volume's account of an originary being-with which finds essentially similar expression in solidarity, the primitive clearing, Mesopotamian walled cities and contemporary "communes, teams, project groups" (45).

Sloterdijk's theory, metaphor or morphology of foam looks much more plausible as coherent social theory, or description, from a top-down ("administrative") perspective of the sort presupposed in the several images Sloterdijk reproduces of foams or foam-like structures (e.g., *Spheres 3: Foams* 236). Its deficiencies are occluded by Sloterdijk's selective and, at key moments in this third volume, excessively abstract presentation. Indeed, it proves frustratingly difficult to determine from his lengthy account what the basic ontological features of the cells, or bubbles, within a foam are supposed to be and to say with confidence what might typically constitute such a cell and its contents. I address three interrelated and, by Sloterdijk unresolved, questions about the structure of the foam-world: (i) does each cell in a foam typically contain one individual human or several?; (ii) if each cell can contain more than one human, how do those within it relate intersubjectively and to what extent is their mode of relating different from the way in which the cells are said to relate to one another in the foam – and how is one geared with the other?; and (iii) to what extent is the nature of human intersubjectivity today adequately captured by the spatial form of being-in-foam?

One of the distinctive features of Sloterdijk's account is that each cell within the foam is said to perform an immunological function by conditioning its own air, or atmosphere. This implies that, in continuity with the originary spheric intersubjectivity postulated in the first volume and developed in the second, there may be several people within it. Indeed, Sloterdijk says at one point that it would be appropriate to envisage the cells in the foam as "human households" (*Spheres 3: Foams* 232), in other words quasi-autonomous administrable units composed of one or more people. Yet in his discussion of Elias Canetti's tribute to Hermann Broch, Sloterdijk says: "Canetti praises Broch's ability to view all people ecologically, as it were: in every person he recognizes a singular existence in its own breathing air, surrounded by an unmistakable climatic shell, integrated into a personal 'respiratory economy'" (171). As Borch has noted, Broch's work – and Canetti's view of it – play a prominent role in the third volume of the trilogy (555), and Sloterdijk's discussion of that work suggests that each cell in the foam is inhabited by just one individual human. So too does Sloterdijk's assertion that foam

> serves to formulate a philosophical-anthropological interpretation of modern individualism that I am convinced cannot be adequately described using previously existing means. Foam theory is connected to the prospect of a new explicatory form for what sociological tradition calls the social bond or "social synthesis" – an explanation that does beyond the classic Kantianizing question of how "society" is possible as a collective of shareholders. (*Spheres 3: Foams* 233)

It hardly makes sense to say this unless Sloterdijk envisages that each cell in the foam is inhabited by just one person. Couture claims that foam theory is a mighty achievement which succeeds in

> overcoming the opposition between the school of liberal individualism (contract theory) and the spiteful conservative school of holistic Romanticism (organicism). The poetics of spherology rearticulates the sense of belonging initially formulated by Romanticism, without sacrificing smaller units (couples, houses, tribes, and networks) in constituting contemporary social wholes. (*Sloterdijk* 104)

While I agree that this appears to have been Sloterdijk's aspiration, in my view his foam theory remains far too vague on key matters of structural ontology to be considered a successful resolution of this conflict.

Foams may be untotalizable and tend toward the ungovernable in the way in which so many households in the sprawl of suburbia – as viewed from a plane, or on a town plan – can each be imagined, with a degree of postmodern latitude, to have their own distinctive inner atmosphere and "values," even though they may readily be agglomerated into purchasing or voting trends by the nudging forces of mass media advertising. This is all just about plausible and coherent from the top-down aerial perspective of a theorist, or administrator, in the instant in which they take their snapshot of the foam. Such foam is far less plausible as a model for contemporary intersubjectivity if you try to envisage that foam-world from the perspective of any human actually inhabiting its cells, singly or severally, over an extended period of time. From this perspective it is evident that each one of us inhabits a plurality of different cells simultaneously: even when we are sat on the sofa in the intimacy of our household cell somewhere in Europe we may be having a telephone conversation with an auntie in Goa, while watching television news images of an earthquake in China and thinking about Descartes, or chocolate cake, or both. It is even clearer that we inhabit several cells sequentially, over the course of a single day, as we move from one spatialized environmental cell to another, each of which – on one reading of Sloterdijk's account – also contains several other humans who similarly live within and move between a plurality of cells and carry with them a similar residue of affectionate and aversive attachments, or neutral associations, with that panoply of other spaces and other people. Trying to probe the foam from the perspective of those who inhabit it suggests that intersubjectivity today is not adequately captured by the foam model, which is an overridingly spatial and administrative model subject to the limitations of three-dimensional space.[2]

Instead of trying to resolve fundamental questions of conceptual design, questions about the basic structure of his foam model, Sloterdijk launches into a rambling re-elaboration of "the anthroposphere" (*Spheres 3: Foams* 338) or "anthropogenic island" (463), which summarizes many of the themes from the first two volumes in nine separate characteristics or "dimensions" (338–463), as though such profusion – bring on the tap-dancing sailor – could distract attention from incoherence in the model's design. While this lengthy recapitulation does not substantively address the key interpretive questions about the ontological structure of the foam, it nevertheless closes with the stark assertion that "each individual cell in the foam must now be understood as a micro-insulation that carries the complete pattern of nine-dimensionality heavily folded within itself" (463). Sloterdijk adds that:

> Every household, every couple, every group of resonances already form a miniature of the whole anthrotope as cells in the foam. Moreover, every cell and every association of cells, that is to say culture, is incorporated into a fluctuating variety of one-sided and reciprocal imitations, crossings and mixtures in which no homogeneous basic form can ever be identified. (463–64)

Foams are unquestionably fascinating in their spatial structure and Sloterdijk shows eloquently how their form may serve in design, architecture and urban planning; that is, wherever spatial considerations are already paramount. Yet to pretend that the bounded spatiality of their cells makes foams adequate as a social or philosophical theory of intersubjective existence is fanciful because (post-)humans today do not exist – and humans never have only existed – at just one point in space: this may be more obvious today when so much of our intersubjectivity is mediated and effortlessly spans the globe but even in the Palaeolithic circle around the fire we were already imagining, or remembering, other places and other people – we existed within that spatially situated sphere and we transcended its bounds. Sloterdijk's dogmatic assertion that each cell is a replication of the complexity of the foam does not resolve the basic ambiguities in his account and does not persuade this reader that it is an adequate model, for if a cell is essentially in its complexity a microcosmic reflection, or "miniature," of the foam in its entirety then the question still remains: what *is* a foam in this figurative sense? Furthermore, if the cells are miniatures of the foam then why not go further and extend the foam metaphor to the personhood of the humans in the foam and see them as foaming composites of their subpersonal, or dividual, qualities? If a foam is a complex aggregate of foams, which are complex aggregates of foams (*und so weiter*) we just have a bare notion of fractal supercomplexity which is said to be spatial but which lacks any determinate spatial pattern or form. Alluring though the metaphor of foam at first appears, ultimately it leaves us with the minimal notion – the mere design – of a composite of semi-autonomous and semi-transparent co-fragile units in space. Because the foam metaphor is so slight a sketch it can be applied very widely, to describe almost any complex organic structure, but this is a weakness rather than a strength of the model. This is not, however, its main weakness. This is that while intersubjectivity today is certainly influenced by spatial form it cannot be reduced to spatial modes of cohabitation, as Sloterdijk does. To attempt to read people off their immediate spatial environment in this way is in keeping with his perspectival preference for top-down snapshots of the foam and reflects an administrative disposition which ironically prioritizes the perspective of the outer world of dead externality at the expense of complex technologies of mediation which allow us to be in intersubjective contact with others, in a shared sphere of interiority, even when it may look from above as though we are neatly contained within our spatial cell. This way of looking is the obverse of the modesty of design espoused by Latour: the tyranny of design's administrative perspective.

In a 2007 interview, Sloterdijk declared: "In my most recent work, I've set about integrating psychoanalysis, the history of ideas and images, systems theory, sociology, urbanism, etc. into a metaparadigm I call General Immunology or, alternatively, Sphere Theory" (Alliez and Sloterdijk 316). This indicates that general immunology was envisaged by Sloterdijk as a compound overarching framework (a "metaparadigm"), involving disciplinary convergence, assemblage or fusion – the plausible focus of and rationale for this convergence being intersubjectivity. I have argued that the predominance of proximate spatiality in the foam model, which prioritizes an administrative top-down perspective, means it is ill-suited to accounting for the dynamic and mediated character of intersubjectivity today. Indeed, it may be that this very insufficiency of the spatialized model is what requires mimetic-imitative resonance to be introduced in order to allow for the agglomeration of different cells at a spatial distance from one another – in other words, resonance is introduced in the third volume to patch the deficiencies of the foam model, which is too dependent on spatial proximity to accurately capture contemporary intersubjectivity. As I turn now to the general ascetology of *You Must Change Your Life*, I suggest that the difficulties I have identified in the foam model that is the culmination of sphere theory, or general immunology, trouble that later book's anatomy of *Homo immunologicus*.

the general ascetology of self-optimization: no pain, no gain

The "general ascetology" of *You Must Change Your Life* [2009] envisages human beings as anthropotechnical animals engaged in "practising, or self-forming and self-enhancing behaviour" (Sloterdijk, *You Must Change* 6, 4). By their repetitions of practising, humans weave the "fabric" of their "symbolic immune systems and ritual shells" (3) and seek "to optimize their cosmic and immunological status" (10). Against the background of the preceding discussion, in this section I start out from the interpretive question of the extent to which such anthropotechnical practising should be thought to take place *within* the protective shelter of an already existing immunological bubble and the extent to which, conversely and as the introductory remarks just quoted seem to imply, such anthropotechnics is essentially a matter of practising *on* or *with* the boundary of that bubble.

Sloterdijk had already suggested, in the trilogy, that human life, both individually and historically, could be thought of as the continual rending and reconstruction of immunological bubbles within "breathed, divided, torn-open and restored space" (*Spheres 1: Bubbles* 46), with the rebuilding of the bubble dependent on a "transfer" of "the integral space" (54), primordially the uterine space. There the matter of the skill, or technique, required to restore the rended shell remained largely implicit in the trilogy's immunology, reaching expression primarily in the first volume's lyrical evocation of the uterine "dowry of memories of the symbiotic field and its enclosing power" (54), on which humans somehow draw – but how, exactly? – as they embark on later reconstructions of their immunological spheres. In *You Must Change Your Life*, Sloterdijk explicates and displaces this question of skill and seems to suggest that these symbolic immunological envelopes not only can, but should, be the object of deliberate projects of anthropotechnical enhancement. Although the language of immunology remains prominent, the emphasis has shifted from the bounded interiority of the spheroid cell in the foam-world to a picture of humans living "in the enclosure of disciplines" (Sloterdijk, *You Must Change* 109). With this shift comes a striking new conceptual vocabulary of verticality, of literally and figuratively "looking up" to transcendent foci of aspiration, and relatedly a celebration of "the constant stimulation of the skilled by competitors" (360), whereby those who devote themselves to self-enhancement through practising inevitably pull away from the common run of humans, who "chronically excuse themselves downwards" (125): "the vast majority of people have no interest in becoming more than they are. If one investigates the average direction of their wishes, one finds that they simply want a more comfortable version of what they have" (176). Almost all of Sloterdijk's scholarly readers see this as a hyperbolic anti-egalitarianism, as, for instance, Couture does in remarking on "the frighteningly concrete meaning that he wishes to give to the figure of the vertical, ascetic, high-performance, and athletic individual" (*Sloterdijk* 91). I do not disagree that the overtones of Sloterdijk's account are troubling but he can be understood to be commenting on the way in which limited aspirations and pessimistic assessments of one's own capacity, or more generally what is called "low self-esteem," demonstrably possess their own prophetic self-efficacy. This could be shown to be compatible with radical (though not social-democratic, distributive) egalitarian thought, even though Sloterdijk himself has no interest in making such a case and seems quite relaxed about distinguishing, with a degree of petty-bourgeois triumphalism, between "winners" and "losers" (38).

How exactly does the vertically aspiring practising life function in immunological terms? The emphasis Sloterdijk places, in his celebration of the "vertical axis," on the positive magnetizing effect of its "higher stressors" (*You Must Change* 60, 87), is tempered by a suggestion, attributed in part to Pierre de Coubertin, that religions not only inspire their devotees to aspire to self-improvement but also serve as "isolators" (91) from the enormity of the very same goals they propose by developing "protocols for regulating traffic with higher stressors and 'transcendental' powers" (87). In other words, positive religious asceticisms simultaneously inspire and protect, forming a shield which augments itself by being repeatedly shattered and regrown. This is in line with the general understanding of symbolic immunology in the trilogy: "Through immune systems, learning bodies incorporate their regularly recurring stressors into themselves" (Sloterdijk, *Spheres 3: Foams* 418). It looks as though devotees gradually ascend towards their god by repeatedly piercing the shell of their own integrity to incorporate parts of that god into themselves. That religious ascetics have often chosen to undertake such studied self-harm in secessionary spaces – monastic communities or individual cells set back in retreat from the world – could thus be understood in terms of the advantage of a surrogate shell during this delicate work, which might be described as "pharmacological" in the sense that it involves "healing harm," in both senses of that expression. For Iwona Janicka, Sloterdijk's work is one of the main ingredients in her anarchist politics of radical social transformation, envisaged in terms of the mimetic spread of exemplary "good habits that produce habitable spheres" (Janicka 81). Her emphasis falls firmly on "the fragility of spheres that we share with others" (104) and the immunological function of bubbles and foams in enabling the development of habits "in a controlled environment" which constitute "good or bad models that will be wittingly or unwittingly imitated" (110). Thus, in Janicka's reading, the development of better habits takes place within the protective and nurturing shelter of the immunological sphere. Compelling though her anarchist vision is in other respects, this is probably a misreading of

Sloterdijk. Ascetic self-work is very clearly work *on* rather than *within* the sphere, work which inflicts a form of self-harm on an outgrown container, the wilful sabotage of a bad habit in order to stimulate growth of new and better form of enveloping protection: no pain, no gain.

Successful practising today, as Sloterdijk understands it, appears to depend to a large extent on the capacity to ignore extraneous factors – presumably including other people – in order to focus on the task at hand: "the art of ignoring is inseparable from successful experimentation – we could even say that the ability to disregard [*Vernachlässigung*] what can be disregarded distinguishes the good experimenter *lege artis*" (*What Happened?* 39). This would effect a personal secession equivalent in function to the anchoritic or cenobitic retreat in religious times, a "recessive self-insulation" (Sloterdijk, *You Must Change* 227) involving the establishment of an "inner protectorate" (229) as the precondition for anthropotechnical care of the self – and Sloterdijk refers here to Michel Foucault's derivation of these technical preconditions for care of the self from Stoicism (227).

Sloterdijk is careful not to mention the fact that there was already significant interest among postmodern management theorists in monastic asceticism (Halsall and Brown 234) when he took up the topic in *You Must Change Your Life*, some of which was influenced by a minority tradition of interpretation, associated especially with François Ewald, which applied Foucault's late work to optimize the business environment, a tradition from which most academic readers of his work in the humanities and social sciences would recoil in horror (251), if they knew of its existence. As Robert Halsall and Mary Brown note, even the language of *metanoia* had already been appropriated by "change consultants" (248) and applied in business schools as a model for the assisted self-conversion of mere institutional superiors into visionary managers. I cannot evaluate this hijacking of Foucault here but I would suggest that knowing about this undisclosed context and about what

Sloterdijk will go on to say some seven years later, in *What Happened in the 20th Century?* [2016], should temper our understanding of the anthropotechnics outlined in *You Must Change Your Life* [2009] in two ways: with regard to spatiality and to the singularity, or plurality, of competitions. Sloterdijk seems to have realized that individual self-secession, as practised today, is unlikely to be able to be spatial, or predominantly spatial, and that although the paradigm makes sense in the context of a single organization and identity (the "visionary manager" in a business, or the virtuoso violinist in an orchestra), most people's social lives are far more complicated because we exist in a multiplicity of different intersubjective spheres at the same time, which makes that book's encomium to the salutary effects of competitive striving seem rather one-eyed, unduly monocontextual. One of the defining features of life under neoliberal capitalism is the simultaneous and unavoidable exposure to a manifold of different competitive, hierarchizing, processes, many of these now algorithmically automated and constantly ticking away in the background; while competition in the singular may hold a certain appeal, "a world of constant, overlapping competitions" and their proliferating plurality of competitive rankings is cumulatively anxiogenic and thus, unchecked, can be presumed to inhibit effective self-enhancement in any one area (Davies 30). This might be thought to imply even greater need for the immunological discipline of closing off, or ignoring, extraneous variables and people. Despite the loose and backward way in which autism is generally used figuratively by Sloterdijk in the trilogy as a pejorative byword for the antisocial, what he seems to be advocating in this later work is the need for a semi-autistic, or autarkic, form of self-centred concentrated attentiveness as a precondition of the successful practising life, but needless to say he eschews the language of autism for this positive possibility. In other words, to be successful at any one thing requires deliberately deciding to be very selective in the races one chooses to run, in the influences one chooses to heed. Yet in the foam-world there is a plurality of practising subjects, each existing in what tends to be an ungovernable relationship with every other, which means that the self-secession of each individual practising subject has, multiplied across the foam, unexpected cumulative side effects:

> if virtually all domains of life become experiments, in the world of work and in that of leisure, in communities as well as in private life, the consequences can easily be gauged: every experimental zone engenders its own surroundings from disregarded variables. As a result, with the increasing consolidation of experiments, we always find that neglected zones [*die Zonen der Vernachlässigung*] increasingly overlap – with more or less severe consequences. In other words, precisely because the globalization of the pursuit of happiness leads to a widespread proliferation of experimental behavior, it must also involve an inflation of negligence. (Sloterdijk, *What Happened?* 39)

The imperative to individual self-optimization that was championed throughout *You Must Change Your Life* is here viewed with some reservation as its sociopathic and ecologically toxic cumulative side effects are quite rightly registered but without this prompting any systematic reconsideration of the earlier work. At the very least this reserve implies – though Sloterdijk refrains from theorizing – the necessity for external shock to snap self-optimizers out of the self-isolated enclosure of their practising and impel them into other spheres and on to other experiences, to begin attending to some of the variables their earlier practising disregarded; such an impetus is vital if anthropotechnical practising in the foam-world is not to equate to narrow individualism with cumulatively sociotoxic side effects.

It may be that Sloterdijk has refrained from systematically reconsidering his earlier work in light of this recently expressed reserve because to do so would involve tugging too hard at some of the weaker strands which hold the fabric of his thought together. In the *Spheres* trilogy it was never decisively resolved, in conceptual terms, whether there was typically one or more people in each cell of the foam that figures contemporary society but the possibility of cohabitation was left open and the gravitational orbit of the trilogy around originary intersubjectivity tended to suppress the individualist possibility of one cell per person, which nevertheless remained as conceptually coherent and plausible as its alternative. Sloterdijk's alleged *Kehre*, from intersubjectivity to individualism, with *You Must Change Your Life*, in fact describes the much more strident assertion of the individualist conception of life in the foam-world that was already present in the trilogy but eclipsed by the countervailing emphasis there on originary intersubjectivity. In analytical terms, if as I have argued it is clear that anthropotechnical practising takes place *on* the boundaries of the cells of the foam, assuming that each cell is inhabited by one person and given that one of the characteristics of foam is the "co-fragility" of its cells, then any individual's self-isolated practising must be presumed to have knock-on effects on other people: if I am piercing my shell to regrow a better one then the foam-world's structure of co-fragility implies that I am simultaneously inflicting violence on the protective envelopes inhabited by others. Putting together general immunology with general ascetology accordingly suggests that if Sloterdijk's global vision of contemporary society is correct then it must also be suffused with violent social antagonism. Since the scenario Sloterdijk prefers to imagine, of one ascetic practiser engaged in one competition at a time, is a misleadingly idealized singular snapshot of the plural overlapping competitions characteristic of life under neoliberal capitalism, the conclusion seems unavoidable that the foam-world of self-enhancers is shot through with antagonistic social violence. I am not criticizing Sloterdijk on this point since in many respects this strikes me as how life under neoliberal capitalism really operates – those who feel the pain seldom enjoy the gain – but it is unfortunate, in my view, that his work does not more fully acknowledge and more systematically explore the cumulatively violent and toxic social obverse of individualized ascetological practising. Instead, the vision of individualized self-optimization he proposes in *You Must Change Your Life* is far too similar to the myth of the heroic entrepreneur, one of the sustaining fantasies of neoliberal capitalism.

conclusion: coming unstuck and becoming unstuck

I have argued that there are significant conceptual weaknesses in Sloterdijk's theoretical models both of spheric general immunology and of practising general ascetology, weaknesses which can be grasped by carefully considering each individually and which become especially vexed when the two are conjoined: the design of Sloterdijk's project quickly comes unstuck. When exposed to the type of critical-analytical scrutiny which he so pugnaciously repels, the work breaks down into an agglomeration of perspicuous local observations, a profusion of details and rhetorical flourishes from which no overarchingly coherent systematic conceptual sense can be made.

I have argued that foam is too spatial and administrative a model to adequately capture human intersubjectivity; I also pointed out that on crucial points of ontological structure Sloterdijk's design for the foam model is frustratingly ambiguous and sketchy. In particular, whether each cell in the foam today can, or typically does, contain just one individual remains unclear. Nevertheless, I have shown that: (i) there is no *Kehre* between Sloterdijk's general immunology and general ascetology because the individualist possibility was already present in the *Spheres* trilogy as one of two plausible understandings of the foam-world, but in that trilogy it was conjoined with a lyrical countervailing emphasis on originary intersubjectivity which tended to distract attention from that individualist reading – in *You Must Change Your Life* intersubjectivity is absent, which leads some readers to think he has turned into an individualist; (ii) in *You Must Change Your Life* the practising subject self-enhances by rending its own protective envelope and rebuilding a better and stronger one; (iii) since Sloterdijk has not explicitly repudiated or significantly qualified the account given of cells in the foam as co-fragile, it follows that individual practising in the foam-world is never wholly individual but must always also involve rending other people's protective envelopes; (iv) although Sloterdijk's idealized focus in *You Must Change Your Life* is narrowly on the individual practising subject engaged in a singular struggle, isolated later remarks suggest he is aware that there must be cumulatively toxic and violent social side effects of singular acts of self-enhancement; (v) his reluctance to think about the violence of social antagonism implied by anthropotechnical practising in the foam-world is consistent with the way his general ascetology of individual self-optimization mimics neoliberal capitalism's sustaining fantasy of heroic self-entrepreneurship and neglects to consider the intersubjective downside of individual success but does not dispel the question of equality; and (vi) the idea that successful practising involves a degree of autistic self-closure to other variables in the social world also implies the need for a motive force to bring practising individuals out of their self-absorption, to move them on to other spheres and other struggles but this motive force is left untheorized, though it is perhaps performed.

The difficulty in reading Sloterdijk arises more between than within his works, in part because he never goes back over his own earlier theoretical practising to explicitly reconsider it in a sustained discussion, though he often makes allusions to earlier work which convey an impression of continuity. There are few regrets, self-corrections or second thoughts, or few are expressed. His work actively repels critique: "The scenery of the critical intelligentsia is [...] populated by aggressive and depressive moralists, problematists, 'problemaholics,' and soft rigorists whose predominant existential stimulus is *No*" (Sloterdijk, *Critique* 126) Even if, on close analysis, the design of his theoretical models is more flawed and less coherent than first appears to be the case, I can still find reason to admire his undertaking, independently of this menacing pre-emptive strike. I accordingly end with Sloterdijk's own troubling tribute to cynical-kynical resourcefulness, which extolls

> the outsmartable nature of resistances, the bypassable nature of obstacles, the postponable nature of difficulties, the reframable nature of deficiencies, the contestable nature of recriminations, the reformulable nature of accusations, the manipulable nature of standards, the subvertible nature of tasks, the replaceable nature of losses, the numbable nature of pain and the avoidable nature of head-on encounters with forces that can only bring defeat. (*Spheres 3: Foams* 689)

It seems churlish to close with gripes about the coherence of Sloterdijk's overall project, to cling to its continuity errors and design flaws without acknowledging that the relentless forward motion of his writing and its sphere-forming capacity is its own extraordinary achievement. To wish to see Sloterdijk turning around himself in eddies of self-doubt would be to scorn the tonic potential of his work and to refuse to consider, in the sheer ambition of its irrepressible and sometimes irresponsible forward motion – its brazen effrontery, even – its compelling anthropotechnical lesson in becoming unstuck. Watching that work unfold is like watching Guido and Fellini becoming creatively unstuck by their own practising, making the film from their very inability to make the film. All the better if the impetus of Sloterdijk's example resonates through the foam to draw people out of their self-isolated spheres of practising, encouraging them to work free of self-stifling hesitancy and the enervating downward pull of too-modest expectations or the imagined obligations to past unhappiness and injury: "The unkindnesses of yesterday compel you to nothing" (*Critique* 547).

disclosure statement

No potential conflict of interest was reported by the author.

notes

1 I borrow the image of the ants on the carpet from Sloterdijk (*What Happened?* 43), who in turn borrowed it from Rumi.

2 It may be that the foam model could be developed to better capture the reality of contemporary intersubjectivity by allowing the foam to froth over into other dimensions of space, in the way that mathematical models of networks of association of the sort frequently deployed at the commercial and military forefronts of "surveillance capitalism" (Zuboff) commonly do.

bibliography

Alliez, Erik, and Peter Sloterdijk. "Living Hot, Thinking Coldly: An Interview with Peter Sloterdijk." *Cultural Politics* 3.3 (2007): 307–26. Print.

Borch, Christian. "Foam Architecture: Managing Co-isolated Associations." *Economy and Society* 37.4 (2008): 548–71. Print.

Couture, Jean-Pierre. "A Public Intellectual." *Sloterdijk Now*. Ed. Stuart Elden. Cambridge: Polity, 2012. 96–113. Print.

Couture, Jean-Pierre. *Sloterdijk*. Cambridge: Polity, 2016. Print.

Davies, William. *The Limits of Neoliberalism. Authority, Sovereignty and the Logic of Competition*. London: Sage, 2016. Print.

Elden, Stuart. "Worlds, Engagements, Temperaments." *Sloterdijk Now*. Ed. Stuart Elden. Cambridge: Polity, 2012. 1–16. Print.

Ernste, Huib. "The Geography of Spheres: An Introduction and Critical Assessment of Peter Sloterdijk's Concept of Spheres." *Geographica Helvetica* 73 (2018): 273–84. Print.

Halsall, Robert, and Mary Brown. "Askesis and Organizational Culture." *Organization* 20.2 (2012): 233–55. Print.

Hoban, Wieland. "The Language of Give and Take: Sloterdijk's Stylistic Methods." *Sloterdijk Now*. Ed. Stuart Elden. Cambridge: Polity, 2012. 114–32. Print.

Janicka, Iwona. *Theorizing Contemporary Anarchism. Solidarity, Mimesis and Radical Social Change.* London: Bloomsbury, 2017. Print.

Latour, Bruno. "A Cautious Prometheus? A Few Steps Toward a Philosophy of Design with Special Reference to Peter Sloterdijk." *In Medias Res. Peter Sloterdijk's Spherological Poetics of Being.* Ed. Willem Schinkel and Liesbeth Noordegraaf-Eelens. Amsterdam: Amsterdam UP, 2011. 151–64. Print.

North, Paul. "Absolute Teacher, Sloterdijk." *boundary 2* 43.4 (2016): 1–69. Print.

Rancière, Jacques. *The Ignorant Schoolmaster. Five Lessons in Intellectual Emancipation.* Trans. Kristin Ross. Stanford: Stanford UP, 1991. Print.

Sloterdijk, Peter. *Critique of Cynical Reason.* Trans. Michael Eldred. Minneapolis: U of Minnesota P, 1987. Print.

Sloterdijk, Peter. "The Plunge and the Turn." *Not Saved. Essays after Heidegger.* Trans. Ian Alexander Moore and Christopher Turner. Cambridge: Polity, 2017. 1–48. Print.

Sloterdijk, Peter. *Rage and Time. A Psychopolitical Investigation.* Trans. Mario Wenning. New York: Columbia UP, 2010. Print.

Sloterdijk, Peter. *Spheres 1: Bubbles.* Trans. Wieland Hoban. South Pasadena: Semiotext(e), 2011. Print.

Sloterdijk, Peter. *Spheres 2: Globes.* Trans. Wieland Hoban. South Pasadena: Semiotext(e), 2014. Print.

Sloterdijk, Peter. *Spheres 3: Foams.* Trans. Wieland Hoban. South Pasadena: Semiotext(e), 2016. Print.

Sloterdijk, Peter. *What Happened in the 20th Century?* Trans. Christopher Turner. Cambridge: Polity, 2018. Print.

Sloterdijk, Peter. *You Must Change Your Life!* Trans. Wieland Hoban. Cambridge: Polity, 2013. Print.

Thrift, Nigel. "Peter Sloterdijk and the Philosopher's Stone." *Sloterdijk Now.* Ed. Stuart Elden. Cambridge: Polity, 2012. 133–46. Print.

Van Tuinen, Sjoerd. "'Transgeneous Philosophy': Post-humanism, Anthropotechnics and the Poetics of Natal Difference." *In Medias Res. Peter Sloterdijk's Spherological Poetics of Being.* Ed. Willem Schinkel and Liesbeth Noordegraaf-Eelens. Amsterdam: Amsterdam UP, 2011. 43–66. Print.

Zuboff, Shoshana. *The Age of Surveillance Capitalism: The Fight for the Future at the New Frontier of Power.* London: Profile, 2019. Print.

andrea capra

STAYING WITH THE DARKNESS
peter sloterdijk's anthropotechnics for the digital age

In an interview which first appeared in the French journal *Le Monde*, Peter Sloterdijk defined himself as "an optimist who achieved optimism at the second attempt" (*Selected Exaggerations* 264). Naturally inclined to pessimism (ibid.), as well as a friend and admirer of the great Romanian thinker of hopelessness Emil Cioran,[1] Sloterdijk demands from the reader the seemingly paradoxical task of confronting the *marche funèbre* of history with a smile: if the answer to the question posed by the title of Sloterdijk's 2016 book *What Happened in the 20th Century?* must irrevocably deal with the atrocities of the century, little is achieved by a passivist perspective of complete world-secession which, as articulated in *You Must Change Your Life*, is not (anymore) an adequate response to the globalized emergence of the state of crisis that Sloterdijk calls "The Great Catastrophe."

The Great Catastrophe bears the traits of what in former times was ascribed to transcendent powers: it remains concealed, and yet it makes its presence visible through the "diffusely and ubiquitously growing realization that things cannot continue in this way" (Sloterdijk, *You Must Change* 442). Remaining, or perhaps even becoming, an optimist in a catastrophic epoch is an exquisitely acrobatic task. In Sloterdijk's jargon an acrobat is one who masters the doctrine of "the processual incorporation of the nearly impossible" (123): an improbable task is accomplished in any acrobatic exercise, and consequently the ceiling of improbability gets higher and higher. Acrobaticism is a form of "natural anti-naturalness": it demands a full metabolization of the artificial, which in turn, once fully integrated as a technique of subject-formation, mutates into (first) nature.[2] The acrobat effortlessly brings his performance to completion, and the smile with which he bows in front of the applauding crowd shows a *sprezzatura* that must belong to his praxis. It should thus be clearer why being an optimist in catastrophic times is far from being a contradiction in terms: it is instead the successful outcome of an acrobatic confrontation with the pressing issue of our time, which demands us to "embrac[e] the monstrosity of the universal in its concretized form" (448).

This is the answer, eleven years after its publication, to the question which closes *Bubbles*, the first volume of the *Spheres* trilogy: "Where are we when we are in the monstrous?"

(Sloterdijk, *Bubbles* 630). When we are in the monstrous, we are in a state of confrontation which "demands of us a permanent stay in the overtaxing-field of enormous improbabilities" (*You Must Change* 448) – indeed, as Sloterdijk argues, the human is the animal of which too much is demanded (443). Sloterdijk's philosophy is of Janusian nature: one face, echoing Walter Benjamin's interpretation of Paul Klee's *Angelus Novus*, is the tragic one that gazes back at the horrors of history, and with disgust for what has been seen calls for an extreme form of spiritual secessionism from a world that resembles a "slough of filth" (219).[3] The other face is the one of the monstro-(anthropo)technician (Sloterdijk, *Not Saved* 104), bearing the traits of the creature who engages with his surroundings through the spiritual, material, cultural, and religious tools at his disposal, and in embodying a post-passive, battle-ready attitude (Sloterdijk, *You Must Change* 197) deploys them in his struggle for affirmative subjective and collective formation.

What follows establishes a dialogue between Sloterdijk's contributions and some of the problems of *anthropos* in the era of digital technology defined by increasing opacity and indecipherability. My target will be twofold: I first side with the tragic face of Janus, and give an account of what according to Sloterdijk constitutes the pivotal transition of the twentieth century, meaning how philosophy's "basic emotion changed from wonder to horror" (*What Happened?* 56). To shed light on this transition, I will focus on Sloterdijk's conception of the monstrous (*das Ungeheure*), as my analysis will show it to be defined by boundlessness, complexity, and excess, and discuss how the human being shows both monster-slayer and monstrous tendencies. Secondly, after having revisited the question "what happened in the twentieth century," I will discuss how Sloterdijk's understanding of the monstrous is helpful in assessing what is happening and what will happen in the twenty-first century concerning digital culture. This section will reflect on our current technological and societal predicament, which increasingly manifests the monstrous traits of simultaneity, unknowability, and opacity. Here, I put Sloterdijk's work in dialogue with recent contributions that deal with the creation of opacity due to computational and digital technology, and processes of blackboxing (Bridle; Beyes and Pias). Finally, I discuss how Sloterdijk's anthropotechnical horizon gives us a useful framework in dealing with the aporias of the current technological predicament, insofar as his technophilic attitude maintains both an affirmative outlook concerning mankind's role in shaping the world even if confronted with an increasingly invasive digital technology, and an awareness that "every unconcealment remains bound up with a flipside of concealment" (*Not Saved* 129), thus accommodating the possibility of untethering technological advancement from promises of absolute clarity.

what happened in the twentieth century?

In the opening section of the essay "The Domestication of Being," published in German in 2001 with the volume *Nicht gerettet. Versuche nach Heidegger*, Sloterdijk discusses what he identifies as the darkening of philosophy, which occurred in the twentieth century due to its transition from wonder to horror. This mutation, Sloterdijk argues, is catalyzed by Martin Heidegger: "Heidegger modernizes wonder, turning it into horror and thus basing philosophy as a whole upon a darker logical affect" (*Not Saved* 91). The trope of the beginning of philosophy in wonder dates back to Plato's *Theaetetus*. In this dialogue on the nature of knowledge, Socrates benevolently smiles at the curiosity of his young interlocutor Theaetetus, who is baffled by the puzzling state of affairs that being alive and being in the world constitutes: "I see, my dear Theaetetus, that Theodorus had a true insight into your nature when he said that you were a philosopher; for wonder is the feeling of a philosopher, and philosophy begins in wonder" (Plato, *Theaetetus* 155d). The same experience of puzzlement and complexity, and the desire of the subject to unravel the intricate knots of reality ignited for Aristotle too the blaze of philosophy: "It is through wonder that men now begin and originally began to philosophize; wondering in the first place at obvious perplexities, and then by gradual progression raising questions about the greater matters too" (Aristotle, *Metaphysics* 1.982b). The sense of wonder as related to philosophy is, according to this genealogy, more tied to the multifaceted experience of being perplexed rather than the unambiguously positive one of marveling at something. Or better: it is a commixture of the two, an interplay of curiosity and concern which creates the conditions of possibility of any exploratory analyses of the intricate and confusing experience of thinking about the world. Theaetetus' reaction once confronted with Socrates' aporias in the abovementioned dialogue speaks about the bewilderingly inebriating nature of wonder: "By the gods, Socrates, I am lost in wonder (*thaumazō*) when I think of all these things. It sometimes makes me quite dizzy" (Plato, *Theaetetus* 155c). From its Hellenic origins, the sense of wonder courses through centuries of Western philosophy in variously mutated forms: for Descartes, as he writes in his *Passions of the Soul*, it constitutes the first of all passions (*l'admiration*), or, putting specific emphasis on the Germanophone tradition, one observes its transitions from Kant's *Bewunderung* to Hegel's *Verwunderung*, until it reaches Heidegger, the Grecophilic philosopher par excellence, who bases his critique of Western metaphysics on his sense of fundamental ontological wonder – "das Wunder aller Wunder: daß Seiendes *ist*" (*Wegmarken* 305), the wonder of all wonders: *that* entities *are*.[4]

Sloterdijk discusses how the darkening which occurred in the twentieth century comes about when wonder "becomes terror-mimetic and transitions to meditation on the monstrous" (*Not Saved* 91). Although the two terms "wonder" and "horror" may appear almost as antithetical experiential poles, this mutation does not fundamentally change the nature of *thaumazein*: the tint of uneasiness that is found in Plato and Aristotle is brought to a fuller and more totalizing expression in the century haunted by the detonations of the battles of Marne and Verdun and by the screams of the torture chambers of the Gestapo – two examples of the "convulsions of the age [that] have spread into the innermost recesses of philosophical discourse," with the former penetrating phenomenology, and the latter existentialism's fundamental tenants (ibid.). The radicalization (from the Latin *radix*, root) of philosophy must be taken literally: after a period of forgetfulness of the question of Being, the twentieth century sees a forced return to the wondrous roots of philosophy only to find them blackened by the monstrosities of a century which irrevocably mutated their nature. This century, of "extreme situations" as Sloterdijk defines it in the first section of "The Domestication of Being," calls for a reconsideration of the basic observation that nourished since its birth the development of philosophy: the realization that "beings *are*," that there is something rather than nothing, turns from the wonder of all wonders to the horror of all horrors (ibid.). The "sublime sangfroid" that Sloterdijk ascribes to Hegel was still a possibility in the nineteenth century, and it was indeed a necessary condition to "conceptualize a spirit that had the virtue of looking steadfastly at the sun and at death while engaged in its learning process" (*What Happened?* 57). On the contrary, the post-1945 epoch comes to the awareness that it "has lost the strength of this elevated indifference" (ibid.). Such a momentous change does not only provide a vantage point from which one retrospectively analyzes the mutations of the philosophical discourse as it relates in particular to history. In fact, Sloterdijk argues that since the beginning of the twentieth century the overwhelming presence of the horrible constitutes the most powerful source of creativity, as first and foremostly demonstrated by the breakthrough of expressionism, which "was the beginning of a long conjecture of hyperbolic worlds of expression that were invoked to correspond to the monstrosities of the history that was transpiring" (*Not Saved* 92): the expressionists belong to the offspring of Theaetetus, as they too are lost in the experience of *thaumazein*, and seek to give voice to the astonishment produced by a confrontation with their surroundings. Yet, similarities notwithstanding, for Socrates the very fact that the *thaumazein* which belongs to the philosopher is a source of delight, whereas its modernized form in Sloterdijk's account abandons its positive underpinnings and becomes reactive to the nearby terror, which, in return, stimulates the creation and the development of artistic and philosophical endeavors.

In 2005, Sloterdijk returns to the mutation from wonder to horror in a public lecture titled "What Happened in the 20th Century?," which will then be published in 2016 in the eponymous volume. In this contribution the discussion of the "age of extremes" (a formulation that Sloterdijk takes from Eric Hobsbawn's 1994 book *The Age of Extremes*) is continued with reference to the mythological figure of Medusa, whose petrifying gaze constitutes a paradoxical remedy against the "phantomization" of the recent past. With "phantomization" Sloterdijk here refers to the ways in which the past century, with its corollary of atrocities, seems to be undergoing a process of mnemonic disappearance typical of late-stage capitalism:

> I would like to refer to the synergies of triumphant consumerism with its imagery of the beautiful life and how this is further developed by neoliberal doctrines – which leads to the jettisoning of the greater part of our dark and disturbing memories. (*What Happened?* 55)

Rather than embracing a purely forward-looking attitude, one which instrumentalizes the memory of the twentieth century by turning it into a commodifiable and quickly disposable repository of violence and tragedy, the task of the thinker should be to "pause beneath the petrifying gaze of the Medusa and contemplate it as an icon of present-day being" (56), thus embracing a stance that preserves the vivid awareness of what triggered the transition Sloterdijk speaks about. Such awareness is the prerequisite for any analysis of the contemporary epoch that holds to the continuity of the phenomenon of the darkening of philosophy, and in so doing modernizes the question concerning of what happened in the twentieth century, and makes it even more relevant for thinking about what is happening and what will happen in the twenty-first.

Sloterdijk identifies the tendency towards simplification and a procedural reduction of complexity as one of the main causes of the explosion of violence in recent history: if on the one hand the twentieth century witnessed the fuller manifestation of the monstrous as defined by the emergence of "a totality that allows neither full understanding nor comprehension" (Oosterling 359), on the other hand the dominant discourses of the epoch all engaged in a "furious struggle against the emergence of complexity" (Sloterdijk, *What Happened?* 57). Indeed, once confronted with totalitarianism and the "fundamentalism of militancy and the myth of a 'new beginning' through revolution" (ibid.), the middle ground of complexity had to endure the relentless onslaught of a variety of political and ideological extremisms. Once this characterization of the twentieth century is put in relation to Sloterdijk's reading of human nature, it becomes clear that the monstrous does not assume solely negative connotations. Sloterdijk draws the connection between the monstrous – *das Ungeheure* – and the human from Hölderlin's translation of the first line of the "Ode to Man" choral passage in Sophocles' *Antigone*: *Ungeheuer ist viel. Doch nichts ungeheurer als der Mensch*[5] (πολλὰ τὰ δεινὰ κοὐδὲν ἀνθρώπου δεινότερον πέλει, lines 332–33). The human being, according to Sloterdijk's anti-essentialist stance, "does not designate any object concerning which one could formulate direct (edifying or lamenting) statements but rather only presents a conceptual container that [...] holds 'vast complexities'" (*Not Saved* 98): the mutable nature of human beings is constructed by their perennial confrontation with the physical and cultural-symbolic spaces that they inhabit, and by the techniques they employ in their attempts at climatizing them – thus making them more suited for the flourishment and development of both individuals and communities (*Bubbles* 45–53). Modernity is the monstrous byproduct of a creature that possesses monstro-technicist tendencies:[6] with its inclination toward complexity and verticality, the human being is "a danger-seeking monster of disturbance that slanders the status quo and leaves nothing as it was," as Sloterdijk puts it in a subchapter of *You Must Change Your Life* (124) fittingly titled "Nothing More Monstrous than Man: Existence at High Altitude" (123–25).

Let us thus return to the question that closes *Bubbles*: "Where are we when we are in the monstrous?" (630). The answer cannot but be that we are at home, in the space of improbable confrontations that belongs to humanity. Sloterdijk's optimism achieved "at the second attempt" can be understood once his historical pessimism is related to the monstrous milieu of complexity and confrontation in which the humans find their most homely place of belonging, which is indeed not any fixed home, but rather a boundless process of constant adaptation and evolution.[7] What is

> proper to the essence of the human being [is] to execute a breaking out of the environment and a breaking through into ontological cagelessness, for which we never find a better characterization than the most trivial and deepest word of the human language, the expression "world" (*Welt*). (Sloterdijk, *Not Saved* 101)

Modernity is thus the epoch of a full(er) expression of man-made monstrosity.[8]

As Sloterdijk discusses in his essay "The Time of the Crime of the Monstrous," in classic metaphysics "the monstrous is possible only for God," demiurge and puppet-master alike, the ruling and omniscient cybernetician whose existence justifies the complexity of the system, and provides mankind with a transcendent panacea for the system's undecipherability and overwhelmingness – this is why within this framework "sublime theory could only appear as theology" (*Not Saved* 238). On the contrary, "[m]odern theory [...] begins from the monstrous-ness of the humanly possible" (ibid.): the death of God consecrates the human being as both a monster-slayer and as a monster himself, whose task is precisely to secure himself in the monstrous (Sloterdijk, *You Must Change* 333). Friedrich Nietzsche thus becomes the patriarch of the "central logical event of the nineteenth and twentieth centuries: the transformation of metaphysics into General Immunology" (332). Sloterdijk's theory of the *Homo immunologicus* rests on the assumption that mankind possesses a psycho-symbolic immune system whose efficacy is tied to practices on which humans have relied throughout history "to cope – with varying success – with their vulnerability through fate, including mortality, in the form of imaginary anticipations and mental armour" (9). This type of immune system, which in the general human constitution is accompanied by a biological and a socio-political one, is the very essence of all forms of practicing life, and it regulates spiritual, cultural, and technical attempts, of both physical and mental nature, at optimizing human beings' status "in the face of vague risks of living and acute certainties of death" (10).

According to Sloterdijk, the human condition in the world is a condition of disorientation: "we feel lost in the world, and would like to know our location" (*What Happened?* 47). It appears clear that the immunological practice of securing oneself in the monstrous must necessarily assume new connotations after the collapse of the system of beliefs and orientations connected to the regulating presence of God. As we saw, in the twentieth century a first response to this disorientation was a generalized tendency towards simplification. Procedural simplification can be understood as a programmatic effort to reduce the feeling of being lost in the world: clear and univocal messages, bracketing their truth-value or bad faith, can provide an impressionistic sense of orientation in what the individual perceives as increasingly directionless and undecipherable surroundings. The genealogy of this confusion begins with the age of discoveries in the fifteenth century, inaugurated and allowed by the success of the sea-maneuver *volta do mar* performed by the Portuguese sailors. The "sea's about-face," to which we will return in the last part of this essay, allowed the *marinheiros* to distance themselves from the European coasts by abandoning their ships to the great permanent wind circle, the North Atlantic Gyre, thus gaining enough propulsion to reach open sea while, at the same time, being able to return home again, contrary to what was allowed by standard techniques of navigation (Sloterdijk, *Not Saved* 46–47): after this "most momentous" achievement of European intellectual history, the path toward the globalized world – the synchronized world, whose form is produced by simultaneity[9] – had been paved, and with it the conjuring up of a world which, to paraphrase Heidegger, sees the collapse of distances go hand in hand with the absence of nearness.[10] The exorcism that the masses performed in the twentieth century against disorientation, as Sloterdijk writes in a chapter on the Weimer Republic in his *Critique of Cynical Reason*, consisted of "a Yes to socio-political and ideological movements that promise the greatest simplification and the most energic return to 'substantial' and reliable states of affairs" (483). This is a political byproduct of a more deeply seated confusion that belongs to modern man: since "[m]odernity is the time in which those humans who hear the call to change no longer know where they should start: with the world or with themselves – or with both at once" (Sloterdijk, *You Must Change* 323), the directionality of the metanoetic[11] imperative and of the consequentially deployed anthropotechnics – i.e., Sloterdijk's theorem of historical anthropology, according to which the human being is a product, and can only be understood (if at all) through analyses of the methods and relations of his production – shifts from a prevalence of subject centered anthropotechnics, to a prevalence of political and societal centered ones.[12] This shift is the one which occurs between the so-called exercises of the ancients and exercises of the moderns, and in his latest works Sloterdijk declares the historical failure of the latter tendency vis-à-vis the collapse of all the systems of ideological world-revolution (440–41).

Although in recent times the exercises of the modern have been the most prevalent form of anthropotechnics and, indeed, they assumed for the greatest part a collective dimension, the analysis of the transition from wonder to horror requires us to focus also on the positioning of the individual in the times of fuller monstrosity. In fact, historicizing the transition from wonder to horror is only one side of the coin: it is the abovementioned tragic face of Janus, which is carried by the winds of time away from the atrocities of what came before, without ever turning his gaze aside from them. The forward-looking face is the one of the monstro-technician that in modernity has indeed mostly engaged with frustrated attempts in socio-political exercises of collective (trans)-formation. From this historical failure Sloterdijk predicts a return to the individual, as we read in a recent contribution on the philosophical aspects of globalization: "In all likelihood, immunological problems (in the broadest sense of the term, including the biological, social, and spiritual condition of individuals) will in future have to be dealt with more at the individual level than at the collective level" (*What Happened?* 54).

If one holds true to the Medusian predicament that Sloterdijk advocates for the thinker of modernity, how can the (monstrous) subject confront the overwhelming monstrosity of the "synchronized world" (*What Happened?* 45), and thus find immunotechniques that are effective on the individual level? After the disappearance of any remaining metaphysical foothold, mankind's task of securing himself while climbing "Mount Improbable" (Sloterdijk, *You Must Change* 117–19) is faced with a novel threat:

[T]he nature of the Modern Age as the time of a crime so disproportionate that it cannot be fully formulated in conventional theoretical of programmatic texts. There is no theory of the monstrous, only hyperbolic projections. One can utter them, just as the feeling of going insane can be articulated; one can confess them as one confesses to sensing that one has committed a crime of an indeterminable nature in a dream. Like a radical suspicion towards oneself, participation in modernity can only be confessed to. (Sloterdijk, *Not Saved* 245)

According to Sloterdijk, the monstrous presence of man-made modernity is too vast and too atrocious to be fully embraced by any rigorous human theorization. Similar to how Athena is born from Zeus' forehead, modernity is the time when man is faced with the uncanny externalization of the core of *Ungeheuerlichkeit* that belongs to him. Modernity then constitutes an ulterior strophe of the "Ode to Man" from Sophocles' *Antigone*, once this is read as the narration of the unfolding of both the manifold monstrosity that inherently belongs to mankind,[13] and, as Sloterdijk proposes, of humans' audacity and resilience when confronted with improbable difficulties (*You Must Change* 123). To convey and to deal with the disproportion of modernity, one is left with hyperbolic projections or whispered confessions.

Readers of the American author H.P. Lovecraft, once relegated to the outskirts of acceptability and nowadays rightfully celebrated,[14] will not fail to recognize familiar overtones in the above cited passage. In Lovecraft's tales the protagonists are confronted with cities whose geometries escape human beings' capacity for synthetic understanding and with entities whose existence escapes accurate verbal depiction. Lovecraft's descriptive technique of such anomalies is a careful balance between hyperbole and reticence. His protagonists are normally those entrusted with the paradoxical task of giving account of the unaccountable, and their attempts at this impossible task – normally suspended between murmured confessions and rabid exaggerations – precede their spiraling down into madness. This necessarily tangential mention of Lovecraft leads us to the second part of this contribution. Here, I explore the technics that the subject may deploy to confront the monstrosity of an epoch that seems to resist to any exhaustive account which, in return, would allow its climatization and integration into a sphere of controlled understandability. Lovecraft's characters almost inevitably sink into a vortex of insanity once they have to deal with the monstrous, coherent with their creator's uttermost pessimism regarding the agency of mankind vis-à-vis indifferent and overpowering cosmic forces that existentially diminish humanity, and relegate man to a state of complete passivity. This condition, as I will discuss in the next section, is one potential outcome of the confrontation between the individual and the current state of technology. In contrast, Sloterdijk's philosophy celebrates the activated human "as one who is autonomously feeling, practicing and imagining in opposition to the felt, the practiced and the imagined" (*You Must Change* 197). This activated subject refuses to be "overwhelmed without a fight" and is "post-passive, repeating, battle-ready" (ibid.). In the next section of this essay, I discuss how Sloterdijk's reflections on the monstrous map onto some aspects of the current technological development as they are tied to a further increase in the opacity and undecipherability of our world.

what is happening in the twenty-first century?

The opening passage from Lovecraft's tale "The Call of Cthulhu," written in 1926, resonates as disquietingly prophetic for us readers of the twenty-first century:

> The most merciful thing in the world, I think, is the inability of the human mind to correlate all its contents. We live on a placid island of ignorance in the midst of black seas of infinity, and it was not meant that we should voyage far. The sciences, each straining in its own direction, have hitherto harmed us little; but some day the piecing together of dissociated knowledge will open up such terrifying vistas of reality, and of our frightful position therein, that we shall either go mad from the revelation or flee from the deadly light into the peace and safety of a new dark age. (167)

This paragraph speaks the language of Sloterdijk's description of modernity as the time of full monstrosity. Beginning from the age of discoveries of the fifteenth century, and passing through the invention of the steam engine in the eighteenth, in the twentieth century the technological and scientific advancement surpassed a critical threshold which made clear to the human being his monstrosity "as the maker of suns and the maker of life" (Sloterdijk, *Not Saved* 135). Sloterdijk is here referring to two previously unheard-of technologies: nuclear and genetic. The former took most devastating form in the detonation which occurred on August 6, 1945 above the skies of Hiroshima, whereas the latter found a place in general imaginary by the birth of the sheep Dolly, the first mammal cloned from an adult somatic cell. In the same passage of "The Domestication of Being" Sloterdijk raises two questions that the human must now face: "whether what he can and does do is actually he himself and whether he is at home with himself in this activity" (ibid.). The first question concerns authenticity and agency, and asks who is actually in control at this point of the dialectics between man and technology;[15] the second question concerns legibility, and mankind's permanence in what so far had been considered, according to Heidegger's dictum, the "House of Being": language. The "terrifying vistas of reality" opened up by the position of the human being as maker of suns and life are the ones actualized by the externalization of the *Ungeheuerlichkeit*, which, continuing to quote Lovecraft, demands a serious assessment of "our frightful position therein." The human being approaches the reflective surface of modernity only to realize in all clarity that his face bears monstrous traits: the outcome of the mirroring stage turns from wonder to horror, and hyperbolic projections or whispered confessions is all that is left for the creature of "surrealistic effort" (Sloterdijk, *You Must Change* 13).[16] Nuclear and genetic technology show that the human does not exist under the sign of the divine anymore, but rather under the sign of the monstrous: if theology was the hermeneutics of the divine, modern philosophy must necessarily be the hermeneutics of the monstrous.

This is the man of the twentieth century, who, according to Sloterdijk, witnessed the historical failure of both humanism as a transgenerational inhibiting device aimed at human debestialization,[17] and of collective anthropotechnics practiced by simplifying totalitarian systems. The man of the twentieth-first century encounters an even fuller expression of the synchronized world, which, as Indian-American anthropologist Arjun Appadurai argued at the doorsteps of the new century, "involves interactions of a new order and intensity" (1) between what he defines as ethnoscapes, technoscapes, mediascapes, ideoscapes, and finanscapes.[18] In addition to the increasing acceleration of world synchronicity and complexity, the last decades saw the full integration of digital and computational technologies into our lifeworld through, in particular, new media.[19] Sloterdijk affirmed in a recent interview that "[e]xistence in the technical world per se is characterized by ever-greater artificialization. Modern and postmodern humans not only live in the 'house of Being' (as Heidegger called language), but increasingly in the abode of the technosphere."[20]

The constant increase of technological mediations in our everydayness generated the conditions of possibility for the birth of what the geographer Nigel Thrift called the "technological unconscious," defined as a "prepersonal substrate of guaranteed correlations, assured encounters, and therefore unconsidered anticipations" (177). Digital technology has effectively become the substrate of our lives, a regulating presence embedded in a nest of predictability powered by a variety of software-controlled devices that promote a progressive cyberneticization of the world.[21] The experience of interacting with devices and networks[22] that function according to increasingly opaque processes of blackboxing[23] – i.e., with known input and output characteristics but unknown methods of operations – has become so prevalent in our lives that it is nowadays fully part of our unconscious. Another increasingly common phenomenon associated with computation and digitalization that triggers relevant consequences in our modalities of interacting with our devices is the so-called "automation bias,"[24] according to which humans tend to favor outputs coming from automated systems – ranging from spellchecking, to following a suggested route on a GPS device, to autopilots – in making decisions.

While the importance of how new media and technologies in radically changing our world cannot be overstated, it is crucial to keep in mind that most human reactions are not necessarily rooted in the novelty of the technology per se. The automation bias, for example, can also be seen, from a certain perspective, as a permutation of the tendency towards simplification that Sloterdijk identified as typical of the twentieth century: if confronted with a set of complicated and interconnected choices, people tend to favor strategies that can be easily understood and followed, such as the ones proposed by our devices. This speaks of an existing interplay between preexisting cognitive and behavioral schemata and new technologies that regulates the experience of interacting with our digital tools.

In a framework of continuity, all this promotes the strengthening of the monstrous nature of our epoch: the progressive and seemingly inevitable disjunction between the velocity and the complexity of technological and scientific advancement on the one hand, and our understanding of the cybernetic systems that surround us on the other hand. The result of this disjunction takes the form of an increasing opacity that stands between us and our tools as they constitute our world. Again, this is not anything new. In his 1917 lecture "Science as a Vocation," Max Weber had already acknowledged that "[t]he savage knows incomparably more about his tools" (286) than we do – and during the past century, the situation has exponentially gained in complexity. Nonetheless, and this is the crucial point, according to Weber increasing intellectualization and rationalization meant that "one could learn at any time" (ibid.) how any tool functioned: time and memory were thus thought by Weber to be the practical (not theoretical), insurmountable obstacles on the path of individual absolute knowledge in relation to the development of scientific advancement at any given point. Weber continues by denying that any mysterious incalculable force plays any role (as it did for the savage), and therefore "one can, in principle, master all things by calculation. This means that the world is disenchanted" (ibid.). It follows that if everything can be absolutely known through technical means and calculations, if any remaining undertone of fog enveloping the world can eventually be dissipated, then epistemology's main asset becomes time. The so-called project of modernity is thus a promise of constant, ever-growing illumination: an opaque, foggy world is progressively disclosed, and an ever-increasing level of clarity concerning the worldly order of things takes shape. In Jürgen Habermas' words: "The project of modernity as it was formulated by the philosophers of the Enlightenment in the eighteenth century consists in the relentless development of the objectivating sciences" (45).[25]

In keeping with Sloterdijkian understanding of a monstrous modernity, recent contributions from James Bridle (*New Dark Age*), and Timon Beyes and Claus Pias ("The Media Arcane") challenge this linear narrative of the structure of modernity. In assessing the magnitude of the transition constituted by the digitalization of our world, they highlight the shortcomings of any pretention of understanding this new state of affairs according to an aprioristic belief in the ever-increasing growth of transparency and understanding tied to technoscientific advancement. They both promote a search for new ways of speaking about our technologies, and our positions therein.

Bridle suggests that a key feature of survival in our times will be to "think without claiming, or even seeking, to fully understand," and that we should resist considering "darkness as a place of danger, even of death." Instead, the technologically informed darkness of our age should be considered "a place of freedom and possibility, a place of equality" (Bridle 15).[26]

Beyes and Pias too in their essay "The Media Arcane" deal with the seemingly paradoxical question of how, in the epoch of generalized algorithmic prediction and blackboxing, is it possible to think without claiming to understand. With the colonization of our lifeworld by an innumerable array of apparatuses capable of independently communicating with one another and providing reciprocal feedback, a new cybernetic-temporal structure emerges. This expanding cybernetic chronotope integrates into its system, one based on prediction (which lies at "the heart of cybernetics" (Beyes and Pias 92)), the data traces of the subject under the form of big data, and conflates them "with the prediction of forms of subjectification," thus collapsing the "modern concept of an open future" (94). According to the authors, to resist this bleak outlook we must consider new modalities of thinking about digital culture. Since the cybernetic chronotope has brought the discourse of transparency to a harsh stop, in order to "conceptualize an ethics without transparency" they advocate a "reconsideration of the general form of the secret and, particularly, of its premodern varieties and corresponding temporalities so as to gain a vocabulary for thinking about digital cultures as a technologically conditioned nexus of secrets" (102).

In their analysis of digital media, these contributions take issue with the ingrained habit of believing in the existence of a direct proportionality between technological advancement, transparency, and understandability.[27] This becomes particularly clear in the discussion of what Bridle calls "computational thinking" (4): the pervading belief that once something can be turned into a quantifiable problem and reduced to data, it can then be integrated into a model of inherently better understandability and therefore operability. The current reliance of our society on big data speaks about the magnitude of this phenomenon: it assumes that if only we could gather enough quantified and quantifiable information we would have access to a reliable model of the world,[28] and hence to new frontiers of social and individual engineering spanning from political predictability in relation to electoral messages, to a tailor-made selection of goods and routines for the individual. Against complexity we seek to simplify; and a form of scientific reductionism according to which "complex systems can be understood by dismantling them into their constituent pieces and studying each in isolation" (84) has reemerged with the explosion of big data in all fractions of our society, and its corollaries of invasive data mining and mass-spread quantification.

Computational thinking holds the monstrous to be nothing but an illusion: it clings to the presupposition that once the correct model has been crafted, the world can be adequately quantified, and thus known. This tendency presents clear similarities with the sociopolitical response to complexity through simplification that Sloterdijk indicates as a cause of the atrocities of the twentieth century: they both rely on relinquishment of agency and propose a strong faith in a dominating model. The current interplay of surveillance technology, computational devices, and big data, indeed, seems to point to the scenario described at the end of the quoted passage by Lovecraft, when technoscience, thanks to massified data gathering processes, will piece together dissociated knowledges and open up a terrifying vista of reality where the human being will be mined, engineered, and controlled in accordance to a univocal yet complex model, in an ubiquitously surveilled yet fully transparent society – a technologically revamped panopticon–crystal palace hybrid.[29] In the final part of my essay, I will show how Sloterdijk's conception of anthropotechnics as it is tied to his reflections of the clearing [Lichtung] opens up a scenario of human resoluteness in the epoch of technologically mediated darkening.

navigating opacity: on the immunological value of darkness

The late twentieth century and the first two decades of the twenty-first saw, from the shores of the end of history, the full integration of digital culture into the human quotidian: big data and automated, interconnected systems showed us our position as nodes in an intricate cybernetic nexus. Yet, Bridle's admonition about the emergence of a new dark age does not in any way subscribe to any technophobic or reactionary stance. On the contrary, he acknowledges that "[t]echnology is not mere tool making and tool use: it is the making of metaphors," and

> as our current understanding of the world proceeds from our scientific discoveries, so our rethinking of it must emerge from and alongside our technological inventions, which are very real manifestations of the contested, complex, and contradictory state of the world itself. (Bridle 15)

Rather than leading to nihilistic resignation, the realization that our way of interfacing with technology is undergoing a radical transformation becomes an important place of departure for thinking through new ways of efficiently integrating this new state of affairs into our lives. Our response, according to both Bridle and Beyes and Pias, cannot start with the presupposition of minimizing the importance of technology in the construction and understanding of our world.

Sloterdijk shares a similar technophilic attitude regarding the influence of technology in shaping and navigating reality.[30] As practitioners of technology, human beings' anthropotechnical attitudes call for a resolute refusal of the "anti-technological hysteria that holds broad sections of the Western world in its grip" (Sloterdijk, *Not Saved* 141), and which promotes an essentialist stance contrary to the recognition that "everything that happens on the technological front leads to consequences for human self-understanding" (139): this feedback loop suggests that one must become a cyberneticist to be able to remain a humanist (236). In fact, the importance of technology in shaping ourselves and our world is so fundamental as to constitute one of the underpinnings of Sloterdijk's reappropriation of the Heideggerian concept of clearing: "Whoever points to the clearing speaks of the coming to presence [*Vorstelligwerden*] of Being in a living being that resonates physically, neurologically, and technologically on such a high frequency that it can encounter 'the world' as world" (98). Thanks to this trinity of resonances, the human being appears as a worldformer, "if to be world-forming means gathering and further writing the world-text" (128–29). Technology is one of the elements that promotes man's ecstatic posture in the world, and it is inherently integrated into that vast complexity called "human" as it promotes an advancement of the clearing. A thinking that is situated in a reactionary position is one from which "only protest is possible, not further thought" (236): technophobia, according to Sloterdijk, leads to a state of paralysis, whence one can loudly scream one's existential confusion and contempt for an increasingly technologized world, but this revolt is condemned to sterility insofar as it voices the refusal to engage with the technogenic origins of mankind (142). A forgetfulness of such origins leads to the stifling of the "main feature of Dasein in motion – letting oneself fall into the initial tendency, egress into the expanse, the deliberate turn that brings back" (47), which is to say taking full advantage of human beings' openness in shaping and getting shaped by their sojourn in the world.

The *bona consuetudo* (the good habit, "the central anthropotechnic principle" (Sloterdijk, *You Must Change* 255)) of Western modernity has been to act according to the belief that technological advancement progressed hand in hand with understanding and transparency. It also ascribed an inherently positive quality to any increase in information, insofar as this was believed to lead to better decision making.

Today it appears clear that a new *consuetudo* must supplant the one that the Western world has so deeply metabolized, in order to avoid staying with what was once a good habit, but has now turned into an obsolete, if not dangerous one. Attempts at rethinking our current understanding of technology and our presence therein such as the ones discussed in the section above are important exercises both in retracing our place in the monstrous while trying to make it more legible, and in beginning to deal with a state of affairs that demands from us a new way of taking action, if we want to keep acting meaningfully and thoughtfully in the cybernetic systems in which we are more and more embedded. For centuries, under the reign of humanism, language was our way of befriending the world: it drew near to "the foreign and the uncanny, in order to integrate it into an inhabited, understandable sphere that can be lined with empathy" (Sloterdijk, *Not Saved* 132). Today this task is still not extinguished, but "one cannot mistake the fact that language in the technological world (where other techniques of drawing near have taken the lead) is increasingly overwhelmed by this task" (ibid.). Indeed, as Bridle suggests, technological acceleration over the last century, and in particular over the last decades, has radically transformed our planet, our society, and ourselves, but it has "failed to transform our understanding of these things" (2): bracketing the radical mutations undergone by our world, the prevailing tendency – the *mala consuetudo* – is still to think that everything can be enlightened in such a way that brushes aside the darkening engendered by algorithmically processed data and blackboxing.

According to Sloterdijk's onto-epistemological paradigm, trafficking at the outer rims of our climatized spheres is what constitutes the very essence of the clearing: the task of the acrobat who seeks to hold true to the thinking of Being is to strike an improbable balance between our environmental cage and the "pure terror of being held out into the indeterminate" (*Not Saved* 109–10). The state of the clearing is a state of twilight and shadows: there, "it becomes manifest that not everything is manifest. The manifestation is never complete – and the suspicion against what is veiled and not appearing is in principle never to be put to rest" (129). The transition from wonder to horror that begun in the twentieth century demands, and here Sloterdijk is quoting Heidegger, "not closing oneself off to the terror of the untamed [*Ungebändigten*] and to the confusion of darkness [*Dunkels*]" (92). Yet, Sloterdijk's thinking, as the subtitle of *Nicht gerettet* recites, is *nach* (after) Heidegger instead of *mit* (with) or *für* (for) Heidegger. And indeed, in talking about the clearing he challenges Heidegger's ontological reflections on technology insofar as the "human being does not stand in the clearing with empty hands – not like some destitute alert shepherd with his flock, as Heidegger's pastoral metaphors suggest" (142).[31]

To be sure, Heidegger's reflections on technology constitute the background of much of Sloterdijk's thinking on the topic, in particular for what concerns the ambiguous essence of technology: a place of danger, and yet, at the same time, where the saving power grows as well.[32] If on the one hand Sloterdijk maintains much of the vocabulary employed by Heidegger, on the other hand he excavates more deeply the genealogy of, and brings to a more technophilic conclusion, the question regarding what the development of technology implies in terms of humanity's relation to Being – Sloterdijk's proposed technogenesis of the human existence is, indeed, decisively un-Heideggerian.

According to Sloterdijk, "*Humanitas* depends on the state of technology*,*" and since technology has played a constitutive role in the process of hominization, its mutations demand from us an affirmative, battle-ready reaction to the metanoetic imperative that emerges from the new technological predicament: you must change your life, to be better in accordance with your "technogenic provenance" (*Not Saved* 142). In *The Art of Philosophy*, Sloterdijk distinguishes between maintenance exercises and developmental exercises: in the former set the practitioner encounters the same level of difficulty of what he is already used to, whereas in the latter the subject engages with an increased challenge (9). The darkening engendered by the cybernetic chronotope demands that man start a new round of developmental exercises, which, in accordance with the doctrine of acrobaticism, will in return yield the processual incorporation of the nearly impossible. In this case, the nearly impossible is to integrate into our habit what at least for the Westernized modernity stemming from the Enlightenment appears as deeply counterintuitive: the ability, to quote Bridle, "to think without claiming, or even seeking, to fully understand [insofar as this] is key to survival in a new dark age" (6). This new state of affairs revitalizes the necessity of finding adequate practices [*Übungen*] to embrace the mutated monstrosity of the universal in its concretized form.

In the age of polarization between the two hysterias of naive transhumanism and an equally naive technophobia, Sloterdijk's philosophy is a precious case of affirmative, non-nihilistic technophilic thinking[33] that traces the technogenic provenance of mankind and integrates in this genealogy self-shaping practices of individual and collective nature – be they past, present, or still speculative – without demanding from this onto-anthropology any qualitative mutation in assessing the human condition in the twenty-first century. His emphasis on remaining at the outermost rim of our climatized spheres is an invitation to endure the proximity of an "outside" that does not possess any mystical or esoteric undertone, but that instead indicates how the world "attains contour as a composite of evidence and veiling" – as an interplay of light and shadows. The awareness that every unconcealment remains bound up with a flipside of concealment has become lost in Western modernity, particularly in relation to technological and scientific advancement: the immunological response of the Enlightenment was to repudiate darkness by promoting constant illumination and transparency. This tendency now seems to have reached its limits, faced with surveillance societies and the algorithmic processing of the human data: the immunological response turned into the autoimmune disease. As Bridle's and Beyes and Pias' recent contributions emphasize, the new metanoetic imperative is that we must familiarize ourselves with the idea of a residency in darkness, a darkness that is not simply a suboptimal and transitory accommodation which, ideally, needs to be promptly evacuated.

As discussed, the darkness of the cybernetic chronotope is multilayered: it rests both on an ontological opacity which Western modernity desperately tried exorcising, and on a newly created one due to the complex interconnections of systems in the digital epoch. The (re)discovery of the immunological value of darkness emerges as a pressing challenge of our time, and it presupposes, at the same time, a heroic leap forward and a double realization. The first realization is a call for humility, which emanates from the abdication of any pretentiousness of full illumination. The second is a call for alertness, and for resolute vigilance in spite of our dwarfed position as marginal nodes in a complex cybernetic nexus: this translates into an acrobatic effort in preserving a sphere of autonomy and clear-sightedness in an increasingly opaque environment. Indeed, two pressing questions of our time will be the following: how to preserve a realm of political agency, without claiming to fully understand? And: how to break free from the cage of a "future perfect" – i.e., a future already pre-established by computational thinking, which, thanks to its legitimizing narratives, certificates the necessity and inevitability of what is not yet here, but will inevitably occur?[34]

The humanity of the cybernetic chronotope can find a source of inspiration in what Sloterdijk describes at the end of his essay "The Plunge and the Turn." There, he narrates the story of the brave sailors of the century of discoveries to discuss how the crossing of the ocean became a problem for the Portuguese *marinheiros* only through its answer – that is, through seafaring itself. The key of maintaining an affirmative, forward-looking, and battle-ready attitude is, according to Sloterdijk, hidden in this momentous transition of European history. The neo-*marinheiros* of today must reconsider their approach to the issues of our relation with technology through models that promote "unscrewing oneself from ossified and distorted structures and ways of running counter to deaf and fatal routines – movements of turning by which the sense of active, conscious, shared life in the multifariously mobilized world is necessarily changed" (Sloterdijk, *Not Saved* 48). Long before the sailors scientifically learnt that the Euro-American winds formed a system, they sensed "first intuitively, but later in an experienced, practical manner" (46) that they could take advantage of obscure forces to rise to the challenge of seafaring: the *marinheiros* of the fifteenth century embraced the overpowering nature of the ocean, and only thanks to its gyre were they able to accomplish what up to that point was thought to be impossible. Practitioners of the sea without yet being its theoreticians, the sailors triangulated between mankind, nature, and technology to successfully incorporate the improbable into their praxis of navigation.

We can only speculate about what the neo-*marinheiros* of the twenty-first century will look like – and, most importantly, what deeds they will accomplish. Their affirmative attitude will necessarily confront the ambiguous powers of technology: at once, as Heidegger describes, a source of salvation and perdition. The technologically induced darkness already strengthens systems of control and of power scarcely interested in potentially disruptive new maneuvers: the question will revolve around the development of anthropotechnics aimed at improving our immunological status while maintaining an openness towards the monstrous, and finding ways to thrive in our residency in the darkness. A new *volta do mar* will call at once for creative and subversive uses of technology.

The Hong Kong protests that started in 2019 may perhaps offer us a glimpse of what the battle for affirmation in the darkness could look like: on the one hand the protesters took advantage of the recording and live-streaming powers of technology to document police violence while, on the other hand, conducting maneuvers aimed at preserving their anonymity in order to shroud themselves against repressive measures enacted by the state. The protesters, facing the overwhelming resources of a surveillance state, sided with the darkness: their resoluteness also consisted in deploying techniques that denied transparency both as an agenda of warfare and as a value, such as encrypted messaging to safely coordinate the protests, and laser pointers to disturb facial recognition. These are only two examples of methods to keep thinking and acting in ways that resist the dogma of omnipresent transparency as an inherently positive trait of our times. A stay within the darkness thus does not invest immunological resources in the vain struggle to fully dissipate the opacity of our cybernetic chronotope, and yet preserves the meaningfulness and goal-driven nature of our actions. It affirms new modalities of responding to the metanoetic imperative: you must change your life, in order to preserve your existential security without abandoning your ecstatic posture.

This parenthesis regarding the Hong Kong protests is only one example of what dealing with the digital monstrous conjugated as the surveillance state may involve. According to Sloterdijk confronting the other facets of "The Great Catastrophe" will call for a broader rethinking of our techniques, especially concerning global issues such as climate change. If the ocean became a problem for the Portuguese *marinheiros* only through seafaring itself, new and more creative ways of thinking must necessarily emerge in technologically dealing with an issue that, indeed, has emerged only through human accelerated technological advancement itself. As a conclusive yet passing note, which suggests the open-ended, ever-evolving nature of this process of rethinking, it will suffice to mention that in a recent essay on the Anthropocene and on mankind's complicated relation with the planet Earth, Sloterdijk states that "technology has not yet spoken its final word" (*What Happened?* 20). Repurposing again Heidegger's reflections on technology, Sloterdijk is here calling for a novel relationship of "co-production between nature and technology" (ibid.), contrary to our history of technological exploitation of the planet.[35] This absolute imperative will perhaps be better heard once we allow ourselves, after a
hiatus of just a few centuries,
to think again about the decisive
role that darkness played in
mankind's history as practitioners of this world.

disclosure statement

No potential conflict of interest was reported by the author.

notes

1 See Sloterdijk's writings on Cioran in *Not Saved* 251–56 and *You Must Change* 73–82.

2 As Sloterdijk writes in *You Must Change Your Life* on the nature–culture caesura, "[i]n the natural history of artificiality, the nature–culture threshold does not constitute any particularly notable caesura [...] The only privilege of culture in relation to nature is its ability to speed up evolution as climbing tour on Mount Improbable" (119).

3 The topic of world-secessionism is addressed from a religious and individual perspective in Sloterdijk, *Weltfremdheit*. See also Sloterdijk, *You Must Change* 217–42.

4 On the topic, with specific emphasis on Plato, Aristotle, and Heidegger, see Llewelyn.

5 "Many things are monstrous, but nothing is so monstrous as man" (my translation).

6 For a study on Sloterdijk's concept of modernity, see Van Tuinen.

7 As Sloterdijk puts it in *Not Saved* 166, "Humans are the beings that have abandoned their houses."

8 Sloterdijk discusses the "three faces of man-made monstrousness of the Modern Age" (i.e., the monstrous in man-made space, time, and thing) in his essay "The Time of the Crime of the Monstrous: On the Philosophical Justification of the Artificial," in *Not Saved* 237–50.

9 As Sloterdijk puts it: "The globalized world is the synchronized world; its form is produced simultaneity, and it finds convergence in things that are current" (*The World Interior of the Capital* 141).

10 Heidegger, "The Thing" 165–66.

11 On metanoia and call to action, see the following passage from *You Must Change Your Life*: "Metanoia is above all a panic phenomenon; in that it goes hand in hand with the gesture of pulling oneself together in a crisis and getting serious before the looming end" (303).

12 On the topic, see Lucci 171–224.

13 On the topic, see Withy 107–08.

14 For the presence of Lovecraft in recent philosophical production, see Harman.

15 Sloterdijk voices this concern and distinguishes between the outcomes of allotechnology (technologies aimed at outwitting nature) and homeotechnology (aimed at imitating nature) in *Not Saved* 146. He returns to this distinction in *What Happened?* 20.

16 "Wherever one encounters members of the human race, they always show the traits of a being that is condemned to surrealistic effort. Whoever goes in search of humans will find acrobats" (Sloterdijk, *You Must Change* 13).

17 On the topic, see Sloterdijk's essay "Rules for the Human Park," in *Not Saved* 193–216. In particular, "The latent theme of humanism is thus the de-bestialization of the human being, and its latent thesis runs: right readings tames" (197).

18 See Appadurai 7–11.

19 On the topic, and in particular on the novelty constituted by new media in the age of networked computation, see Hansen.

20 Gardels 13.

21 On the topic, with particular reference to Heidegger's philosophy of technology, see Hörl.

22 On the topic of networks, see Galloway; Galloway and Thacker.

23 Bruno Latour defines blackboxing as

> the way scientific and technical work is made invisible by its own success. When a machine runs efficiently, when a matter of fact is settled, one need focus only on its inputs and outputs and not on its internal complexity. Thus, paradoxically, the more science and technology succeed, the more opaque and obscure they become. (304)

24 We owe to Linda J. Skitka and Kathleen L. Mosier some of the first contributions on the topic, as in Mosier and Skitka, "Automation Use and Automation Bias." See also Cummings.

25 The genealogy of a dialectics between known/unknown, light/darkness is vast, and cannot be fully addressed here. The fundamental starting point for the post-World War II period is Horkheimer and Adorno, *Dialectic of Enlightenment*. The works of Élisabeth Roudinesco are a useful reference too: see Roudinesco, *Our Dark Side* and "Freud." Recently, the notion of "Dark

Enlightenment" has been reframed by the philosopher Nick Land in the context of his Neoreactionary manifesto "The Dark Enlightenment."

26 Elizabeth R. Petrick's essay on the history and the use of the concept of the black box by cyberneticians reads as an eloquent document of the seemingly paradoxical task of bringing together darkness and possibility.

27 The topic is discussed by Bernard Stiegler, in terms of calculability, incalculability, disruption, despair, and madness. For a discussion of similarities and divergences of Sloterdijk and Stiegler, with particular emphasis on Heidegger's reflections on technology, see Lemmens and Hui.

28 Bridle's case study of the problems that this tendency created in medical and pharmacological research due to data drenching, Eroom's law, and the replication's crisis shows the shortcomings of this predicament. See Bridle 83–102.

29 On the illusion of transparency and control as it is related to surveillance, see Bridle 161–86.

30 Sloterdijk has been accused of eugenicist tendencies after his talk "Rules of the Human Zoo," which led to his controversy with Habermas. For an account of this controversy, see Couture 74–84.

31 On the topic in relation to Heidegger's conception of authentic and inauthentic (*eigentlich* and *uneigentlich*) life, with reference to Sloterdijk, see Campbell.

32 See Heidegger, "The Question Concerning Technology" 28.

33 Nick Land's philosophy of accelerationism is perhaps the most spectacular example of a nihilistic technophilic attitude: see Land, *Fanged Noumena*. For a very recent inquiry on how these technophilic nihilistic tendencies have been embraced by the Neo-reactionary Movement (NRx), which finds its radiating core in the Silicon Valley, see Pinto.

34 This topic has been taken up by a number of cultural critics, from Fredric Jameson (1991) to Mark Fisher (2009) and Franco "Bifo" Berardi (2017).

35 For a recent analysis of Sloterdijk's reflections on the Anthropocene, see Lemmens and Hui, in particular 36–39.

bibliography

Appadurai, Arjun. "Disjuncture and Difference in the Global Culture Economy." *Public Culture* 2 (Spring 1990): 1–24. Print.

Berardi, Franco "Bifo." *Futurability – The Age of Impotence and the Horizon of Possibility*. London: Verso, 2017. Print.

Beyes, Timon, and Claus Pias. "The Media Arcane." *Grey Room* 75 (May 2019): 84–105. Print.

Bridle, James. *New Dark Age. Technology and the End of the Future*. London: Verso, 2018. Print.

Campbell, Timothy. *Improper Life. Technology and Biopolitics from Heidegger to Agamben*. Minneapolis: U of Minnesota P, 2011. Print.

Couture, Jean-Pierre. *Sloterdijk*. Cambridge: Polity, 2016. Print.

Cummings, Mary. "Automation and Accountability in Decision Support System Interface Design." *Journal of Technology Studies* 32 (2006): 23–31. Print.

Fisher, Mark. *Capitalist Realism: Is There No Alternative?* Winchester: Zero, 2009. Print.

Galloway, Alexander R. "Networks." *Critical Terms for Media Studies*. Ed. W.J.T. Mitchell and Mark B.N. Hansen. Chicago: Chicago UP, 2010. 280–96. Print.

Galloway, Alexander R., and Eugene Thacker. *The Exploit: A Theory of Networks*. Minneapolis: U of Minnesota P, 2007. Print.

Gardels, Nathan. "Controversial Philosopher Says Man and Machine Will Fuse into One Being." *New Perspectives Quarterly* (October 2015): 10–16. Print.

Habermas, Jürgen. "Modernity: An Unfinished Project." *Habermas and the Unfinished Project of Modernity*. Cambridge, MA: MIT P, 1997. 38–57. Print.

Hansen, Mark B.N. "New Media." *Critical Terms for Media Studies*. Ed. W.J.T. Mitchell and Mark B.N. Hansen. Chicago: Chicago UP, 2010. 172–85. Print.

Harman, Graham. *Weird Realism: Lovecraft and Philosophy*. Winchester: Zero, 2012. Print.

Heidegger, Martin. "The Question Concerning Technology." *The Question Concerning Technology*

& *Other Essays*. Trans. William Lovitt. New York: Garland, 1977. 3–35. Print.

Heidegger, Martin. "The Thing." *Poetry, Language, Thought*. Trans. Albert Hofstadter. New York: Harper, 1975. 163–86. Print.

Heidegger, Martin. *Wegmarken*. Frankfurt: Klostermann, 1976. Print.

Horkheimer, Max, and Theodor W. Adorno. *Dialectic of Enlightenment*. Stanford: Stanford UP, 2002. Print.

Hörl, Erich. "The Technological Condition." *Parrhesia* 22 (2015): 1–15. Print.

Jameson, Fredric. *Postmodernism, or, the Cultural Logic of Late Capitalism*. Durham, NC: Duke UP, 1991. Print.

Land, Nick. "The Dark Enlightenment." Web. 26 Feb. 2020. <http://www.thedarkenlightenment.com/the-dark-enlightenment-by-nick-land/>.

Land, Nick. *Fanged Noumena*. Falmouth: Urbanomic, 2017. Print.

Latour, Bruno. *Pandora's Hope: Essays on the Reality of Science Studies*. Cambridge, MA: Harvard UP, 1999. Print.

Lemmens, Pieter, and Yuk Hui. "Reframing the Technosphere: Peter Sloterdijk and Bernard Stiegler's Anthropotechnological Diagnoses of the Anthropocene." *Krisis. Journal for Contemporary Philosophy* 2 (2017): 26–41. Print.

Llewelyn, John. "On the Saying that Philosophy begins in Thaumazein." *Afterall: A Journal of Art, Context and Enquiry* 4 (2001): 48–57. Print.

Lovecraft, Howard Philips. *Tales*. New York: The Library of America, 2005. Print.

Lucci, Antonio. *Un'acrobatica del pensiero. La filosofia dell'esercizio di Peter Sloterdijk*. Rome: Aracne, 2014. Print.

Mosier, Kathleen L., and Linda J. Skitka. "Automation Use and Automation Bias." *Proceedings of the Human Factors and Ergonomics Society Annual Meeting* 43.3 (Sept. 1999): 344–48. Print.

Oosterling, Henk. "Interest and Excess of Modern Man's Radical Mediocrity: Rescaling Sloterdijk's Grandiose Aesthetic Strategy." *Cultural Politics* 3 (Nov. 2007): 357–80. Print.

Petrick, Elizabeth R. "Building the Black Box: Cyberneticians and Complex Systems." *Science Technology and Human Values* (Oct. 2019): 1–21. Print.

Pinto, Ana Teixeira. "Capitalism with a Transhuman Face." *Third Text* 33.3 (2019): 315–36. Print.

Roudinesco, Elisabeth. "Freud, Thinker of the Dark Enlightenment." *Journal of Romance Studies* (Summer 2008): 1–9. Print.

Roudinesco, Elisabeth. *Our Dark Side: A History of Perversion*. Trans. David Macey. Cambridge: Polity, 2009. Print.

Sloterdijk, Peter. *The Art of Philosophy. Wisdom as a Practice*. Trans. Karen Margolis. New York: Columbia UP, 2012. Print.

Sloterdijk, Peter. *Critique of Cynical Reason*. Trans. Michael Eldred. Minneapolis: U of Minnesota P, 1988. Print.

Sloterdijk, Peter. *Not Saved. Essays after Heidegger*. Trans. Ian Alexander Moore and Christopher Turner. Cambridge: Polity, 2017. Print.

Sloterdijk, Peter. *Selected Exaggerations: Conversations and Interviews 1993–2012*. Trans. Karen Margolis. Cambridge: Polity, 2016. Print.

Sloterdijk, Peter. *Spheres. Volume I: Bubbles. Microspherology*. Trans. Wieland Hoban. Los Angeles: Semiotext(e), 2011. Print.

Sloterdijk, Peter. *Weltfremdheit*. Frankfurt: Suhrkamp, 1993. Print.

Sloterdijk, Peter. *What Happened in the 20th Century? Towards a Critique of Extremist Reason*. Trans. Christopher Turner. Cambridge: Polity, 2018. Print.

Sloterdijk, Peter. *The World Interior of the Capital. Towards a Philosophical Theory of Globalization*. Trans. Wieland Hoban. Cambridge: Polity, 2013. Print.

Sloterdijk, Peter. *You Must Change Your Life. On Anthropotechnics*. Trans. Wieland Hoban. Cambridge: Polity, 2013. Print.

Stiegler, Bernard. *Dans la disruption: comment ne pas devenir fou?* Paris: Les Liens qui libèrent, 2016. Print.

Thrift, Nigel. "Remembering the Technological Unconscious by Foregrounding Knowledges of

Position." *Environment and Planning D: Society and Space* 22 (2004): 175–91. Print.

Van Tuinen, Sjoerd. "Critique Beyond Resentment: An Introduction to Peter Sloterdijk's Jovial Modernity." *Cultural Politics* 3 (Nov. 2007): 275–306. Print.

Weber, Max. "Science as Vocation." *Sociological Works*. Trans. Hans H. Gerth and C. Wright Mills. New York: Continuum, 1999. 276–303. Print.

Withy, Katherine. *Heidegger on Being Uncanny*. Cambridge, MA: Harvard UP, 2015. Print.

the unknown quantity: sleep as a trope in sloterdijk's anthropotechnics

robert hughes

THE UNKNOWN QUANTITY
sleep as a trope in sloterdijk's anthropotechnics

I'd like to take this occasion to think about sleeping and, because sleep is also a continuing trope in the work of the contemporary German philosopher Peter Sloterdijk (b. 1947), this paper will let his recent work guide our reflections. By the by, we will find that our excursion through the trope of sleep in Sloterdijk will also illuminate some unexpected but important problems closer to the center of his project. So, we have a twofold aim: to meditate productively on sleep as a kind of unknown quantity in human existence and, in light of what Sloterdijk's writings will bring to these reflections, to refine our understanding of Sloterdijk's larger philosophy of anthropotechnics.

When the humanities take an interest in sleep, most typically that interest is focused on the dream – and it is easy to see why this would be so: dream is the one aspect of sleep that offers itself for elucidation – an elusive tease, so to speak, for our powers of rationalization. Hence, literary critics will read the oracular dreams of Homer's Penelope, for example, and hope to deduce something important about her relation to her suitors, Raskolnikov's dream of a horse brutally beaten to death will crystalize for readers the larger tension, in Dostoevsky's *Crime and Punishment*, between an innocent's anguished intuition of moral truth and (too often) the world's shameful violation of the same, and thinkers of the subject can productively follow (or challenge) Freud's own reading of the dreams of the Wolf Man. To bracket and set aside the aspect of dream in a consideration of sleep is to leave scholars in the humanities with next to nothing to work with. Consider "Rip Van Winkle," Washington Irving's classic tale of a man who falls asleep and awakens twenty years later to find his world astonishingly transformed. Irving's title character is, together with the Grimms' Briar Rose and Wagner's Brünnhilde, one of the most famous sleepers in all of Western literature and what does his mighty

This is an Open Access article distributed under the terms of the Creative Commons Attribution-NonCommercial-NoDerivatives License (http://creativecommons.org/licenses/by-nc-nd/4.0/), which permits non-commercial re-use, distribution, and reproduction in any medium, provided the original work is properly cited, and is not altered, transformed, or built upon in any way.

sleep look like? Like a paragraph return, an indent, and nothing more:

> at length his senses were overpowered, his eyes swam in his head, his head gradually declined, and he fell into a deep sleep.
>
> On awakening, he found himself on the green knoll [...] (Irving 776)

With dreamless sleep, we have a Before, we have an After, but the During – twenty otherwise eventful years in the case of Rip Van Winkle – is a narrative excision nestled into a wordless paragraph break. What is there to be said about dreamless sleep? Irving's tale suggests: maybe nothing at all. Sleep, as Sloterdijk writes, constitutes a "discrete nothing" of our worldly existence (*Weltfremdheit* 373) and "an enclave of worldlessness in the world" (*Foams* 504). The present essay proposes to work through these and related claims in Sloterdijk's considerations of sleep.

As for philosophy more generally, generations of gently nodding philosophy students have only reinforced in their professors an already-existing disciplinary hostility to sleep. Heidegger's *Introduction to Metaphysics* quotes Heraclitus from fragment B73 "One should not act [*poiein*] and talk [*legein*] as if asleep" (136). We see here, at the origin of Western philosophical thought, the basic binary that has dominated our tropes of sleep, from Heraclitus's admonition, through the fateful interruption of Kant's dogmatic slumber, down to Sloterdijk and the present day. And we might note the verticality of the classic tropes – our swinish animal natures issue their low seductions, our heads gradually decline, we sink into unconsciousness, we fall into a deep sleep, we plunge into dream. By implication, the hiatus of sleep constitutes a falling away from our potential participation in divine reason and a somewhat shameful capitulation to our baser animal natures. By contrast, true thinking is cast in terms of wakefulness – and proper action begins with vigilance. So we have a cluster of terms gathering on each side. On the one hand: sleep, the obscurity of night, unthinking unconsciousness, animal corporeality, passive inactivity, and the irrational and idiosyncratic freaks of dream-life. On the other hand: wakefulness, the clear-sightedness of day, true thinking and consciousness, participation in the divine, an active relation to the world and one's communal responsibilities within it.

As for Sloterdijk, readers will recall from *You Must Change Your Life* his chapter on Heraclitus, called "Sleepless in Ephesus," which we will get to shortly. In fact, however, Sloterdijk's devotion to thinking about sleep goes much deeper and much further back than just that. Already in his first book, *Critique of Cynical Reason* (1983), sleep makes a fleeting appearance in his review of the discovery of the unconscious that mortified the human ego's presumptions to self-mastery. Ten years after that, in a 1993 interview, sleep had moved closer to the center of how he thought about his developing interests as a philosopher:

> I no longer work on a theory of protest but on a fundamental theory of the absent person. That means I use anthropological arguments to develop the thesis that humans have turned away from the world to a large degree, and that they always exist also in the mode of absence, in the mode of unknowing, in a nocturnal relation to the world. (Sloterdijk, *Selected Exaggerations* 4)

Several questions later, he clarifies that his philosophical interest in human absence from the world is really "a kind of theory of the night and of sleep" (6). A year later, this time in an interview from 1994, he is already declaring that:

> this may not be a lofty philosophical topic, but the human being as the sleeper is the unknown quantity per se in the history of thought [...] Philosophers do not want to know that they sleep. (16)

Sloterdijk, of course, has given many interviews and said many things over the long course of his rather public life, but these are broad, strong programmatic declarations and, while we won't hold him to them, exactly, I do think they give us warrant to investigate sleep more seriously as it appears elsewhere as a topos in his philosophy. It will not be my claim that sleep is an indispensable trope in Sloterdijk's philosophy and at first it will seem a little odd to follow this marginal feature of his writing. As it will turn out, however, thinking Sloterdijk's philosophy through his various tropes of sleep will help us conceptualize more precisely some of its core features: the narcosis and world impoverishment he identifies in any metaphysics of sleepless day, what he values about the anthropotechnics of practice, how he thinks about the subject, and the extent to which he feels justified in presuming the subject's possibilities for action in the face of powerful constraints. We will see – and this is important – that Sloterdijk does indeed assign an important role to the body in his work as he works his way around the deducible edges of this "unknown quantity" of the sleeper.

Let us begin by noting that what we have already set up – the conceptual field that Western metaphysics associates pejoratively with sleep – is not altogether a strawman that Sloterdijk intends to knock down to make some dazzling contrarian point. If the prevailing schema of sleep and thought in Western philosophy aligns sleep with animality and sleeplessness with divinity, Sloterdijk mostly goes right along with it. For that matter, he doesn't at all contest the superiority of waking and its metaphorical extensions in thought, reason, and divinity. But, while sleep and wakefulness offer themselves to thought very easily as a binary, Sloterdijk plays a more complex game, as *You Must Change Your Life* shows in its section on Heraclitus. The complexity arises from the mapping of a binary figure – sleeping and unsleeping – onto what eventually reveals itself as several sets of ternary vertical structures:

Divine	Unthinkable truth	Unsleeping
Human	Potential thought	?
Animal	Unthinking matter	Sleeping

with a mystery blank right now for how humans are positioned between unthinking, sleep-prone animality and the sleepless, perhaps unthinkable truth of divinity.

Before we make the conceptual distinctions that will split our sleeping–unsleeping binary into a ternary, however, let us spend a little time with Sloterdijk's Heraclitus. *You Must Change Your Life* argues that Heraclitus is concerned with the tension within the human being, who is, on the one hand, mired in habits and passions, and, on the other hand, stretching toward the divine with the fire of reason, the all-pervading logos, and the commonwealth of shared understanding and communal vision that assures the security (and conditions the thought) of the *polis*. If our base possession by habits is shared likewise by animals, this fact, so far as we can tell, is of scant interest to Sloterdijk's Heraclitus. For Heraclitus, animals are hardly worth his time to think about – and little better, for that matter, are the many among his fellow citizens who are basically too sleepy to rouse themselves from the stupor and unthinking confinement of their sleep-world. In Sloterdijk's paraphrase:

> for him [Heraclitus], *hoi polloi* are none other than the people who do not awaken to the shared (*koinon*) in the morning, but instead remain in their private world, their dreamy idiocy [...] Trapped in their own worlds, people do not hear what the non-sleepers have to say to them. If one speaks to them of the all-pervading logos, they merely shrug their shoulders. They see nothing of the One, even though they are submerged in it. (*You Must Change* 171)

The many who do not awaken, who have no interest in the One that transcends and unifies the sundry particulars of the world, and who do not attend to logos – these sleepy shirkers are interesting to Sloterdijk's Heraclitus only for the unhappy challenge they pose for the city striving to secure thought beyond the exigencies of its brute survival and by way of the lowly point of contrast they offer to those of higher spiritual and philosophical ambition. These people may indeed be capable of knowing themselves, of showing good sense, and of fulfilling their duties as sentinels awake and watchful on behalf of the city, but they show every sign of being sleepily indifferent to the task of actually realizing that ascent.

The real interest for Sloterdijk's Heraclitus lies with the few who are awake: people of good sense, people engaged in listening for the transcendental logos, and how these people attend to the unsleeping suprahuman realm of the divine, in comparison with which, even the wisest human is a mere ape, to use Sloterdijk's gloss. But what exactly is the relation between the awakening human and the unsleeping suprahuman divine? It's really not a continuum – more of an absolute, categorical break between the human and the divine. And yet the human, better than a swine, might aspire to scale by degrees his or her finite approximations of infinite divine height. The final unattainability of the divine endpoint of our highest aspirations, the impossibility of finally and decisively shedding our sleep-prone animal materiality – these things lend a certain pathos to the whole project:

> If there is one strong characteristic of the pre-Socratics [...] it seems to me that it lies in the pathos-filled equation of waking and thinking.
> If one had to say in one sentence what constituted thought in the Ionic era, the answer would be: thinking means being sleepless in Ephesus. (Sloterdijk, *You Must Change* 171)

So, if we return to our three vertical columns,

Divine	Unthinkable truth	Unsleeping
Human	Potential thought	Potentially waking
Animal	Unthinking matter	Sleeping

we see the more precise terms of the specific project of aspiring humanity: human beings, considered in their potentiality, are neither sleeping nor sleepless, but engaged in a process of wakening themselves – no longer asleep, as it may be, but incapable of the sleepless perfection of surveillance and truth they attribute to the divine. Hence the pathos of the waking: to have been existentially assigned (and heroically embracing) a glorious project of self-becoming and transcendental participation, but condemned to fall ever short, such that, though the wisest will mount summit upon summit, they do so only ever as ape-like epigones of the gods.

We might try to think more carefully about the relation of humanity to this aspirational ideal, however. When we consider participation in truth, logos, and the One and consider also the two modalities for doing so in our table above – the human and the divine, or, let us say, the human and the specific "divine" ideal that humanity has come to adopt for itself – and when we consider, further, Sloterdijk's tropes of sleep and wakefulness, we find a novel way into this problem. Neither the divine nor the ideal human is asleep, but only the human is waking, properly speaking: never having been in a state of sleep from which they might awaken, the gods in our table seem to be equally foreclosed from sleeping and from waking. If it is true that only humans are capable of awakening and if we postulate that humans and the divine have distinct modes of relating to truth, then we might speculate that the human mode, "thinking" or "philosophizing," is for present purposes a temporal process of questing, working toward, and working-through, and thus is foreclosed to any divinity enjoying an immediate, non-processual, atemporal participation in truth and the Heraclitean One. To put the point a little bit differently, perhaps human thought works toward the light of truth from a position that recalls what we read above from Sloterdijk's 1993 interview: whatever else might be said to the credit of their conquests in knowledge, human beings "always exist also [...] in the mode of unknowing, in a nocturnal relation to the world" – and this very human dualism of knowing and unknowing marks a categorical distinction from the mode of absolute and purely positive knowing that our culture has assigned to its gods.

In *Weltfremdheit* (1993), his book from the time of that interview, Sloterdijk describes the gods as necessary figures in the development of civilization and thought. Approaching the gods from a speculative anthropology, he poses a pre-history of humanity in which communal life was lived in hordes and gods were posed as local energy fields or as guardian spirits of a specific ethnos. In this account, a people would enter into history when it attained to the luxury of thinking beyond brute survival – and this became possible when human groups started to pool their collective powers of wakeful watchfulness, such that some could develop more expansive, more complex, more powerful insight into the world, while others stood sentinel on behalf of this community project. Such an "originary communism of attention" (336) expanded humanity's scope of vision beyond the immediacy of its needs – and, correspondingly, it inspired an expansion in their conception of the gods, who came to resemble a metaphysicalized and radicalized version of the vigilant sentinel. When gods came to be posed as ever-wakeful, all-seeing, and all-knowing witnesses of the world, the world itself came to be reconceived: less limited to the exigencies of need and immediate locality, it became a world thoroughgoingly subject to vision and knowability. Inspired, then, by the powers it had attributed to its own creation, humanity ventured their own expositions of the world, occupying ideal positions of limited local instances of the gods' all-encompassing comprehension of the world as a whole. This is why Heraclitus is a signal figure for this aspect of Sloterdijk's work: Heraclitus articulated a vision of divinity as inhabiting an eternal day beyond the world's nychthemeral alternation of day and night. And the object of metaphysics, at first a defense and a contest and a struggle engaged with the adversarial night, became in the modern period an aspiration to bring the world and life in its entirety into the uninterrupted light of day – and to transform philosophy into a luminous thought devoid of night.

The attribution of sleeplessness to the gods has been, in Sloterdijk's account, both a blessing and a curse therefore. It has transformed our world into a sphere that we understand to be thoroughly penetrable by wakeful watchfulness and susceptible to knowledge – and the result has been a previously unthinkable advance in our conception of the world. But adopting a "divine" perspective on a world as if under perpetual light, with its implicit ontology of eternal presence, has perhaps in some respects alienated us from a truer, more worldly vision of the nychthemeral world. In truth, the world in itself is "a rhythm of coming and going" (Sloterdijk, *Weltfremdheit* 367) and our own existences as part of that world are "a constant pulsation between a *Dasein* and a *Fort-sein*" (374) – waking and sleeping, of course, but also day and night, presence and absence, the revealed and the hidden, the concrete figures and the discrete nothings, the rising of the world and its withdrawal. When we depolarize being, when we denocturnalize it by situating it within perpetual light, wakeful watchfulness loses its preeminence among human virtues, humanity comes to suffer a kind of "narcosis of light" (369), human civilization loses the communitarian project that has bound it together from the beginning, and the world, bereft of its proper hiatus, begins to lose its appearance as itself. So imitation of divine wakeful watchfulness serves us well – but only up to a certain point, beyond which it begins to lose contact with the very nature of the world it purports to witness.

Strikingly, the operative limit in the human relation to any divinity conceived along these daylit lines is one that Sloterdijk poses not in traditional terms of human finitude and the gods' inimitable omniscience; rather, it's a problem of world – a kind of category mismatch between the gods' unsleeping world of perpetual light and the human world of nychthemeral and circadian rhythms. So we might supplement our table with a fourth column on different varieties of world, metaphysically considered:

Divine	Unthinkable knowledge	Unsleeping	Unremitting day
Human	Potential thought	Potentially waking	Nychthemeral alternation
Animal	Unthinking matter	Sleeping	Unremitting night

The implication is that the sleepless vision of the gods is not quite suitable for the rhythms of our world and philosophy would be advised to take this into account. It remains true: Sloterdijk himself is a champion of day and wakefulness and he shares Heraclitus's aversion to the dark seductions of sleep. But he also contests any metaphysics that refuses due recognition to the dimension of night and sleep. Our world, unlike the divine world and unlike any metaphysics modelled on it, has this twofold nature. As we see in *Weltfremdheit* and as we will see as we further explore his anthropotechnics, Sloterdijk pursues his philosophy of awakening in a finally insuperable tension with our worldly aspect of night and sleep – a tension sustained and not to be overcome by any act of wishfulness.

But let us leave aside fantasies of our own potential for god-like sleeplessness, unwavering thought, and constant vigilance to meditate a short while on what would be entailed in the actuality of human wakefulness unrelieved by our periodic falls into the world of sleep. Sloterdijk himself pursues this theme in relation to the Romanian philosopher and essayist, Emil Cioran (1915–95).

In *You Must Change Your Life*, Sloterdijk devotes a chapter to Cioran as offering a valuable rebalancing to Sartre's emphasis on existentialist engagement. Cioran, by implicit contrast to Sartre, is described as pursuing an existentialism of refusal and incurability, even as he also lived an experimental life disciplined by a creative and paradoxical refusal of directed action, and a kind of commitment to airing the dark, depressive moods that colored and overwhelmed his existence – a life led on the principle of "the healthiest way to be incurable" (82). Sloterdijk's curious admiration for Cioran will be important to us as an index of the capaciousness of any definition of the Sloterdijkian hero. Cioran was "the first master of not-getting-anywhere," as Sloterdijk calls him (78), one who scaled "the heights of despair" – to borrow the strangely formulated title to one of Cioran's books – and did so without ever aiming to overcome these heights. So, when readers consider the values implicit in the Sloterdijkian hero, they will want to do so in such a way that this heroism can make room for an unconventional figure like Cioran. Sloterdijk admires two things in particular about Cioran: (1) his open-eyed, unflinching perception of the more venomous truths of existence and (2) his rigorous commitment to his own inventive mode of living and persisting, notwithstanding life's most venomous truths. It seems not to matter to Sloterdijk that this mode is one of committed refusal and a special purity of *ressentiment*. I offer this by way of reminder and anticipation. Our main interest right now in Sloterdijk's Cioran is found in a different text.

Some years before *You Must Change Your Life*, Sloterdijk published a collection of essays on Heidegger, under the title of *Not Saved*. Its penultimate chapter is scarcely on Heidegger at all, however, and is in fact devoted to the inimitable Cioran and his insomnia. The following passage suggests Sloterdijk's main claim:

> Cioran's Archimedean point, from which he unhinges the normative view of the world and its philosophical and ethical superstructure, is the discovery of the privilege of sleeping [...] His unparalleled clear-sightedness in the disenchantment of all positive and utopian constructs has its basis in the pervasive stigma of his existence – in a sleeplessness that was undoubtedly of a psychogenic origin and which marked him for years in his formative phase. This is what lends an envenomed *epochē* to the thinker, Cioran. The insomniac knows, in contradistinction to the critic, that he is not the master of his premises [*daß er nicht der Herr seiner Prämissen ist*].[1] (*Not Saved* 252–53)

Right away, we should note that Sloterdijk is following Cioran to think about sleep in a somewhat different register than was the case when Sloterdijk was reading Heraclitus. Sloterdijk's Heraclitus was thinking of sleep as a trope for thoughtlessness; Cioran is evidently concerned with sleep itself as an animal necessity and as conditioning the moods that color one's relation to the world. So Heraclitus and Cioran each use sleep as an occasion to meditate about somewhat different conceptual complexes. That said, Heraclitus and Cioran are both concerned with the sleep-prone animal substrate of the human potential for thinking and taking proper action and this is how we will bring these thinkers together under the name of Sloterdijk.

But, to return to our quote, Sloterdijk wants us to consider how there is a kind of normative view of the world, and by extension of its "ethical superstructure," that pays insufficient regard to the necessity of sleep. Philosophers, as we have already read, "do not want to know that they sleep" and ignorance on this precise point, Sloterdijk suggests, permits philosophers to imprudently erect their positive and utopian constructs. One of the norms apparently undergirding these constructs, the supposition that man is the master of his own premises, is unhinged by Sloterdijk's Cioran. His insomnia has taught him a bitter truth and, from this truth, we might deduce the relevant basic outlines of the subject.

In some respects, this is an old critique of an even older norm. In his *Critique of Cynical Reason*, Sloterdijk reminds his readers that the sovereignty of consciousness in the human subject had come under critical challenge long before Freud and he draws specific attention to the special interest taken by the late Enlightenment and the Romantics in the somnambulist and the subject under hypnosis – Sloterdijk reports that hypnosis[2] was sometimes known in the late eighteenth century as "magnetic sleep" or "artificial sleepwalking":

> Somnambulant phenomena provide provocative proofs that consciousness does not know everything about itself. In the state of magnetic lucidity, a zone of knowledge speaks that remains inaccessible to surface consciousness [...] In the process of enlightenment, human beings become more and more deeply involved in the self-evidence of the enigma that "there is still something else there." Like an internal gremlin, it manifests itself in such a way that it cannot be directly grasped. If one looks closely, it has already disappeared. It follows consciousness like a shadow or like its double, who never agrees to an encounter with the first ego. But it constantly follows the first ego without ever revealing its name. Its emotional mode of appearance is the uncanny and the fear of going mad – two properties that are not the exclusive property of romanticism. (*Critique* 49)

Sloterdijk's early consideration here of the philosophical importance of sleep speaks eloquently to the Romantics' sense of a shadowy psychological agency internal to the subject that is alternate or alien to the ego and its mere "surface consciousness." What is different about his more recent treatments, including his essay on Cioran, is a new emphasis on how this alternate agency is insinuated in the very flesh of the subject. For the more recent Sloterdijk, this is not a contest between two disembodied agencies for mastery of the flesh.

To conceive of the subject in terms of disembodied intelligence and sovereign will would be a mistake for a number of powerful reasons – most immediately, for the insomniac, because the human potential for thinking, our capacity for participation in logos, is predicated on a reasonably well-rested organism. Parents know too well the misery of seeing their little angels lapse into demonic irrationality when deprived of normal sleep. Some more moderate degree of this affliction will manifest itself likewise in the everyday life of adults. Sloterdijk's point, however, is broader and deeper than just this parental (and materialist) truism, because sleep here is beginning to function as a trope for something bigger than just the necessity of rest – although rest is pretty important by itself. Sleep also operates as an index of a vaster, but scarcely known component of human existence: an "unknown quantity," a black box, so to speak, of automatic functioning that is partly organismic, yes, but also partly psychosomatic, as Cioran's psychogenic insomnia will testify. The fruitlessness of the insomniac's appeal for the relief of rest exposes Cioran to a truth that the rest of us close our eyes upon: that we are dominated by automatic processes and that these processes are, collectively, the true master of the existential premises inhabited also by our thinking selves. We would do well to take it into account, therefore, as we think about the subject and as we consider Sloterdijk's investigations into anthropotechnics. When we consider the forces that condition and constrain anthropotechnics and when we consider the constituent structures that might be harnessed and turned into motors of anthropotechnic ascent, we will have to work from something not far from Sloterdijk's own premise that "99.9 per cent of our existence comprises repetitions, mostly of a strictly mechanical nature" (*You Must Change* 406).

The role of habits and the technics of their harnessing will be familiar as the main topic of *You Must Change Your Life* and I won't belabor the point, beyond laying down a few markers. Sloterdijk assigns the first philosophical working-through of this problem to Heraclitus and the pre-Socratics. What they grasped – and what the moderns have sometimes forgotten – is that it is never a question of inscribing good habits upon a blank-slate animal organism, nor of detecting and removing a few pernicious habits in order to restore a natural good-functioning. Rather, the human being is always, post-infancy let us say, the site of a massive, already-existing complex of habits and inertias. The significance of this fact is enormously far-reaching. We see that training and anthropotechnics, for example, are always a dual matter of both working within the context of existing complexes of habit, whether good or (more usually) bad, as well as seeking to establish new habits through repetition and practice. Put another way, the subject who aspires to vertical ascent must find a way to put the unknown quantity of his or her automatic, habitual functioning, however nocturnal, however obscure, into the service of self-improvement. Anthropotechnics becomes a matter, perhaps above all else, of managing one's own black box. It's not a question of being more consistently "woke" or of becoming super-humanly aware of the minutest processes of interior life, but rather of acknowledging one's aspect of sleep, acknowledging the black box that does not answer to ego or the will, and tricking and training it to work in concert or in coincidence *with* one's purposes instead of *against* them. It's not a matter of shining a light into this darkness, illuminating its mechanisms and making them totally amenable to one's independent will – because, in any case, insomnia shows us that the will itself is not a thing separate from the automatisms of the body. Rather, anthropotechnics is a matter of harnessing, through practice, the still obscure operations of our subjective automata to take the subject to its own vertical elsewhere.

To develop his thinking on these topics in *You Must Change Your Life*, Sloterdijk turns to two figures that fascinated the imagination of the nineteenth century: the automaton and the somnambulist, or sleepwalker. What is shown by the late-Enlightenment and Romantic cultural fascination with the automaton and the somnambulist? To Sloterdijk, this cultural phenomenon suggests a modern working-through of the fact that human beings are "possessed" by habits and inertias and it suggests the new idea that this possession might usefully be thought of as "a taking over of humans by the embodied mechanism" (*You Must Change* 169). The figure of Olimpia will be a familiar automaton to fans of Offenbach's opera, the German Romantic tales of E.T.A. Hoffmann, and Freud's essay on the uncanny. Olimpia dances with untiring, clockwork perfection, she coos demurely and unthreateningly into the ear of our neurotic hero, Nathanael, and she utterly seduces his mad fantasy, up until the uncanny moment when she is revealed to be an android built by an ingenious mechanician. Freud thought that the uncanny power of the tale derived from our recognition that the hero's sufferings mirrored our own in various ways. But we might, after Sloterdijk, wonder whether the uncanny effect, like the hero's final derangement, comes also in part from the recognition that it is Olimpia, the android, who is really our secret figure of readerly identification – our recognition that there operates in the most intimate obscurity of our own lives, a mechanism whose internal working remains quite mysterious to us, though, with some reflection we can see the effects it is constantly producing in our lives, from our overdetermined objects and perversions of desire, to the movements and gestures and characteristic habits of our bodies. In the maturity of the mechanical age, but still in the morning of the computer age, just as new cybernetic horizons began to promise androids that could do more than dance and coo, L. Ron Hubbard, in Sloterdijk's account, offered an update on much the same perspective: Hubbard's dianetics expressed a revision of the mind–body dichotomy with the view that "many of the phenomena one had previously attributed to the mind-and-soul side of the totality of being [*Seinsganzen*] in fact belonged on the material-mechanical side" (*You Must Change* 99). The result of these insights of the modern period is that "every individual was now confronted with the stimulus of understanding themselves as a composite of android and real human" (358).

We might be tempted to place machines (including computers) together with the divine on our table of ternaries. They are, after all, unsleeping and unthinking and perfectly knowledgeable so far as they go. What, then, to make of the machinic aspects of our own "totality of being"? Sloterdijk at one point describes the android as one's inner statue and recalls the Stoic teacher's injunction to students to activate their inner statues and to conform their dispositions to its perfect and regular form (*You Must Change* 357). God and the machine are perhaps not so far apart for these purposes, though thinkers in the wake of Plato may be unenthused, if I can put it that way, to locate their divinity in this unthinking aspect of the subject, with its vague sense of the correct opinion contrasted by Socrates' Diotima with truly thoughtful understanding (*Symposium* 202a).

At any rate, Sloterdijk tropes the somnambulist in tandem with the android and he argues that they fulfill much the same function in our imaginative self-conception. Even if the wetware organicity of the human body removes sleepwalking more decisively from the potential realm of human invention and manufacture (so far as the nineteenth century was concerned), still, for Sloterdijk, sleepwalking seems to reveal a human body animated by an inner android, a sense-making mechanism completely, unaccountably, and scandalously separate from ego and consciousness:

> It is not without reason that somnambulism [...] was the central psychopathological symptom of the nineteenth century. The sleepwalker presents the inner android acting independently after the subtraction of the ego's consciousness. (*You Must Change* 358)

There is a strange and delightful action–reaction video on YouTube, plausibly genuine, of a sleepwalking father filmed by his tweenage daughter and then shown, upon waking, the video of his sleepwalking self, rummaging through the fridge and nattering on about the tooth-fairy and the birds who are going to eat his teeth. The father's dopey, open-mouthed astonishment in watching his own animated body and his daughter's charming hilarity are completely worth anyone's five minutes of time. Another short action–reaction video, this time a minute and a half in length and even more plausibly genuine, features a middle-aged mother whose grown son shows her a video of herself sleepwalking and talking senselessly about a "tomato cage," as she watches, hand covering her mouth in incredulous amazement and frank fascination. How to account for this? And how to account for the nearly ten million views this video had amassed by mid-2017? Here is Sloterdijk:

> The constant back and forth between the poles of the android id and the human ego gave rise to the soul drama of the mid-Modern Age, which was simultaneously a technical drama. Its topic is best summarized in a theory of convergence, where the android moves towards its animation while increasing parts of real human existence are demystified as higher forms of mechanics [...] The ensoulment of the machine is strictly proportional to the desoulment of humans. (*You Must Change* 359)

I don't want to place too much emphasis on Sloterdijk's analogizing of the psychoanalytic id as a twentieth-century conceptual elaboration of our inner android, though one can see where he is coming from. What I do want to highlight is the way that somnambulism, as a figure of popular fascination and as a psychopathological symptom of our continuing age of Enlightenment, makes visible something that captures our uncanny intuition that we – our egos – are not altogether in the driver's seat of a subjectivity that is, after all, heterogeneously composed.

We might elaborate this by way of the body. This dimension of Sloterdijk's thinking is easily missed in *You Must Change Your Life* and one might easily come away from that book feeling that there isn't a strong sense of the body in Sloterdijk's work. Tracing the trope of sleep, and Sloterdijk's insistence on it as an undismissible and significant fact of our being in the world, will surprise us, therefore, with a sophisticated place for the body in his work. And what exactly is the body as it appears in Sloterdijk's work? It seems to be what he called earlier "the unknown quantity per se" – a kind of stupid materiality, stupid in the sense of having something of the unimaginable, unsymbolizable real about it: my body is undoubtedly mine in some sense, it is the primordial Gestalt figure of my self for my self, after all, and yet it remains to some degree uncooperative with my efforts to tame it in the name of consciousness and will. And for all my efforts to recruit it into the service of my fantasy life, it will stubbornly insist on its own unruly way, in defiance of, or in utter indifference to my will. The body can be a rigorous teacher of unwelcome wisdom; the maladies of sleep – we have mentioned insomnia and somnambulism – will teach the lessons we have already outlined: that we are not altogether what we suppose ourselves to be, that we are possessed by a complex of powers that pays scant regard to our will, that in the intimate–extimate interiority of our bodies, in the animation of our stupid need- and symptom-prone flesh, there are unknown quantities and unknowable mechanisms that perform their work sometimes to our detriment and downfall, though perhaps potentially to our upliftment. But there is one more lesson we have touched upon but might elaborate more fully: the way that sleep as a trope invites us to complicate the presumed mind–body binary. This paper has already discussed this in terms of insomnia – how the functioning of the mind is vulnerable to the moods and colors imposed upon it by the needs and symptoms of the sleep-prone body and is thereby shown to be more thoroughly co-implicated with the functioning of the body than we sometimes suppose. But let us explore this problem a little further by way of anthropotechnics, leaving sleep to the side for a short while.

We might approach this by way of what Sloterdijk called "the ensoulment of the machine" and "the desoulment of humans" at the end of the last quotation. One of the ways to think about what such formulations summon to thought passes by way of the question of desire and how desire might be shaped by the mechanisms of habit. We typically assign desire to the province of our true selves, in possible tension with our recalcitrant body-machine. Thus, one will say, for example, "I really *want* to exercise, *but* I cannot manage to wake up early enough to fit it into my daily routine [...]" Still, it bears emphasizing that often anthropotechnics is a problem equally of the recalcitrant soul – in order to improve our piano playing or our chess game, in order to coax our tummies into some less gelatinous form, in order to pursue any kind of training to strengthen our capacities, we will need to practice, of course, but even before we practice, and conditioning any practice, we will need to *want* to practice. This, I take it, is the most foundational problem of anthropotechnics. Sloterdijk cites the lesson of Nietzsche's Zarathustra to propose that "the vast majority of people have no interest in becoming more than they are" (*You Must Change* 176). But we might state this more precisely still: the issue is not that people don't admire the acrobat or the person who achieves highly – in fact we do admire her, but we too often admire her without being inspired to action ourselves. We perhaps wish we could do the same – mere wish is cheap enough, as everyone knows – but we do not desire it with sufficient intensity to assign it a time and a place for practice in the everyday course of our existence. But if there are those who "have never heard or seen any trace of [the call for self-improvement]," there are also those others who do indeed "hear the imperative that catapults them out of their old life" (191). It is a problem of hearing the imperative *as* an imperative worth heeding and being thereby motivated within oneself to take action:

> What is genuinely thought-provoking is the question of how, in the course of this secession, the complex of acquired habits as such could become thematic, and the thought of supra-ordinary things powerful [*mächtig*] within individual humans. (191)

Thought-provoking indeed! How to install that inner catapult in the soul? How indeed to cultivate within the human being the sense that the labor and occasional tedium of self-improvement is worthwhile and perhaps not so tedious after all, that there is a time in everyday life to be reserved for running through piano scales or meditating upon chess puzzles or finally taking advantage of that gym membership? The answer suggested by Sloterdijk's anthropotechnics, I think, is that desire too can be strengthened and shaped through exercise and repetition or through some kind of disciplined practice and the inscriptions of habit. Sloterdijk cites the essential transferential function of the trainer, for example, whose indispensable task is to excite our own desire to improve and thereby overcome our swinish tendencies to inertia: "My trainer is the one who wants me to want [to change my life]" (*You Must Change* 55). The cultivation and technics of desire, from a certain perspective, appear to form the linchpin of the whole project Sloterdijk describes.

Against the subject's exalted desire for ascent and against the heroic effort to overcome animal inertia, we see only ethico-existential disappointment in the capitulation of will and desire and the consequent retreat into passivity. Sloterdijk tropes this kind of subjective capitulation, in one interview, as hibernation. As we examine the implications of Sloterdijk's hibernation trope, we will find that it is inconsistent with some of what has already been established elsewhere by his consideration of sleep more generally. But let us follow this through more deliberately.

Sloterdijk's core value, at least in this aspect of his philosophy, is arguably the value of vertical ascent as such; it is unsurprising, then, that he generally takes a dim view of hibernation and any refusal of the call to rally one's energies, to commit to the discipline of a project of ascent, and to creatively raise the horizons of one's life.[3] In 2011, two years following the publication of *You Must Change Your Life*, in a lengthy conversation with Ulrich Raulff, Sloterdijk mused on hibernation as a trope of capitulation and retreat:

> Strangely enough, there are countless people who see the statement "There is absolutely nothing we can do" as good news. Whereas others resist this thesis with every inch of their being, fans of fatalism welcome it as absolution from the requirement to do anything [...]
>
> The tendency to hibernate at the nadir of the will doesn't only exist in the form of the desire to overcome [one's attachment to worldly] things [as in pre-modern cults of fatalism]. The quietist acceptance of fatality was just as attractive for countless people in the twentieth century. Many people are happy to obtain proof that nothing can be done [...] I suspect this doesn't only apply to the fatalism of ordinary people who want a quiet life; a large part of the intellectual movements of the twentieth century also felt the longing for hibernation. (*Selected Exaggerations* 302)

After Raulff introduces the term "hibernation" (referring to Roland Barthes), Sloterdijk twice takes it up to exploit it as a trope for a retreat from the demand for action. Such a retreat is surely understandable in human terms – a little relief from the multiple, sometimes overwhelming ethical demands of life, and from the little failures they necessarily entail, can be more than welcome. Nor, in any case, can one accept every call for self-improvement – one perhaps commits to a small number of them at most and refuses the rest in the name of ascetic discipline. And yet, such "quietist" passivity and indeed a will to "hibernate" also disappoint our hero for their sense of bad faith: shouldn't we rather open our eyes, get out of our beds, face the day, and take up at least some of our responsibilities, instead of burying our faces in our pillows, clenching our eyes shut, and giving ourselves up to slumber until the rigors of winter pass in the due course of time? Sloterdijk celebrates activity and denigrates passivity more directly in *You Must Change Your Life*:

> anyone who takes part in a programme for de-passivizing themselves, and crosses from the side of the merely formed to that of the forming, becomes a subject. The whole complex known as ethics comes from the gesture of conversion to ability. Conversion is not the transition from one belief system to another; the original conversion takes place as an exit from the passivist mode of existence in coincidence with the entrance into the activating mode. (195)

Sloterdijk declares one of his fundamental ethical values here: that one should seize hold of one's existence and assume an active role in shaping the form that that existence will take. The subject, says Sloterdijk in a discussion of the late Foucault, is "someone who is *active* as the carrier of a sequence of exercises" (*You Must Change* 156; my emphasis). The kind of existential heroism Sloterdijk announces as a value here will be familiar to readers of philosophy since Nietzsche and I won't belabor the point.

We should, though, observe a tension produced by Sloterdijk's casual appropriation of the trope of hibernation and his recourse to the language of existential heroism – a tension that will move us to refine our conclusions about Sloterdijk's use of sleep as a trope in his work on anthropotechnics. Let us leave aside, for present purposes, the special case of Emil Cioran with his uniquely heroic transformations of passivity and refusal. We can grant Sloterdijk's Heraclitean point above that, in the ordinary course of events, passivity[4] and inertia give the subject little aid and much hindrance in the pursuit of self-improvement. But the whole language of passivity and activity, of hibernation at "the nadir of the will," is too much the language of agency and ego. This language indeed has its place – the subject would be nowhere without an ego and its seemingly inevitable supposition of self-sovereignty and the more or less free exercise of the will. Moreover, Sloterdijk's whole project grants a key role for the "self" in the self-improvement of a subject who commits to one field of ascent (or several), closes out extraneous or debasing distractions, and, through ascetic self-discipline and training, endeavors to raise his or her horizons of competence and thereby creatively alter the form of his or her life. In a sense, the whole project of an anthropotechnics is the formation or construction of a superior self.

And yet, in truth, we can no longer use this binary of activity and passivity, this language of will and capitulation, these admonitions against fatalism and hibernation, quite so freely, now that Sloterdijk has restored to our understanding of the subject much of what is implied by the various appearances of sleep. This subject may indeed be defined by a potential for striving, thought, and self-becoming, for divine or transcendental participation, and for all varieties of awakening. But this subject is also defined, and no less rigorously, by his or her sleep-prone corporeality – which is to say, by a need for periodic and proper rest, by a merely mortal temporality, and by automatic processes and unknown quantities of the body and spirit, that countermand the ego's supposed mastership of its subjective premises.

Sleep is important as a trope in Sloterdijk's work, then, because sleep serves as an index of the mystery of the automatic processes of the body and spirit that dominate our existence. It works as an example and an index of the fact that we are dominated by a plethora of inertias and programmings that are proper to the subject and yet opaque and scandalously separate from consciousness and ego. The exigencies and maladies of sleep remind us, then, that our anthropotechnical projects will be constrained and conditioned by this finally inescapable fact – and this needs to be taken into the philosophical account[5] and the practical mechanics of self-improvement. The automatic processes of the subject, including sleep, must be dealt with – accommodated, harnessed, overwritten, redirected, managed, but without hope of final mastery – for any ambitious project in anthropotechnics. So there are real limits to any ethics of striving existential heroism, given our sleep-prone animal substrate and given that the subject is significantly constituted through his or her automatic processes. In short, however the subject comes to think about the call, relayed by Rilke, to change one's life, this thinking and this ascent must also and inevitably yield to what Rilke called in a letter to Lou Andreas-Salomé "that great god: Sleep!": mild yet imperious, sublimely silent, careless of human time, but full of a depth and a mystery that nourishes the immense night (Rilke and Andreas-Salomé 341).

disclosure statement

No potential conflict of interest was reported by the author.

notes

1 The German *Prämissen*, like the English *premises*, refers equally to real-estate property (considered in an official context) as to the givens of a logical proposition. Sloterdijk could intend either or both, but the first and most likely sense is surely one of property, implying a subject who "houses" a cacophony of contending voices and interests and whose ego is not the undisputed lord of this manor. That said, it is an attractive possibility for meditation that Sloterdijk may have had additional meanings in mind, related to the givens of the existence into which we are thrown, or related to the human relation to logic itself.

2 In *Spheres, Vol. I: Bubbles* (2011), Sloterdijk discusses mesmerism at much greater length, but his interest there lies in the way that the eighteenth and nineteenth centuries were exploring figures of the human susceptibility to "magnetic" interpersonal influences, rather than (as with our interest in the present essay) in the revelation of an unknown and finally unmasterable agency proper to the subject, but external to consciousness.

3 In the example of Cioran, "the first master of not-getting-anywhere," Sloterdijk acknowledges that even passivity, transformed by creativity and self-discipline can be put to the purpose of ascent. This is also a salutary reminder that Sloterdijk is remarkably non-prescriptive, non-dogmatic about the content of his religion, so to speak, even as he celebrates a general mood of heroic exertion for its own sake. His pantheon of various heroic figures – amateur athletes, Unthan the armless violinist, Zarathustra's nameless acrobat, the insomniac Cioran in his unexpected way – suggests a celebration of discipline and the love of long, hard, labor as well as a capacious sense for the many possible fields of heroic endeavor. Some readers will wish to know what this labor and exertion go to produce, but my sense of Sloterdijk is that he makes a principled stop here: the exertion is the thing. The true product is not a superior violinist or a superior acrobat; the true product is self-improvement as such, measured on an individual scale.

4 Of course, passivity per se cannot be always and everywhere a bad thing in Sloterdijk's philosophy, even aside from the somewhat perverse figure of Cioran. Human beings are, for example, simultaneously the agent and the object of action in the case of self-discipline and self-improvement. They are, in this sense, the passive objects of the work that they actively perform upon themselves. Sloterdijk develops this point in his remarks on the "auto-operative curvature" of the self-improving subject.

5 It surely goes without saying that the philosophical account is not the only possible frame for working with these matters. It is easy to imagine, for example, that a trainer might seek to rally the desire and commitment of the self-improving subject by falsely flattering the ego's pretensions to mastery. Such a ruse, when successful, would serve as a salutary caution against the fatalism that, Sloterdijk also warns us, might accompany a too-heavy emphasis on the automatisms that dominate much (though not all) of subjective life. There is a delicate balance to be struck, for the philosopher, between properly acknowledging the limitations and unknown quantities of the subject and allowing that there is, even so, some range of freedom and agency for the subject. Moreover, to reiterate a key point developed earlier in this essay, Sloterdijk's philosophy urges us to the view that this is not a static standoff of forces:

anthropotechnics necessitates that the subject find ways to put his or her automatic processes to work in support of (or in coincidence with) the ego's projects for self-improvement.

bibliography

Heidegger, Martin. *Introduction to Metaphysics*. Trans. Gregory Fried and Richard Polt. New Haven: Yale UP, 2000. Print.

Irving, Washington. "Rip Van Winkle." 1819. *History, Tales and Sketches: Letters of Jonathan Oldstyle, Gent.; Salmagundi; A History of New York; The Sketch Book of Geoffrey Crayon, Gent.* New York: The Library of America, 1983. 769–84. Print.

Plato. "Symposium." *The Collected Dialogues*. Ed. Edith Hamilton and Huntington Cairns. Princeton: Princeton UP, 1963. 526–74. Print.

Rilke, Rainer Maria, and Lou Andreas-Salomé. *Rilke and Andreas-Salomé: A Love Story in Letters*. Trans. Edward Snow and Michael Winkler. New York: Norton, 2008. Print.

Sloterdijk, Peter. *Critique of Cynical Reason*. 1983. Trans. Michael Eldred. Minneapolis: U of Minnesota P, 1987. Print.

Sloterdijk, Peter. *Not Saved: Essays after Heidegger*. 2001. Trans. Ian Alexander Moore and Christopher Turner. Malden, MA: Polity, 2017. Print.

Sloterdijk, Peter. *Selected Exaggerations: Conversations and Interviews 1993–2012*. 2013. Ed. Bernhard Klein. Trans. Karen Margolis. Malden, MA: Polity, 2016. Print.

Sloterdijk, Peter. *Spheres, Volume I: Bubbles – Microspherology*. Trans. Wieland Hoban. Los Angeles: Semiotext(e), 2011. Print.

Sloterdijk, Peter. *Spheres, Volume III: Foams – Plural Spherology*. Trans. Wieland Hoban. Los Angeles: Semiotext(e), 2016. Print.

Sloterdijk, Peter. *Weltfremdheit*. Frankfurt: Suhrkamp, 1993. Print.

Sloterdijk, Peter. *You Must Change Your Life: On Anthropotechnics*. 2009. Trans. Wieland Hoban. Malden, MA: Polity, 2013. Print.

andrea rossi

UNTITLED (NEGATIVE EXERCISES)

Index

Note: Page numbers followed by "n" denote endnotes.

aesthetic imperative 29–31
allotechnics 93, 96–97
anthropology 47, 71
anthropotechniques 77
Aristotle 12, 45, 126
art 4, 6, 9, 12, 29–31, 40, 42, 44–46, 49, 53–54, 58, 61, 70, 72, 74
art history 44–45
ascetic life 15, 72, 81
Athanasius 13–14, 18
Augustine 17–18
Aurelius, Marcus 10–12, 14–15, 17
authority 10, 24–26, 28–31, 35, 49, 54, 64, 67, 79
automatic processes 148, 153–54
Ayles-worth, Gary 2

bad habits 73, 119
Baudelaire, Charles 15
being-in-spheres 51, 112–14
being-in-the-world 1, 24, 27, 31, 33–34, 79, 81, 83, 98, 102, 112
black box/blackboxing 138n23, 148–49
breeding 4, 71, 93

Christianity 24, 56, 72, 94
Cicero 10
Cioran, Emil 147, 153
civil disobedience 12
climate change 2–3, 23, 35, 137
coming-to-the-world 34, 83
commitment 68–70, 147
communism 43
complexification 54–55, 58–59
complexity 53, 68, 116, 125, 127–28, 131–34, 144
confessions 17–18, 130
consciousness 11, 45, 73–74, 78, 83, 143, 148, 150–51, 153
contemporary society 112, 120
cosmos 14, 63, 79, 84, 86, 114
cultural techniques 2, 9
culture 6, 15, 55, 59, 86, 95, 99, 101, 111, 114, 116

darkness 132–33, 135–37, 149
Dasein 5, 23–24, 32–34, 134, 146
deserts 13, 15–16, 94
detachment 68–71
digital culture 125, 133
disorientation 26, 128–29
dreamless sleep 143

ecological catastrophe 27, 102
ecstase-technology 32
ego 12, 15, 74, 109, 148–51, 153
Einsamkeit 13
Epictetus 11–12, 18
epoche 68, 71
ethics 22–23, 28, 30, 42–44, 46–47, 52, 54, 56, 75, 94, 96, 100, 153–54; of technology 28
experience of freedom 11, 70
experimental life 56, 147

fatalism 95, 152–53
foam metaphor 116
foam model 112, 116–17, 121
foam theory 115
foam-world 109, 111–12, 115, 118, 120–21
Foucault, M. 2, 9, 14, 69, 77, 79, 81, 119
freedom 11, 16, 26–28, 30, 57, 68–70, 74–75, 93, 99, 132

Gelassenheit 23–25, 33–34, 40
general ascetology 4–5, 27, 46, 112, 117, 120–21
general immunology 5, 25, 27, 48, 53, 102, 111–12, 117, 120–21, 128
generosity 100, 109

Habermas, Jürgen 132
Hadot, Pierre 4, 10–12, 15
Heidegger, Martin 126
Heraclitus 46, 143–44, 146–47, 149
hibernation 152–53
homeotechnics 92–93, 96–97, 102–3
human freedom 26–27

humanism 22, 31–32, 75, 96, 131, 135
humanity 1–2, 4, 6, 22, 26–28, 32–33, 59–61, 94–97, 102, 128, 130, 142, 145–46
human life 43, 64, 72, 117
human nature 4, 28, 127
human subjects 95, 148

immanence 47, 51, 53, 55, 63–64
immune systems 6, 25, 27, 30, 53, 118, 128
immunology 5, 30, 51–52, 61, 94, 112, 118
imperatives 22–23, 25, 27, 33, 46, 67
inertias 72–73, 75, 149, 152–53
insomnia 147–49, 151
intelligence 31
intersubjectivity 98, 114, 116–17, 120

James, William 55–61, 63
Jonas, Hans 25–28, 34, 61

Kant, Immanuel 2, 14, 16, 24–27, 30, 47–49, 58–59, 67, 75

language 27–28, 30, 32, 39, 52, 67, 71, 118–19, 130–31, 135, 153
Latour, Bruno 138n23
life-stultifying asceticism 41–42, 69

Mauss, Marcel 9
meditative cybernetics 31
metaphysics 25, 32, 35, 42, 47, 80, 82–85, 94–95, 128, 143–44, 146–47
modernity 3, 6, 22, 24–25, 29–30, 39–40, 45–46, 51–52, 55, 58–59, 85–86, 128–32
modernization 2–4
monstrosity 29–31, 79–81, 124, 126, 128–31

natural history 32–34
neoliberal capitalism 119–21
networks 28, 62, 115, 131
new technologies 2, 4, 31, 35, 132
Nietzsche, Friedrich 2, 25, 28–29, 38, 41–42, 45–47, 53–61, 68, 80, 86, 100

objective 11, 42, 57–58, 61, 69–72, 78, 92
objective representation 10
originary intersubjectivity 112, 120–21
otherness 63, 92–93, 97–98, 101, 103

passivity 73, 152–53
Petrick, Elizabeth R. 139n26
Plato 10, 13–14, 18, 43, 81, 125–26, 150

Pliny 10
political agonism 82, 85–86
political order 79–80, 82, 84
possession 12, 15–16, 149

Rancière, Jacques 110
Raschke, Carl 70
religion 3, 6, 38, 43–44, 47, 49, 52–55, 57–58, 60, 64, 82, 94–95, 101–2
renaissance 42, 45, 49, 58–60
replaceability 32, 34
Rimbaud, A. 15

Sartre, Jean-Paul 70
secondary anthropotechnics 95–97, 101
self-formation 4, 74
selfhood 73–74
self-improvement 31, 103, 112, 118, 149, 151–53
self-mobilisation 77, 85, 87
sleepless 43, 144–45
sleepwalking 150
Socrates 14, 40, 78, 80, 125–27
solitary-nomadic life 15
solitude 2, 9–16, 18–19, 58, 98
somnambulant phenomena 148
somnambulism 150–51
subjective representations 10
subjectivity 68, 74, 82, 87, 92–93, 97–98, 151
sublime 16, 23, 48, 61

technology 2, 4, 6, 9, 23–25, 28–29, 31–35, 87, 93, 96–97, 130–32, 134–37; essence of 24–25, 32–34
tertiary anthropotechnics 101, 103
thaumazein 126–27
theory of society 53, 55, 60
Thoreau, Henry David 12
thymotic communities 100, 103
Tours, Joseph Moreau de 15
traditional ethics 28
transformations 33, 58, 60, 78, 86, 128, 153
transparency 132–34, 136–37
Trottein, Serge 2
true human life 27, 61, 64, 67

wakefulness 31, 143–46
world history 78
world-secessionism 138n3
world of traditions 82, 84
world religions 60, 64
Worms, Abraham von 13